WRITERS EXPRESS

A Handbook for YOUNG WRITERS, THINKERS, and LEARNERS

Written and Compiled by
Dave Kemper, Ruth Nathan, Carol Elsholz, Patrick Sebranek

Illustrated by **Chris Krenzke**

WRITE SOURCE®

GREAT SOURCE EDUCATION GROUP
a Houghton Mifflin Company
Wilmington, Massachusetts

Acknowledgements

We're grateful to many people who helped bring *Writers Express* to life. First, we must thank all the students from across the country who've contributed their writing and their ideas.

Also, thanks to some of our favorite authors and teachers who helped make *Writers Express* a reality.

Sandy Asher, Nancy Bond, Roy Peter Clark, Toby Fulwiler, Will Hobbs, Stephen Krensky, Gloria Nixon-John, Susan Ohanian, Anne-Marie Oomen, Marie Ponsot, Peter and Connie Roop, Lorraine Sintetos, Vicki Spandel, Paula and Keith Stanovich, Peter Stillman, Charles Temple, Toni Walters, and Allan Wolf

Another thank-you goes to our team of educators, editors, and designers: Laura Bachman, Colleen Belmont, Laurie Cooper, Marguerite Cotto, Sherry Gordon, Julie Janosz, Beverly Jessen, Kathy Juntunen, Pat Kornelis, Lois Krenzke, Ellen Leitheusser, Dian Lynch, Verne Meyer, Candyce Norvell, Randy Rehberg, Kelly Brecher Saaf, Linda Sivy, Lester Smith, John Van Rys, Sandy Wagner, and Claire Ziffer.

International Standard Book Number: 0-669-47163-1 (hardcover)
  5 6 7 8 9 10 -RRDC- 05 04 03 02 01

International Standard Book Number: 0-669-47165-8 (softcover)
  5 6 7 8 9 10 -RRDC- 05 04 03 02 01

Express Yourself!

Writers Express **is divided into five major parts . . .**

The Process of Writing • Use this section to answer your questions about writing, from selecting a subject to proofreading a final draft.

The Forms of Writing • Would you like to start a personal journal, write a poem, do a research report, or create a tall tale? Then this section is for you!

The Tools of Learning • If your study, reading, or test-taking skills could use a little pumping up, turn to "The Tools of Learning."

Proofreader's Guide • Do you have a question about punctuation? Spelling? Capitalization? Here's where you find the answers.

Student Almanac • Ten full-color maps, the metric system, a historical time line—*Writers Express* is truly an all-school handbook!

Table of Contents
The Process of Writing

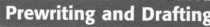

The Forms of Writing

The Tools of Learning

Proofreader's Guide

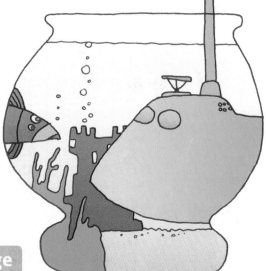

Student Almanac

Using Language

Exploring Science

Improving Math Skills

Using Maps

Making History

Why Write?

One day last summer, my friend and I discovered a big old fishing boat that had washed up on the beach. We adopted the boat for the summer. We had a great time making up adventures about being shipwrecked on a deserted island, discovering a new country, and being ocean scientists.

As more friends joined us, we began sharing things we knew about boats and ships and the ocean. Then we decided to use our great adventure stories and write a play about them. We acted it out right in the boat for our families and friends. It turned out great! Everyone was amazed that we could write a play and act it out. So were we!

The Express Connection

This story is not unusual. Kids have been writing and acting out plays for a long time. Writing is a great way to express what you think or feel or imagine. That's *why* people write, and that's why we've created *Writers Express* for you. We also hope it helps you become a better reader, thinker, speaker, and all-around student. Not bad for one little book!

Getting Started

A Basic Writing Guide

A Handy Handbook

Your *Writers Express* handbook gives lots of good advice about writing. But there is only one way to learn how to write, and that is to do it—every day if you can. Your handbook gives you help to get started, tips to keep going, and ideas for making your writing as good as it can be. Keep it handy whenever you are writing.

This chapter has questions and answers about writing. The questions are ones that many writers ask. The answers will help you find your way through the writing process and around the first part of the handbook.

Questions & Answers About Writing

1 ## What can I write about?

Write about a subject that you know about or can learn about. Also, write about something that really interests or excites you. Your subject could be something you have written about in your journal.

What you write about depends on why you are writing (your purpose) and who you are writing to (your audience).

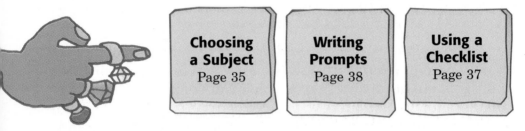

Choosing a Subject	Writing Prompts	Using a Checklist
Page 35	Page 38	Page 37

2 ## How do I get started?

First of all, be sure you know your subject well. Gather the information you need for the kind of writing you will be doing. If you know a lot about the subject already, you can write freely or make a list to get your ideas going. If you need to gather new information, you can read books or magazines or find information on-line. You can also interview someone who knows about the subject.

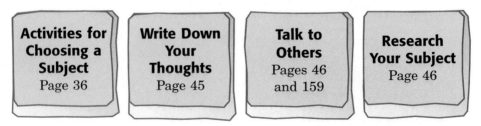

Activities for Choosing a Subject	Write Down Your Thoughts	Talk to Others	Research Your Subject
Page 36	Page 45	Pages 46 and 159	Page 46

3 How do I know what to say about my subject?

You can't write everything you know about a subject, so you have to decide on a focus, or main idea. You also need to make a plan and know what form of writing you will be using.

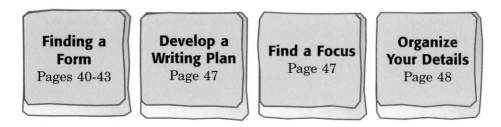

Finding a Form
Pages 40-43

Develop a Writing Plan
Page 47

Find a Focus
Page 47

Organize Your Details
Page 48

4 How should I write my first draft?

First, follow your plan. Then write your first draft freely and honestly, as if you were talking to a group of friends. Get your ideas down and don't worry about making everything perfect the first time.

One Writer's Process
Pages 12-17

Writing a First Draft
Pages 50-53

The Parts of a Paragraph
Page 76

5 How can I make my writing interesting?

You make your writing interesting by writing with style and using your writing voice. Your voice is your special way of expressing your ideas and feelings. As you continue to write, your voice will develop naturally.

Traits of Effective Writing
Page 19

Adding Details
Page 83

Using Writing Techniques
Pages 124-127

Tips to Make Your Writing Stronger
Pages 58-59

6 Why do I have to do more than one draft?

You don't always have to do more than one draft. However, when you are going to share your writing with others, it is important to take time to revise your writing and make it the best it can be. There are many ways to do this.

What Is Revising?
Page 56

Revising Checklist
Page 57

Guidelines for Sharing Writing
Pages 62-63

Publishing Your Writing
Pages 68-73

7 **How can I find all the errors in my writing?**

You probably can't find all the errors. Otherwise you wouldn't have made them! One way to find errors is to ask a teacher or classmate to work with you. You can also use your handbook (there are many checklists) and a dictionary to check for grammar, spelling, and punctuation rules. (Remember, even if you are using a spell checker on your computer, you will need to do some double-checking.)

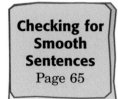
Checking for Smooth Sentences
Page 65

Checking for Word Choice
Page 66

Proofreader's Guide
(**SEE** yellow pages.)

Editing and Proofreading Checklist
Page 67

8 **How do I know if my writing is good?**

You can use a simple checklist to evaluate your writing. If you can say *yes* to each of the following questions, you can feel good about your work:

- Did I choose a subject that I knew a lot about or one I was interested in?
- Did I follow a plan to guide my writing?
- Did I focus on a specific subject?
- Did I make changes until my writing was as good as it could be?
- Is my final draft correct and neatly formatted?

Checklist for Good Writing
Page 23

Five Tips for a Super Portfolio
Page 33

Steps in the Writing Process

Wishful Thinking

Suppose you could plot out your next writing assignment on a special computer pad, like this:

> **Subject:** **Class trip**
>
> **Purpose:** **To report on our performance at the nursing home**
>
> **Form:** **Newspaper story**
>
> **Audience:** **Students at Pierce Elementary**

Then you plug your keyboard into the pad, set it on "superwriter," and eat a piece of pizza while your story is being written. Just press a few buttons, and your writing comes out exactly the way you ordered it!

It would be nice if reports and stories could be written by a computer, but it's not that simple. You must do your own writing step-by-step—from planning to revising to publishing.

The Steps in the Writing Process

Prewriting

Prewriting refers to all the thinking and planning you do before you write your first draft. It includes thinking about your purpose, gathering information, choosing a form (paragraph, letter, report), making a plan, and deciding who your audience will be (friends, adults, younger students).

Writing the First Draft

Writing the first draft means getting all your ideas down on paper. As you know, writers often write more than one draft.

Revising

Revising means changing and improving your writing. It's your opportunity to think about what you've written and then add, cut, or change ideas. It's also a good time to share your writing with others and get their reactions or ideas.

Editing and Proofreading

Editing and proofreading refers to the final changes you make in your writing. It's a careful line-by-line check of your writing to catch and correct any errors.

Publishing

Publishing is a way of sharing your writing. It includes everything from posting your writing on the wall of your classroom to posting it on the Internet. (**SEE** pages 68-73.)

Note You may repeat some steps. For example, even after the first draft, you may need to do more planning.

The Writing Process in Action

These two pages give you an overview of the writing process. You will also find chapters for each step of the writing process in this section of your handbook.

Prewriting Planning Your Writing

Choose a Subject ● Pick a subject you know about or can learn about. If you're interested in your subject, your reader will be, too.

Gather Details ● Gather the information you need to make your writing interesting. You can do this by reading books, using the Internet, or interviewing other people.

Make a Plan ● You can make lists, create an outline, draw a picture, or do a word web.

Focus ● You can't tell everything in your writing, so decide on one main point to focus on.

Writing the First Draft

Write Freely ● Write your first draft freely, getting *all* your ideas on paper.

Picture Your Audience ● Write as if you were talking to the people you are writing to. This will give your writing a personal voice.

Follow Your Plan ● Your writing should have a beginning, a middle, and an ending.

Wait to Edit ● Don't stop to check spelling and punctuation now, or you may forget to include all the important information.

Revising *Improving Your Writing*

Read Your First Draft Aloud ● Ask yourself, "Does it make sense? Does it have enough details?"

Share Your Writing ● Ask a classmate, a parent, or a teacher to read and react to your writing.

Make Changes ● Add, take out, or move information if you need to make your writing clearer. (**SEE** pages 15 and 243 for examples.)

Double-Check ● Use the revising checklist on page 57.

Editing and Proofreading

Check Your Writing ● Check for errors in capitalization, punctuation, spelling, and grammar. (**SEE** pages 64-67.)

Get Help ● Work with a classmate or your teacher to check your writing for errors.

Think About Your Writing ● Make sure you used interesting words and smooth sentences.

Dictionary

Write a Final Copy ● Prepare a neat final draft of your writing.

Proofread Once More ● Check your final draft for any additional errors.

Publishing

Share Your Work ● Turn to pages 68-73 for suggestions about publishing your writing.

One Writer's Process

One Step at a Time

We often think that our favorite authors have no trouble writing. They just think of a story idea, sit down at the keyboard, and within minutes—presto—it's done! As any writer will tell you, though, it's almost never that simple, even for the pros.

Luckily, however, writing can be broken down into steps, making it more manageable. By following the writing process one step at a time, you can become a better writer.

In this chapter, we'll take you inside one writer's process—to see how she plans her writing and improves it as she goes along.

Prewriting Planning Your Writing

For one of her assignments, Hillary Bachman was asked to write a character sketch. She chose to write about her favorite teacher. Here's how she used the writing process to go from choosing a subject to completing a final draft.

Choose a Subject ● Hillary started by thinking about all of her favorite teachers, past and present. She thought of Mrs. Thompson, Mr. Schwarz, Mrs. Juarez, and Mr. Vetter. The one teacher that really stood out was Mr. Vetter, so she decided to write about him.

Gather Details/Make a Plan ● Then she gathered her ideas about Mr. Vetter in a cluster. This gave her a basic plan for her writing.

encourages us
helpful
answers our questions
we learn a lot

coach — **Mr. Vetter** — **math teacher**

makes learning fun

friend

gives good advice
always friendly
tells funny jokes

Writing the First Draft

Hillary kept her cluster in front of her. As she wrote her first draft, she remembered other details to include. Here is the beginning of her paper.

A Great Teacher

Hillary starts with words from her cluster.

Funny, helpful, and friendly--what am I describing? Is it one of your classmates or your best friend? Beleive it or not, I'm describing a teacher! His name is Mr. Vetter. We call him Mr. V.

One thing that really like about him is the way he makes learning fun.

She continues by giving details about Mr. Vetter.

If math seams boring, he will make it fun by saying something that is so funny so you want to learn. Once I sneezed really loud in the middle of class. Right away, Mr. V. said "googolplex."* It sounded just the same as gesundheit or bless you.

Mr. V. is also . . .

*Googolplex refers to a very large number.

Revising Improving the Writing

After reading over her first draft, Hillary tried to make her writing clearer and more complete. (The comments written in blue were made by a classmate.)

Hillary rewords the first sentence.

A Great Teacher

Who is ⟩

↳ Funny, helpful, and friendly, what am I ?

describing? Is it one of ~~your~~ my classmates or ~~your~~ my

best friend? Beleive it or not, I'm describing a my math

teacher! His name is Mr. Vetter. We call him Mr. V.

She follows the advice of her writing partner (in blue).

One thing that I really like about him is the way

he makes learning fun. ⟵ Why is this sentence all alone?

If math seams boring, he will ~~make it fun by~~

She rewrites a wordy sentence.

we
saying something ~~that is so~~ funny so ~~you~~ want to

learn. Once I sneezed really loud in the middle

of class. Right away, Mr. V. said "googolplex." It

sounded just the same as gesundheit or bless you.

Good example!

Mr. V. is also . . .

Editing and Proofreading

Next, Hillary made sure that her writing was easy to read. She checked it for errors, especially punctuation and spelling. After writing a neat final draft of her paper, Hillary proofread it again.

A Great Teacher

Who is funny, helpful, and friendly? Is it

one of my classmates or my best friend? Beleive

it or not, I'm describing my math teacher! His

Hillary combines two short sentences into one smooth sentence.

name is Mr. Vetter. We call him Mr. V.
, but we

One thing that I really like about him is the

seems
way he makes learning fun. If math seams

boring, he will say something funny so we want

She adds a comma and capital letter to the quotation.

to learn. Once I sneezed really loud in the

middle of class. Right away, Mr. V. said

G
"googolplex." It sounded just the same as

gesundheit or bless you.

Mr. V. is also . . .

Publishing

Hillary produced this neat final copy on her computer. She shared it with her classmates and teachers. She made her paper as clear and correct as it could be.

Final Character Sketch

A Great Teacher

Who is funny, helpful, and friendly? Is it one of my classmates or my best friend? Believe it or not, I'm describing my math teacher! His name is Mr. Vetter, but we call him Mr. V.

One thing that I really like about him is the way he makes learning fun. If math seems boring, he will say something funny so we want to learn. Once I sneezed really loud in the middle of class. Right away, Mr. V. said, "Googolplex." It sounded just the same as gesundheit or bless you.

Mr. V. is also a great encourager because when you don't understand something, he will help you out step-by-step and say, "Good job!" And, if you have a question, he will always answer it. Mr. V. says, "No question is trivial." He will tell you exactly what you need to know. I've had many good teachers, but Mr. V. is the best.

Traits of Effective Writing

Throw a Strike

A baseball pitcher needs speed and accuracy to throw a strike. A writer needs bright ideas and the right words to write an excellent paper. You can use the traits of effective writing explained in this chapter to help you "throw a strike."

Take time to learn about these traits of successful writing and how to make them work for you. Practice often, and you'll be throwing writing "strikes" in no time!

Your favorite authors use the traits of effective writing that are explained in this chapter. That's how they produce their best stories.

Traits of Effective Writing

Always keep the following traits in mind when you write. If you follow them, you will do your best work.

1 **Stimulating Ideas:** Good writing includes important ideas, accurate information, and interesting details. It also has a clear message or purpose.

2 **Logical Organization:** Good writing is well organized. The opening catches the reader's attention. The middle is well developed and answers the reader's questions. The ending ties things together and leaves the reader with something to think about.

3 **Personal Voice:** In the best writing, you can hear the writer's voice. Voice is the special way a writer expresses ideas and feelings. Voice depends on who you are writing to: the audience.

4 **Original Word Choice:** Good writing contains well-chosen words, including vivid verbs (*fizzle, cringe, wheeze*), specific nouns (*Dalmatian, shack, mango*), and colorful adjectives (*clumsy, brilliant, tender*).

5 **Smooth Sentences:** Good writing flows smoothly from one sentence to the next. Sentences begin in different ways; some are short and others are long.

6 **Correct, Accurate Copy:** Good writing is free of errors in capitalization, punctuation, spelling, and grammar.

Note Depending on the type of writing you are doing, you can choose many different ways to design and publish it. (**SEE** pages 68-73 and 264-269.)

Writing Traits in Action

On the next three pages, you will see a writing sample for each of the traits of effective writing. Try comparing your own writing with the samples to discover your strengths and weaknesses in these areas.

 Stimulating Ideas: In this paragraph, the author presents accurate and interesting information about an amazing discovery made by children.

> **Six children in Australia found a giant fossil egg while they were playing in the sand dunes. The 2,000-year-old egg is probably from an extinct Madagascar elephant bird. The egg may have floated across the ocean from Madagascar to Australia. It's so large that 150 chicken eggs could fit inside it!**

■ Reading this paragraph makes you want to read more about this discovery. It may even encourage you to find Madagascar and Australia on a globe or map.

2 Logical Organization: In this brief paragraph from *Sea Snakes,* the author, Sneed B. Collard III, organizes his information logically so the reader can follow it.

> **Sea snakes are not giant, people-eating monsters. Compared to land snakes like anacondas and pythons, sea snakes are quite small. Most grow no longer than three feet. The biggest ones measure about eight feet. But what is a sea snake?**

■ Notice how the opening sentence grabs your attention. Then each sentence that follows adds new information about the subject. The last sentence leads you right into the next paragraph to learn more about the sea snake.

3 **Personal Voice:** In *Belinda's Hurricane* by Elizabeth Winthrop, you clearly hear the author's voice as she writes about the love between Belinda and Granny May.

> Belinda loved Granny May. They fit together like two old armchairs that sat on either side of her fireplace. They collected shells and glued them onto little boxes. . . . They got up early in the morning to go fishing in the yellow rowboat. They went to bed late after a big bowl of ice cream with fudge sauce and a game of Parcheesi. Every clear night, they slept with their windows open, so the gulls would wake them up again in the morning.

■ These descriptions of Belinda and Granny May put the reader in touch with Belinda's feelings about her grandmother. The author's words are easy to read and easy to listen to.

4 **Original Word Choice:** In the following paragraph, the author chooses words that give a clear picture of the volcanoes in the Hawaiian Islands.

> When the first people arrived in the Hawaiian Islands, they were puzzled. The mountains would suddenly rain fire and melted rock down on them. The melted rock would slowly pour down the mountainside and swallow up everything in its path. Soon legends grew up to explain the fiery mountains. They said that Pele (pā'lā), the goddess of volcanoes, lived in the mountains.

■ The phrases *rain fire* and *swallow up everything in its path* use colorful words that show action. The words make the volcanoes seem like living beings. The strong verbs *rain, pour,* and *swallow* help you to picture the action of the volcanoes.

5 **Smooth Sentences:** In this passage from "The Living Desert," you find an interesting description of the desert tortoise. From the very beginning, one sentence seems to flow right into the next.

> **Consider the desert tortoise. In the spring, it drinks rainwater and feeds on cactus fruit and tender new plants and flowers. It stores water inside its upper shell, and it adds to its fat reserves. Although the next rain may be months away, the tortoise can live through times when food and water are scarce by using its stored supplies.**

■ In this paragraph, the author uses a variety of sentence lengths and beginnings. This variety adds to the smooth flow of the paragraph.

6 **Correct, Accurate Copy:** In *The Medusa and the Snail,* author Lewis Thomas writes playfully about punctuation. He helps you think about not only how to use it, but how you may *feel* about it as a reader. For instance, he suggests that seeing too many exclamation points can become distracting.

> **Exclamation points are the most irritating of all. Look! they say, look at what I just said! How amazing is my thought!**

■ Thomas clearly makes his point. But he never could have done it so well without the humorous use of his own exclamation points. Good writers use punctuation marks correctly to make meaning clear; they don't overdo it.

Checklist for Good Writing

How can you tell if something you read or write has the traits of effective writing? You can use the following checklist.

✔ Stimulating Ideas

___ Did I present important, interesting information?

___ Did I hold the reader's attention all the way through?

✔ Logical Organization

___ Did I include a clear beginning, middle, and ending?

___ Did I use specific details to support the main ideas?

✔ Personal Voice

___ Did I show my enthusiasm for the topic?

___ Is my writing easy to read aloud or listen to?

✔ Original Word Choice

___ Did I use strong verbs, specific nouns, and colorful adjectives?

___ Did I help the reader picture what I am writing about?

✔ Smooth Sentences

___ Did I mix short sentences with longer ones?

___ Did I show variety in my sentence beginnings?

✔ Correct, Accurate Copy

___ Did I follow the basic rules of spelling, capitalization, grammar, and punctuation?

Writing with Computers

Tools of the Trade

People can't work or play without the right tools. A family doctor couldn't examine a patient without a stethoscope or tongue depressor. (Say ahhh!) A mechanic without socket wrenches and screwdrivers might as well close up shop. And a spelunker, someone who explores caves, would be lost without a flashlight and hardhat.

All "Keyed Up"

One tool that many writers could not do without is the **personal computer.** Writers will tell you that a computer allows them to say a lot in a short amount of time. They will also tell you that revising and editing first drafts is easier on the computer.

Remember the golden rule of the computer age: "Always save your work!"

Computers in the Writing Process

A computer can be fun. It can also be an important tool for writing. Here are some ways a computer can help you with the writing process.

Prewriting

A computer can help you plan your writing. You can freewrite ideas and rearrange them easily in the order you like best. You can also use your computer to research your subject. Depending on the computer you have, you may be able to access information from CD-ROM's, your local library, and the Internet. (**SEE** pages 264-269.)

Writing the First Draft

When you write your first drafts on a computer, you can add and delete ideas as they come to mind.

Revising

A computer is especially handy for revising. You can move words, sentences, and even whole paragraphs. Making changes to your writing is easy (even fun).

Editing and Proofreading

Many computers have grammar and spell checkers. But these checkers cannot catch everything. For example, they don't know that you meant "two" when you typed "too." It's a good idea to print out a copy of your work to edit and proofread.

Publishing

A computer allows you to save your work, print out copies, and share them with others. With some help, you might also post your work on the Web. (**SEE** pages 267 and 269.)

Computer Tips

Keep the following things in mind as you write with your computer.

Protect your files. Make sure to "save" often while working on a computer.

■ Remember, what you type is just on the screen. If something goes wrong, it could be lost forever!

■ Save your information on a backup disk.

■ Protect your disks. Keep them away from heat, cold, dirt, liquids, and magnets, or your work may be lost.

Get "help." When you have a question, you can do one of three things:

■ You can look for an answer using the computer's "help" function.

■ You can ask a teacher or classmate for his or her help.

■ You can use your handbook to look up computer terms.

Designing Your Writing

A good page design makes your writing clear and easy to follow. (**SEE** pages 202 and 203 for a sample.)

● You should use appropriate margins and line spacing.

● Use simple type fonts that are easy to read. (Don't use more than two fonts per page.) Also, use a 12- or 14-point type size.

● You can use tables, graphs, and pictures to add interest to your writing.

● Make titles and headings short and to the point.

● Avoid single words at the bottom or top of a page.

● Print out a copy to judge your overall page design.

Computer Writing Terms

Character • A letter, number, or symbol.

Cursor • A pointer on the computer screen that shows where the next character will appear.

Directory • The list of files on a disk.

Drag • To move items across the screen by using the mouse.

Drive • The device a computer uses to read and save information.

File • A computer document.

Font • A set of typeface characters that share the same design or style. Fonts help create the look of a page.

Graphic • A picture, chart, or table.

Keyboard • A device used to type letters, symbols, and numbers into the computer memory. The information is displayed on the monitor.

Memory • The chips in a computer that store information and programs.

Menu • A list of choices in a computer program.

Modem • (<u>mo</u>dulator <u>dem</u>odulator) A device used to send computer information over telephone lines.

Monitor • A video screen that displays information from a computer.

Mouse • A hand-controlled device that moves the computer's cursor across the screen and sends commands to the computer when it is clicked.

Printer • A machine that can make a paper copy (also called a "hard copy") of information from a computer.

Program • A set of instructions for a computer to follow.

Save • To copy a file onto a disk or hard drive for storage.

Word Processing Program • A special computer program for writing, revising, editing, and printing files.

Computer Keyboard

You can practice keyboarding right on this page! The hands on the opposite page show you which fingers to use on the different keys. To get started, place your fingers on the home row of keys. (The home row is the blue row of keys.)

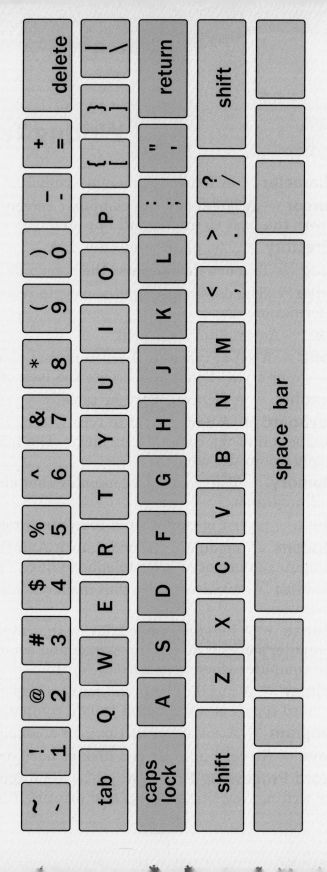

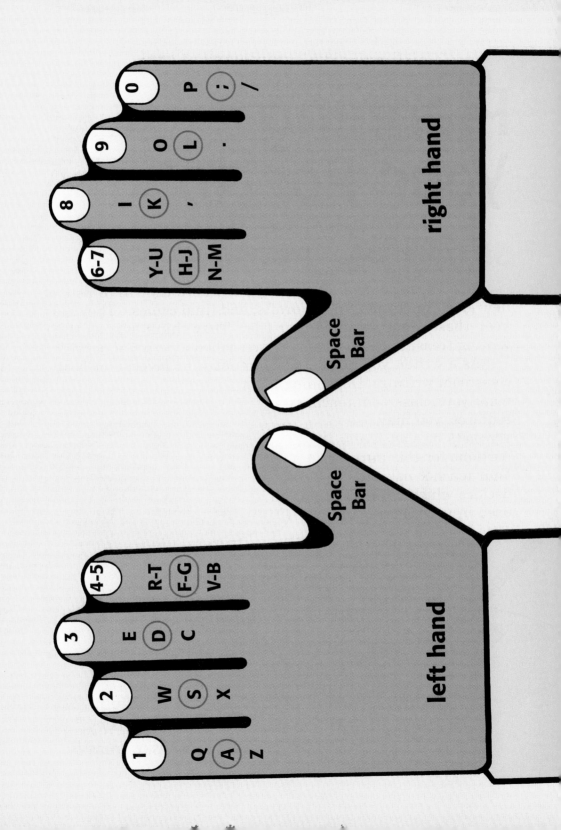

Planning Your Portfolio

Sharing Your Treasures

Most writers have a special place where they save lists of new ideas, quotations, early drafts, and final copies. They may keep these ideas in a folder or file. They think of it as their writing treasure chest. This is often called a *personal portfolio*.

As a writer, you need a place to put your favorite or best classroom writing. Depending upon what your classroom teacher requires, you may use a *growth* or a *showcase* portfolio for this purpose. Your teacher usually decides which one will be used in your classroom.

"Writing is a way of expressing yourself. It is a way of passing on stories and history."
—CHRIS CERNANSKY, STUDENT

Personal Portfolios

A personal portfolio is a collection you keep for yourself. It may have different sections like the ones listed below.

New Ideas ● In this part of your portfolio, you can collect interesting thoughts and descriptions of things you have seen. These can be written on notebook paper or even on a dinner napkin! This section is a good place for writing ideas.

Important Drafts ● This section includes writing projects that aren't finished—prewriting activities and first drafts you want to save. You can keep them here until you are ready to write the final drafts.

Writing Just for Me ● The writing in this section may never get published. It includes personal letters and special pages from your journal or writing notebook. Sometimes ideas for new writing projects come to you as you reread this section.

Finished Writing ● This is the writing that is as good as you can make it. Some of this work has already been published or handed in. It's writing you want to save.

New Ideas

Important Drafts

Just for Me

Finished Writing

Express Yourself Accordion files, boxes, or folders work well for personal portfolios. You can decorate your portfolio with paintings, sketches, quotations, photos, or a collage.

Classroom Portfolios

There are different kinds of classroom portfolios. Two popular kinds are the *showcase portfolio* and the *growth portfolio.* Your teacher can help you decide which kind is right for you.

Showcase Portfolio

In a showcase portfolio, you show off your best work. Your best work may include writing that you like very much or writing that you worked especially hard on. Your teacher will help you, but in the end, it's important that you decide which pieces are your best.

Growth Portfolio

If you've ever looked at a photo album, you know that people change over time. Writing is like that. It changes as the writer changes. A growth portfolio contains writing you have done throughout the year. It shows how your writing changes from September to December to May. By the time you get to May, you may look back at your September writing and say, "Wow! Did I write that? Can that really be mine?"

> *"I used to think of writing as my most dreaded fear. Now it's what I look forward to. . . . When I look over my work, I feel honored that I wrote it."*
>
> —Kristen Tomlinson, student

Note There's a difference between a writing folder and a writing portfolio. A writing folder usually contains ALL the writing you've done. A portfolio is different. It is a group of writing samples you collect for a special purpose.

Five Tips for a Super Portfolio

1 ## Date everything.
This is very important, especially in a growth portfolio. Knowing when you wrote each piece will help you see how your writing has changed over time.

2 ## Keep your portfolio small, but not too small.
Adding a new sample of your writing every four to six weeks is usually about right for a growth portfolio. More samples than that can make your portfolio hard to manage, and fewer samples won't tell enough about you.

3 ## Attach a self-evaluation to every piece.
Besides telling what you like about the writing, mention one or two problems you had and how you solved them. Also give reasons for choosing each sample—it's fun for readers to know this information.

4 ## Write a letter of introduction.
Tell who you are and what kind of portfolio you've made. Suggest some things to look for, like interesting details, good spelling, strong voice, or humor.

5 ## Keep on schedule.
Do not wait until the night before your portfolio is due to quickly write eight pieces and throw them together. That would be like grabbing anything out of your closet to pack a suitcase. You won't like the result.

Think It Over

Portfolios, like the people who make them, are unique. Your portfolio will not look exactly like anyone else's—and that is a good thing. The writing you choose should tell the story of you, as a writer.

Prewriting and Drafting

Choosing a Subject

Find the "Write" Subject

Imagine that your teacher asks you to write about a memorable experience. You say to yourself, "No problem. I'll write about . . . " But then no ideas come to mind. So what do you do? You can choose from the following:

- **check** your journal or writer's notebook for ideas,

- **talk** about the assignment with your classmates and teacher, or

- **try** one or more of the activities listed in this chapter.

> "I like to write about something I know a lot about. Then I learn even more about it."
>
> **—KENDRICK PARKS, STUDENT**

Activities for Choosing a Subject

CLUSTERING Begin a cluster by writing a word or phrase connected with your assignment. Then list related words and ideas around it. Circle and connect new words as shown here:

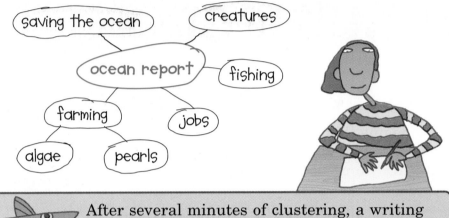

Note After several minutes of clustering, a writing idea or two may begin to take shape. Pick one of those ideas and freewrite about it.

FREEWRITING Choose an idea related to your assignment and write freely for 3 to 5 minutes. *Do not stop to make corrections or look up facts—just write.* As you write, one or two subjects may come to mind.

LISTING Freely list any ideas that pop into your head when you think of your assignment. Brainstorm with a classmate for an even longer list of subject ideas.

SENTENCE COMPLETION Complete a sentence starter in as many ways as you can. Make sure that your sentence starter has something to do with your assignment. Here are some samples:

I remember when . . .   I really get excited when . . .
One thing I know about . . .   I just learned . . .
I wonder how . . .   School is . . .

USING A CHECKLIST Look at a checklist for possible subjects. A good place to start is this basics-of-life checklist:

agriculture	education	food	love
animals	energy	freedom	machines
art/music	environment	friends	money
books	exercise	health	plants
clothing	faith	housing	science/technology
community	family	laws	work/play

Here's how to use this checklist:

■ Choose one of the categories or groups. *(food)*

■ Decide how this category relates to your assignment. *(memorable experience)*

■ List possible subjects. *(my most memorable meal, a kitchen disaster, meeting a new friend in the cafeteria)*

MAKING A LIFE MAP Start your life map with your birth and work up to the present. Then choose the experiences you want to write about.

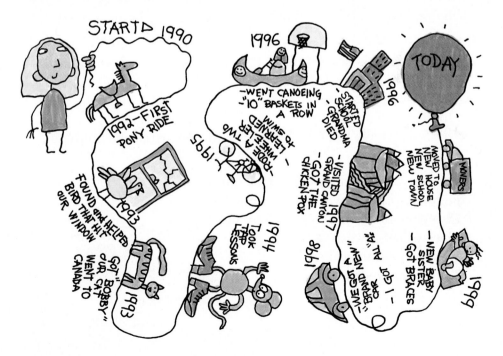

Sample Writing Subjects

When you need a subject or starting point for a writing assignment, check these pages for ideas.

Writing Prompts

The following prompts will be helpful when you are writing about a personal experience.

Best and Worst

My best day
A great memory
My worst moment
My biggest accomplishment
My saddest experience

It could only happen to me!

It sounds unbelievable, but . . .
I felt so foolish.
I looked everywhere for . . .
Why do I keep losing things?

What if . . . ?/Why?

What if animals could talk?
What if I had three wishes?
What if we have to move?
Why is it important to win?
Why do we have to go so fast?

First and Last

The first time I . . .
My last visit with . . .
My first goal
The last place I want to go
I like to be the last one . . .

I was just thinking . . .

I believe in . . .
I worry about . . .
Things that make me angry
Talk about being scared!

School Days

I've never worked so hard.
I'd like you to meet . . .
Where did I put my
   assignment?
My favorite school day is . . .

Quotations

"Be yourself. Who else is better qualified?"
"Following the crowd can lead nowhere."
"Everyone needs a place to hang out."
"More is not always better."
"We all make mistakes."
"Take life one day at a time."

Types of Writing

The following subjects are organized according to the four basic types of writing. They will be especially helpful when you need an idea for a specific kind of writing.

EXPOSITORY

How to . . . make a taco, care for a pet, simplify your life, earn extra money, get in shape, be a good friend, stop hiccups, run a race, saddle a horse, teach . . . , choose . . . , build . . . , fix . . . , grow . . . , save . . . , find . . .

The causes of . . . rust, acid rain, friendship, hurricanes, happiness

Kinds of . . . music, commercials, clouds, heroes, cars, pain, groups, restaurants, fun, streets, stores, books

The definition of . . . love, learning, a good time, friendship, a team, equality, a teacher, courage

PERSUASIVE

Issues: school rules, homework, recycling paper, bicycle safety, air bags, something that needs improving, something that's unfair, something everyone should see or do, something worth supporting

DESCRIPTIVE

People: a relative, a teacher, a classmate, a neighbor, yourself, someone you spend time with, someone you wish you were like

Places: your room, a garage, a basement, an attic, a rooftop, the alley, the gym, the library, a barn, a lake, a river, a yard, a park, the zoo, a museum

Objects or things: a poster, a stuffed animal, a video game, a book, a drawing, a junk drawer, a photograph, a letter, a pet, a souvenir, a model, a key, a dream, a Web site

NARRATIVE

Stories: getting caught, getting lost, getting together, making a mistake, being surprised, making the news, learning to . . . , being scared, winning

Finding a Form

Consider Your Audience

Finding the right *form* for your writing is just as important as finding the right subject. If, for example, you are asked to write about a serious topic, it would be a good idea to select a traditional essay or report form rather than a poem or tall tale.

Narrow Your Choices

When you are selecting a form, be sure to ask yourself who you're writing to (your audience) and why you're writing (your purpose). Then ask yourself which type of writing you need to do. Will you be telling a story *(narrative)*, explaining something *(expository)*, describing a person or thing *(descriptive)*, giving your opinion about something *(persuasive)*, or trying to learn something *(writing to learn)*? Then choose the form you think would work best.

> Your handbook is filled with nearly 50 different forms of writing. This chapter will help you find just the "write one."

Choose a Type of Writing

If you know which type of writing you will be doing, use the lists below to help you choose a specific form. (You can find models and guidelines for each form on the pages listed.)

Narrative To Tell a Story

Narrative Paragraphs (79)
Narrative Writing (106-111)
Writing in Journals (136)
Writing Personal Narratives (139-142)
Biographical Writing (152-155)
Writing Friendly Notes and Letters (144-145)
Writing Fantasies (210-214)
Writing Tall Tales (217-219)
Writing Realistic Stories (221-225)
Writing Stories from History (227-231)
Writing Plays (233-237)

Expository To Explain Something

Expository Paragraphs (76, 80, 340, 342)
Expository Essays (89-93)
How-To Writing (172-175)
Writing Social Notes (148-149)
Writing Newspaper Stories (160-162)
Writing Business Letters (177-180)
Writing Memos (182-183)
Writing a Summary (186-187)
Writing a Classroom Report (193-203)
Multimedia Computer Reports (205-207)
Writing a Speech (205-207, 312-317)
Writing Lists (96, 334, 339)

Descriptive To Describe Someone or Something

Persuasive To Express an Opinion

Think It Over

Writers often combine these general types when they write. In other words, **narrative** writing can be **descriptive, expository** writing can be **persuasive,** and so on.

Writing to Learn To Learn Something

Other Forms You Might Try

You can learn a lot about writing by experimenting with different forms. For example, by writing travelogues, you may learn how to write better descriptive paragraphs.

Anecdote • A little story used to make a point.

Bio-Poem • A poem about someone's life.

Cartoon • A simple drawing with a humorous message.

Commentary • A personal opinion about the state of the world around you.

Dramatic Monologue • A one-way conversation in which someone tells a lot about him- or herself.

E-Mail (electronic mail) • A message sent between two people using computers.

News Release • An explanation of a newsworthy event using the 5 W's.

Oral History • Writing down tape-recorded or filmed conversation about an earlier time period.

Parody • A funny imitation of a serious piece of writing.

Pet Peeve • A personal feeling about something that really bugs you.

Petition • A formal request addressed to someone in power.

Profile • A detailed report about a person.

Proposal • Writing that asks for approval of an idea, a report, or a schedule.

Time Capsule • Writing that captures a particular time period.

Travelogue • Writing that describes a trip or travel pictures (slides, video, film).

Gathering Details and Making a Plan

Think Ahead

Once you have chosen a subject, it's time to gather details and make a plan for your writing. Here are some basic ways to do both:

- write down your thoughts,
- research your subject,
- develop a writing plan, and
- organize your details.

Some writing forms, like reports, call for lots of gathering and planning. Others, like friendly letters or journal entries, come from details you have in your memory, and take less planning.

Write Down Your Thoughts

To gather thoughts about your subject, try one or more of the following strategies:

Listing ● Make a list of any ideas that pop into your head as you think of your subject.

Freewriting ● Write freely for at least 5 to 10 minutes, exploring your subject in as many different ways as you can. (Don't forget to include personal experiences.)

5 W's of Writing ● Answer the 5 W's—*Who? What? When? Where?* and *Why?*—to collect information about your subject.

Focused Thinking ● To think carefully about a subject, write freely about it in two or three of the following ways:

Describe it.	**What do you see, hear, feel, smell, taste?**
Compare it.	**What is it like? What is it different from?**
Apply it.	**What can you do with it? How can you use it?**
Break it down.	**What are its parts? How do they work?**

Subject Talk ● Make up a dialogue in which two people (real or imaginary) talk about your subject. Keep the conversation going as long as you can.

Crazy Questions ● To help you see your subject in a new way, try answering questions like these:

Writing About a Person
What type of clothing is this person like?
Which city or place should this person visit?

Writing About a Place
What does this place like to do?
What song does it like?

Writing About a Thing
What does this thing do on weekends?
What does it look like upside down?

Research Your Subject

Sometimes you will need to gather facts from other resources. This is especially important for essays and reports.

Reading ● Learn facts and details by reading about your subject in books, encyclopedias, and magazines.

Viewing and Listening ● Watch TV programs, on-line sources, and videos about your subject.

Surfing ● Explore the Internet for up-to-date information.

Using a Gathering Grid ● Use a gathering grid like the one below to keep track of all of your gathering notes. (**SEE** the finished gathering grid in "Writing a Classroom Report," page 195.)

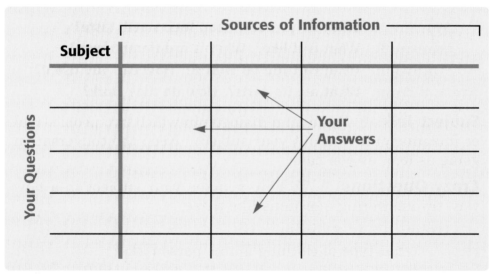

Talk to Others

Here are some person-to-person ways to gather facts:

Interviewing ● Ask someone questions about your subject.

Discussing ● Talk with classmates, teachers, or other people who know about your subject.

Develop a Writing Plan

Once you have picked your subject and gathered your details, it's time to develop a writing plan. Successful sports teams start out with a game plan. It helps them to focus and stay organized throughout the game. A writing plan can help you do the same thing with your writing. Here's a plan:

Subject: **Who or what am I writing about?**

Purpose: **Why am I writing? (To explain? To describe?)**

Form: **What form will I use (poem, letter, play)?**

Audience: **Who are my readers?**

Voice: **How should my writing sound (serious, funny, friendly, informative)?**

A Sample Plan

Imagine that you must write an essay for school. Here is one way to use the plan:

Subject: creatures in the ocean

Purpose: to report information

Form: observation report

Audience: classmates

Voice: informative, serious

Find a Focus

When you have finished your plan, you will probably have a focus in mind. A focus is the most important or interesting part of your subject—it should be specific. (**SEE** page 77.)

Subject: **Creatures in the ocean**

Specific Focus: **Seeing ocean creatures from a submersible**

Focus Statement: **From our submersible, we saw a whole world of ocean creatures.**

Organize Your Details

Once you have a plan and a clear focus, it's time to organize your details. Graphic organizers can help you gather and organize details for writing.

Detail Diagram

Collect and organize details for informational paragraphs and essays. (**SEE** pages 76, 80, and 91.)

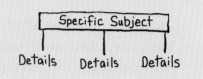

Sensory Lists

Collect ideas for descriptions and narratives. (**SEE** pages 101, 104, 110, 189, and 334.)

Venn Diagram

Collect details for two subjects you are comparing. (**SEE** pages 92-93 and 335.)

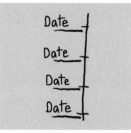

Time Line

List details in chronological order (according to time) for essays and reports. (**SEE** pages 437 and 478-487.)

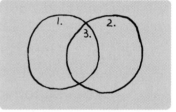

Cluster

Add and connect ideas about the subject that you want to explore. (**SEE** pages 13, 193, and 334.)

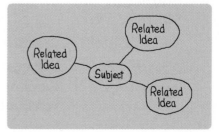

Outline

An outline arranges information from general to specific. A *topic outline* contains only words and phrases. (See the sample below that is based on the first draft on pages 51-53.) If you want to include more detail, write a *sentence outline*. (**SEE** page 197.)

Sample Topic Outline

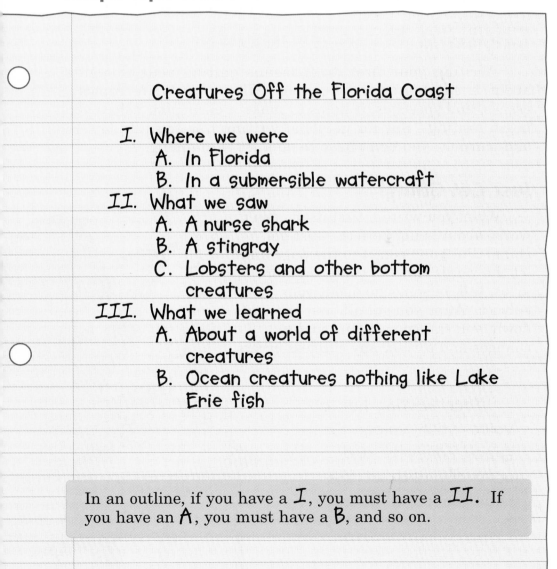

Creatures Off the Florida Coast

  I. Where we were
    A. In Florida
    B. In a submersible watercraft
 II. What we saw
    A. A nurse shark
    B. A stingray
    C. Lobsters and other bottom creatures
III. What we learned
    A. About a world of different creatures
    B. Ocean creatures nothing like Lake Erie fish

In an outline, if you have a I, you must have a II. If you have an A, you must have a B, and so on.

Writing a First Draft

Capture Your Thoughts

Writing your first draft means getting your thoughts about a subject down on paper. When you write reports, essays, and speeches, it helps to make a clear plan before you begin writing. But for personal writing like friendly letters and journals, you don't have to do a lot of planning.

Just Get Going!

When you write a first draft, don't worry about being perfect. Just get going. Put your pencil to the page and let the words flow. If you need more ideas, talk to someone about your subject. After you get all your thoughts down, you can go back and make changes and correct any careless errors.

Your writing has a voice—your voice. So speak honestly and naturally and let the real you come through.

The Parts of a First Draft

Writing a first draft is a time for getting your ideas on paper. Unless you know a lot about a subject, you will have to find plenty of facts before you start writing. Also keep your main point or focus in mind. Here are some tips.

- Plan a beginning, a middle, and an ending for your writing.
- Use a plan as a general guide, but add ideas as you go along.
- Wait until later to check for mistakes—your first draft doesn't have to be perfect.

Writing the Beginning

When you are writing a story, an essay, or a report, you need to plan an opening paragraph. Here are some ways to begin.

- Begin with an interesting fact about the subject.
- Introduce one of the main points you plan to cover.
- Start with a question.
- Use a quotation from someone.
- ✔ Share a brief story.

> Believe it or not, I once dove into water full of sharks. But I wasn't a bit afraid. That's because I was inside a submersible watercraft with my dad and a guide. It was connected to the surface by a cable and an air hose. I had a chance to do this when I was visiting my grandparents in Florida. I'll never forget the sights of this underwater wonderland.

Developing the Middle Part

The middle part of your draft should include specific details about your subject. Here are some ways to do that.

Explain: Support your main ideas with information.

Define: Give the meanings of important terms.

Argue: Use facts and examples to prove something is true or false.

Describe: Share specific details about the subject.

Compare: Use examples to show how two things are alike.

Contrast: Use examples to show how two things are different.

It got dark as we dove down, and the lights on our craft lit up the sea. What a scene we saw. Brilliant-colored fish—small and large—were darting in front of the thick glass window. A nurse shark bumped into the window with a thud, and a huge stingray floated gently along. I kept looking for an octopus! Lobsters and other bottom dwellers skittered away. With the help of our guide, we wrote the names of all the creatures and fish we could recognize. We listed 27 in all.

Tip Try developing your subject in more than one way. For example, in the paragraph above, the writer did some explaining and some describing.

Writing the Ending

The ending of your draft is important because it is your reader's last look at your ideas. Here are some ways to end your writing.

- Remind your reader of the main idea.
- Write a summary of all the main points.
- Say something to keep your reader thinking about the topic.

From our submersible, we saw a whole world of ocean creatures. There were strange kinds of animals and plants that most people never see. Some of the creatures were weird looking. They were nothing like the fish we see in Lake Erie. I would recommend a dive under the ocean for anyone who gets a chance.

Some Special Drafting Tips

If you are having trouble

- **getting started** . . . try talking through your writing as if you were telling a story. You can even make a tape recording to hear how it sounds.
- **keeping your writing going** . . . write for short periods of time. Just keep writing for three minutes at a time. See what happens.
- **ending your writing** . . . wait for a while. Then read through the writing you have done. This fresh look at your writing may give you an idea for your ending.

Revising and Editing

Revising Your Writing

Smile!

Ever see yourself in a photograph and say, "Yikes! Look at that weird expression on my face"? You wish you could fix that expression—or at least put a smile on your face. But the photo has been snapped, and you are frozen in time.

Take Your Time

Unlike a photograph, writing is not created in an instant. In the hands of a good writer, it changes over time. In fact, writing is more like painting a picture. You can keep adding colors and shapes until it looks just right. Changing writing—*revising*—means adding a bit here, taking off a bit there, and moving things around until the piece turns into something great—an essay, a poem, a mystery, a story, or a biography for someone to read and enjoy.

> "Writing a story takes time and energy, but it feels really good when it's done."
>
> **—LAUREN BRYDON, STUDENT**

What Is Revising?

Revising simply means *changing* and *improving*. In writing, revising includes changes like these:

- adding details,
- changing the order of sentences or paragraphs,
- taking out information you do not need, and
- rewriting something that is not clear.

How to Get Started

When your first draft is done, you're ready to revise. Here are some ideas to get you off to a good start.

Read and share. Read your rough draft aloud to yourself. Then read it to one or two classmates. Jot down any ideas or questions that come up during this sharing session. (Use the response sheet on page 63.)

Take a break. This step is easy! Put your rough draft in a folder for a while. Later, when you read it again, changes will occur to you that you did not think of before.

What to Look For

Look for the strong parts. Always find one or two things you like in your draft. You may like a portion of dialogue or a certain descriptive sentence. Put a star next to these parts. It's good for the spirit.

Look for the weak parts. Also look for parts that need work. Important details may be missing, or your sentences may sound confusing. (The checklist on the next page will help you revise your work.)

Revising Checklist

Use this checklist either by yourself or with classmates.

✔ **Did I follow a writing plan?**

___ Did I use a graphic organizer or an outline?

___ Did I have a clear purpose (to explain, to describe, to persuade, to tell a story)?

___ Did I keep my audience in mind?

✔ **Do I need to add information?**

___ Is my topic sentence strong, clearly stating my main idea?

___ Did I choose details that will help the reader understand my idea or story?

___ Did I answer the important questions about this subject?

✔ **Do I need to cut any information?**

___ Did I tell so much that my writing lost its focus?

___ Did I repeat information?

___ Did I include information not related to my subject?

✔ **Do I need to rewrite some parts?**

___ Will my beginning get the reader's attention?

___ Are any of my ideas unclear?

___ Did I show, not just tell? (**SEE** page 58.)

___ Will my ending give the reader something to think about?

✔ **Do I need to reorder any parts?**

___ Did I tell things in an order that makes sense? (**SEE** pages 19 and 59 for ideas on organizing writing.)

___ Does my most important point stand out?

Tips to Make Your Writing Stronger

1 Show, don't tell.

When you help readers feel, hear, smell, taste, or see things through your writing, you are "showing" them a clear picture of your subject.

■ **Showing:** In *Charlotte's Web*, author E. B. White describes the barn where Wilbur the pig and his spider friend, Charlotte, live. White used *showing* details to place his readers right there with Charlotte and Wilbur:

> **It smelled of hay and it smelled of manure. It smelled of the perspiration of tired horses and the wonderful sweet breath of patient cows . . . And whenever the cat was given a fish head to eat, the barn would smell of fish.**

■ **Telling:** If the author had decided to tell, not show, his description might have sounded more like this:

> **The barn was full of interesting smells of many kinds. The smells came from all the animals and things in the barn.**

2 Choose details that paint a picture.

Always make sure you have included enough details in your writing.

■ This passage shows details that bring the game to life.

> **It rained so hard in the last inning of the game, we were soaked to our underwear. When their team's best batter launched a mighty hit, our right fielder slugged through ankle-deep mud and snagged a ball none of us could even see! We forgot our wet hair and let out a thunderous cheer. We had won 8 to 7.**

■ This passage tells just the "basics" about a baseball game.

> **Our baseball game was fun. It rained. We won.**

3 Put some power into the beginning, middle, and ending.

Your writing should be clear and complete from start to finish—from the beginning, through the middle, to the ending!

■ **Beginning:** The beginning must get your reader's attention and also give a hint about what's coming.

> **"Listen everybody. Let's keep our buses clean."**

■ **Middle:** The middle is your chance to put in the interesting details that answer a reader's questions. Stick to the point. All the ideas in the middle (body) should support or explain your subject.

> **How will we keep the buses clean?**
> **Who will help?**
> **When will we begin?**

■ **Ending:** Don't just say, "The End." That's boring! Leave your reader with an interesting thought or question to ponder.

> **"I've seen too many gum wrappers, paper wads, and old tissues, thank you! I hope you have, too."**

4 Add a snappy title.

A good title makes your reader curious about your subject. Compare these titles and ask yourself, "Which one grabs my attention?"

Facts on Ants	**or**	**Big Brains in Tiny Bodies**
Holiday Disaster	**or**	**Cookies Can Be Dangerous**
A Day I'll Remember	**or**	**Swimming with Sharks!**

Revising with Partners

Share and Learn

Sooner or later, writers need a real audience—someone to listen to what they've written. Do you ever nudge your friend at school and say, "Hey, Josh, listen to this"? Or at home, do you ever ask your mom or dad what they think of your writing? If you do, you are acting like a real author.

Getting Started

When you share your writing, you give others a chance to react to your work. Their responses may please you or surprise you. Either way, they can help you turn your first draft into a great piece of writing that people will want to read.

> "I was happy when I heard my suggestions for revising in Noah's final writing."
>
> **—RAMA PATEL, STUDENT**

Why Writers Share

Except for journals, diaries, and other personal writing, most writing is done for an audience. So it's very important for a writer to know how a real audience will react. It helps when a writer works with a partner to find answers to questions like these:

- Will my readers understand my words and ideas?
- Will they think the "funny" parts really are funny?
- Will they have any questions?

What Partners Do

The partner's main jobs are (1) to listen carefully, (2) to offer encouragement, and (3) to give advice. Good writing partners

- **point out parts of the writing that they feel are strong,**
- **ask questions about anything that is unclear, and**
- **give honest answers to the writer's questions.**

How to Help One Another

Partners can help you throughout the writing process. Their advice is really important when you are ready to revise your writing. Partners can help you find the parts that work well in your writing, as well as the parts that don't work so well.

Writing partners can also help you when you are ready to edit and proofread your work. They will often catch the spelling or grammar errors that you miss.

Note Partners should not "fix" a paper the way an auto mechanic fixes a car. Partners should give suggestions for improving your writing, but it is up to you, the writer, to decide what changes to make.

Guidelines for Sharing Writing

During sharing time, authors take turns reading their drafts aloud. Partners listen, and sometimes they take notes or use response sheets (next page).

Tips for the Writer

- Come prepared with a draft you want to revise.
- Practice reading your draft out loud so that you can read it smoothly.
- Speak slowly and clearly. Don't rush.
- Ask questions like "Does my beginning get your attention?" "Does this title fit my story?"
- Listen to your partner's comments and suggestions.

Tips for the Partner

- Listen carefully.
- Point out what you like about the writing.
- Ask about anything you do not understand, such as a word you don't know or a sentence that seems out of place.
- Be kind and polite. (Sharing makes some people nervous.)
- Make suggestions in a thoughtful way.

   Don't say, "Your writing is boring!"

   Do say, "I want to know more about that scary bear."

Express Yourself Compliments are great. However, specific compliments work best. "Good job, Scott!" makes Scott feel good. But it's more helpful to say, "That description of your dog Charlie bumping into the post was crystal clear!"

Sample **Response Sheet**

A partner can help a writer with revising by filling out a response sheet like this one.

Response Sheet

I noticed these strong parts in your writing . . .

I liked this part of your writing . . .

Here's an idea to make your writing better . . .

Editing and Proofreading

Polish Your Writing

Editing and proofreading are the steps you take to get your writing ready to share or publish. Remember, editing and proofreading should be done only *after* you have revised the main ideas (content) of your first draft.

Make Every Word Count!

The guidelines in this chapter will help you check your writing for style and correctness. All of your sentences should read smoothly, and they should be free of careless errors. Learn to make every word count in your writing.

> "I think about what I write and put great care into picking the words I use."
>
> **—CATHERINE FERRANTE, STUDENT**

Checking for Smooth Sentences

Combine sentences. If you use too many short sentences one after another, your writing may sound choppy. You can correct this problem by combining some of your sentences.

Short sentences: **The dog followed Mary.**
She stayed calm.

Combined with a conjunction:
The dog followed Mary, but she stayed calm.

Change sentence beginnings. If too many of your sentences begin in the same way, your writing may sound boring. You can correct this problem by changing the way you start some of your sentences.

Three sentences beginning with the subject "I":
I slowly ate the eggplant. I washed it down with milk to cover the taste. I tried to hide it when my mom wasn't looking.

How to Change Sentence Beginnings

Start with a modifier:
Slowly, I ate the eggplant.

Start with a phrase:
To cover the taste, I washed it down with milk.

Start with a clause:
When my mom wasn't looking, I tried to hide it.

Correct sentence errors. There are three basic sentence errors to watch out for in your writing: *sentence fragments, run-on sentences,* and *rambling sentences.* (**SEE** page 115.)

Checking for Word Choice

Use powerful verbs. As writer Will Hobbs says, "Verbs power sentences, making them fly or jump or sink or swim." They help make your ideas come to life for your readers. Here are two sentences from *Bearstone* by Will Hobbs. The powerful verbs (in red type) give a clear picture of the action.

> **The big fish flip-flopped against Cloyd's leg. He nudged it back into the water with his foot, then leaped across the Rincon stream.**

Use specific nouns. Some nouns like *car, fruit, flower, store,* and *candy* are general and don't give readers a clear picture. Other nouns like *minivan, kiwi, sunflower, food court,* and *peppermint* are specific and give readers a much clearer picture. Always try to use specific nouns in your writing.

Choose colorful modifiers. Well-chosen adjectives and adverbs add color to your writing.

> **Using adjectives: She wandered into the deep shade of the giant cottonwoods.** (The adjectives *deep* and *giant* make the picture clearer.)
>
> **Using adverbs: Rover ran wildly after Tim, who headed directly for the house.** (The adverbs *wildly* and *directly* add to the action.)

Helpful Hint: Modifiers are very important, but be careful not to overuse them. Too many adjectives and adverbs can make your writing sound artificial.

Select the right word. Make sure that the words you use in your writing are correct. For example, it's easy to confuse words that sound the same—*there, their,* and *they're; know* and *no.* (**SEE** pages 402-411 for a list of words that are often confused.)

Editing and Proofreading Checklist

Use this checklist when you edit and proofread your writing.

✔ Sentence Fluency

___ Did I write clear and complete sentences?
___ Did I write sentences of different lengths?
___ Did I begin my sentences in different ways?

✔ Word Choice and Usage

___ Did I use powerful verbs, specific nouns, and colorful modifiers?
___ Did I use the correct word (*to, too,* or *two*)? (**SEE** pages 402-411.)
___ Did I use subjects and verbs that agree in number? (**SEE** pages 116 and 413.)

✔ Punctuation

___ Did I end sentences with correct punctuation marks?
___ Did I use commas in a series (*Larry, Moe, and Curly*)?
___ Did I place commas before coordinating conjunctions (*and, but, or, so, yet*) in compound sentences?
___ Did I punctuate dialogue correctly? (**SEE** pages 378, 379, and 386.)

✔ Capitalization

___ Did I start each of my sentences with a capital letter?
___ Did I capitalize the names of specific people, places, and things?

✔ Spelling

___ Did I check for spelling errors (including the ones my computer spell checker could have missed)? (**SEE** pages 398-401.)

Publishing Your Writing

"Attention, Please!"

Publishing is a very important part of the writing process. It lets other people read and listen to your ideas. And it can make all of your planning, drafting, and revising worth the effort.

You can publish your writing in many different ways. Reading a finished story to your classmates is one way. Selecting a poem for your classroom portfolio is another way. This chapter offers you a choice of more than 30 ways to publish your writing.

> Publishing gives a writer a special reason to work hard and produce something to be very proud of.

Publishing Tips

Publishing is the final step of the writing process. It gives others a chance to read and enjoy your writing. The following list will help you prepare for that final step.

Think of your purpose and audience. When you are getting ready to publish your writing, you must keep your purpose and audience in mind.

- If you are writing to your grandfather to make him laugh, send one of your funny poems or stories.
- If you are sending an e-mail to a friend, make sure you follow the e-mail form on your screen. (**SEE** pages 146-147.)
- If you are choosing a writing sample for your portfolio, use the directions set up by your teacher to prepare the piece properly.

Present a neat finished piece. Remember, a clear final copy makes your writing attractive and easy to read.

- If you are doing a handwritten piece, use blue or black ink and write on one side of the paper.
- If you are composing on a computer, use fonts that are easy to read. (Don't get too fancy!) Also, leave one-inch margins on the top, bottom, and sides of the paper.
- If you are adding art, photos, or other graphics, be sure they are large enough for the reader to understand and enjoy.

Check for style and correctness. Use the checklist on page 67. Then, if possible, have at least one trusted person check your work before you hand it in or send it.

Follow all publication guidelines. Be sure to follow your teacher's directions for final drafts. If you are entering a writing contest or sending your writing to a magazine, follow the directions given by the publisher.

Send It

Greeting cards

Letters to public figures

Requests for information

Thank-you letters to field-trip guides, bus drivers, and so on

Letters that complain about or praise a product or service

Letters to pen pals in other schools, towns, or countries

Notes or memos to parents about school activities

Web It

See the Internet chapter, pages 264-269, to find more details about publishing on-line.

On-line magazines

Writing contests

Favorite Web sites

E-mail connections

E-pals

Bulletin board postings

Perform It

Plays for school and community audiences

Puppet shows

Radio broadcasts over the school public-address system

Talking books for the visually impaired

Tape-recorded or videotaped interviews

New words for familiar music

Presentations at PTA or school board meetings

Introductions of guests at assemblies

Videotaped documentaries for local TV stations

Print It

All-school or classroom anthologies

Stories for doctors' waiting rooms

Manuals on how to do certain things

School-survival guides for younger students

Programs for school productions

Newspaper reports about class trips or projects

Brochures for local travel agencies

Fliers for area chamber of commerce

Submit It

Many magazines and Web sites feature student writing. Write to or e-mail one that you think might publish your work. Ask your teacher or librarian for help.

Owl

Topics: Environment/Science/Nature

Forms: Letters, drawings, poetry, short short stories

Address: *Owl*, Editor
179 John St., Suite 500
Toronto, Ontario
CANADA M5T 3G5

E-mail: <tamara@cow.on.ca>

Creative Kids

Topics: Writing/Art/Photography

Forms: Essays, short stories, games, fiction, riddles, poems, true stories

Address: *Creative Kids*
Submissions Editor
P.O. Box 8813
Waco, TX 76714

Include an S.A.S.E. (self-addressed stamped envelope).

Skipping Stones

Topics: Multicultural/Nature

Forms: Fiction, songs, games, true stories, poems, essays, nonfiction, personal responses to current events

Address: *Skipping Stones*, Editor
P.O. Box 3939
Eugene, OR 97403

E-mail: <skipping@esn.org>

Web: <www.nonviolence.org/skipping>

Highlights for Children

Topics: General

Forms: Fiction, poems, true stories, letters to the editor

Address: Children's Mail
803 Church Street
Honesdale, PA 18431

Midlink

(on-line publishing)

Topics: Monthly Thematic Projects/Illustration

Forms: stories, essays

Web: <longwood.cs.ucf.edu/~Midlink/>

Stone Soup

Topics: Writing/Art

Forms: Stories, poems

Address: *Stone Soup*, Editor
P.O. Box 83
Santa Cruz, CA 95063

Web: <www.stonesoup.com>

KidNews

(on-line publishing)

Topics: Writing

Forms: Reviews, profiles, features, creative writing, sports, news

Web: <www.kidnews.com>

Bind It

To make your own book, follow these six basic steps. Be sure to add your own personal touches as you put your book together.

 Put the pages to be bound in order. Add extra pages for  titles, table of contents, and so on.

 **2** Staple or sew the pages together.

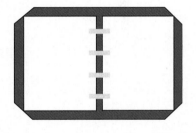

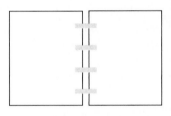

3 Cut two pieces of cardboard 1/4 inch larger than the page size. Tape them together.

4 Place the cardboard on cover material (cloth or contact paper). Turn the edges of the material over the cardboard.

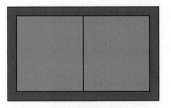

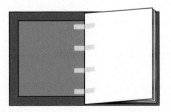

5 Attach construction paper or contact paper to the inside of the book cover.

6 Fasten the bound pages of the book into the cover with tape. Cover the tape.

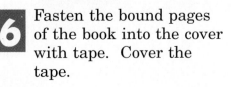

Building Paragraphs and Essays

Writing Paragraphs

What Is a Paragraph?

A paragraph is a group of sentences that tells about one subject or idea. Each sentence in a paragraph must give information about the topic. Also, the sentences must be in the right order, so your readers can understand the information. A good paragraph presents a complete and interesting picture.

Learning to write good paragraphs will help you write good essays, stories, letters, and other forms of writing.

Four main reasons for writing paragraphs are to describe, to tell a story, to explain, or to persuade.

The Parts of a Paragraph

A paragraph has three parts. The *topic sentence* states the main idea. The sentences in the *body* of the paragraph are all connected to the main idea. The *closing sentence* sums up the paragraph's message.

Sample **Paragraph**

The Topic Sentence

The Body

The Closing Sentence

Trees may be the most important form of plant life on earth. Trees add beauty to the landscape and give shelter to wildlife. Tree roots prevent soil erosion and help store water. Different types of trees provide wood, paper, food, medicines, and other useful products. Though it is something you cannot see, one of the most important things trees do is help clean the air. Trees absorb carbon dioxide and produce oxygen. And it's oxygen that people need to breathe. People can thank trees for a lot more than shade!

A Closer Look at the Parts

The Topic Sentence

The *topic sentence* tells the reader what the paragraph is about. A good topic sentence does two things: (1) it names the subject, and (2) it gives the focus or main point.

Formula: **An interesting subject**
            + a specific focus or main point
            = a good topic sentence

Topic Sentence:

Trees (an interesting subject) **may be the most important form of plant life on earth** (a specific focus).

The Body

The sentences in the *body* include the information or details the reader needs in order to understand the topic. The following sentences include plenty of specific details.

Trees add beauty to the landscape and give shelter to wildlife. Tree roots prevent soil erosion and help store water. Different types of trees provide wood, paper, food, medicines, and other useful products. . . .

Organize your sentences in the best possible order. There are three main ways to organize your sentences: *time order, order of location,* and *order of importance.* (**SEE** page 84.)

The Closing Sentence

The *closing sentence* reminds readers of the topic or sums up the information in the paragraph.

Closing Sentence:

People can thank trees for a lot more than shade!

Types of Paragraphs

There are four kinds of paragraphs.

- To describe something, write a **descriptive** paragraph.
- To tell a story, write a **narrative** paragraph.
- To explain something, write an **expository** paragraph.
- To express your opinion, write a **persuasive** paragraph.

Sample Descriptive Paragraph

In a **descriptive** paragraph, you describe a person, a place, a thing, or an idea. When you write a descriptive paragraph, use words related to the five senses. Tell your audience about the colors, smells, and sounds related to the subject. This will help your readers feel as if they are right there with you.

The topic sentence sets the scene.

Details give smells, sights, and sounds.

The best details are saved for last.

A few blocks from my city neighborhood, there's a tree that I love to visit. Whenever I ride my bike closer to the woods, I can see the tree towering above the others. I can smell the moss and ferns growing under its branches. My tree's trunk is so wide around, I can't reach my arms around it! Its bark forms funny patterns as it crawls up the tree, and the tips of its branches reach for the sky. On a windy day, small branches crack and break off as the leaves rustle together. I often sit under this tree, watching the squirrels and listening to the birds. I love my tree.

Sample **Narrative Paragraph**

In a **narrative** paragraph, you tell a story about a personal experience. Try to pull your readers into the story and keep them wondering what will happen next. Be sure to include enough details to make your experience come to life.

The topic sentence introduces all the characters.

Details give the story suspense.

The closing sentence sums up the story.

Last Tuesday, I invited Danny, Julio, Renatta, and Mishiko to ride over to climb my favorite oak tree. We've all climbed the tree together before, but this time we decided to see who could climb the highest. Julio and Renatta climbed a little bit higher than usual, and I climbed almost to the end of one huge branch. Mishiko climbed even higher than I did, but it was Danny who won our little contest. Unfortunately, I don't think he realized how high he had climbed, until he looked down. He froze. He clung to the branch he was on and was afraid to climb down. What if he had to stay up in the tree all night? Renatta took off on her bike to tell her mom. Her mom called the fire department. An engine with an extension ladder, sirens and all, arrived to rescue Danny. It was very exciting, and we all sure learned a lesson that day!

Note To be sure you have included all the important details in your narrative paragraph, ask the following questions: *Who? What? When? Where? Why? How?*

Sample Expository Paragraph

Your main purpose in an **expository** paragraph is to give information about a subject. You may give directions, present ideas, or explain how to do something. An expository paragraph uses transition words such as *first, then, after,* and *finally.*

The topic sentence states the subject.

The details are listed in the order they happened.

The closing sentence explains that the project was completed.

This summer, my four friends and I put up a tree house. Our parents helped us plan and gave us a hand with the building. Our first step was to agree on a design for the tree house. Then we had to buy materials. We made a list of places that carried building supplies, took the money we had saved, and went shopping. After that we took all our purchases to the oak tree and got to work! First, we used a rope to raise the wood up into the tree. Next, our parents helped us make a frame for the floor. We nailed boards to the frame. Then the walls and roof went up. Finally, to celebrate, we had a picnic in our new tree house!

Think It Over

Before you begin writing, it's helpful to list the facts or examples you are going to include in your paragraph. That way, you can put your supporting ideas into the best possible order before you begin.

Sample Persuasive Paragraph

In a **persuasive** paragraph, you give your opinion on a subject and try to get your reader to agree with you. Always give facts and examples to back up your opinion. Otherwise, you won't *persuade,* or convince, your readers.

The topic sentence states an opinion.

The body gives reasons.

The closing restates the opinion.

Kids need a place to call their own, and a tree house is the perfect place. A tree house gives my friends and me a chance to get away from the pressures of school, homework, and little brothers or sisters. We can decorate our tree house any way we want. (I like bright green and orange paint myself.) We can express ourselves! A tree house is a good place for thinking, playing music, looking at the sky, or just being with friends. Sure, if we didn't have this kind of place, we'd find other ways to amuse ourselves. We'd go to the mall or the arcade, play video games at home, or just veg out in front of the TV. But doesn't a tree house sound like a better place for kids to spend their time?

Express Yourself Read your paragraph out loud so that you can listen for missing information. Also turn to page 347 in your handbook for more ideas about using facts and opinions in your writing.

Writing a Paragraph

Prewriting Planning Your Paragraph

■ Even before you choose a subject, ask these questions:

Subject:	*Who or what will I write about?*
Purpose:	*What part of my subject will I focus on?*
Audience:	*Who will be reading my paragraph?*
Form:	*What kind of paragraph will work best?*

■ After you answer these questions, start gathering details.

For a . . .	you'll need . . .
descriptive paragraph	lots of details about how things look, sound, smell, feel, and so on.
narrative paragraph	details about an experience: how it began, problems that came up, how it ended.
expository paragraph	details that give information or explain the subject you're writing about.
persuasive paragraph	facts, figures, and examples to back up your opinion.

Writing the First Draft

Put your information in order. The topic sentence usually comes first. Next comes the body—the sentences that tell about the topic sentence. Your closing sentence should sum up the paragraph or tell what it means. (**SEE** pages 76-77 and 84.)

Revising Improving Your Paragraph

Read your paragraph as if you were reading it for the first time. Did you include details that support your topic sentence? Do your sentences read smoothly?

Adding Details

Details, facts, and examples bring a paragraph to life.

Personal Details

Many of the details you use in your paragraphs will be personal details—things you know from your own experience.

Details from Your Senses ● These are things that you see, hear, smell, taste, and touch. You will need a lot of these when writing a descriptive paragraph.

> On a windy day, small branches crack and break off as the leaves rustle together.

Details from Your Memory ● These details come from memories of things you've done and experienced. In descriptive and narrative writing, such details can bring the past to life. In an expository paragraph, they can help you explain how to do something.

> First, we used a rope to raise the wood up into the tree.

Details from Your Imagination ● These details are things you hope for, wish, and wonder about. Such details can make narrative paragraphs interesting and fun.

> What if he had to stay up in the tree all night?

Details from Other Sources

When you write a paragraph, use what you already know about the subject. Then add details from other sources.

- **Ask someone you know** for the answers you need—teachers, parents, neighbors, friends.
- **Ask an expert.** For example, if you are writing about the flu, you could talk to a doctor or a nurse.
- **Study resources** such as newspapers, magazines, books, and the Internet.
- **Write, call, or e-mail** companies or government offices.

Putting Things in Order

The sentences in the body of a paragraph must be organized so that readers can follow all of your ideas. Here are three ways to organize your sentences.

Time Order It is easy to follow ideas when the facts are explained in the order in which they happened. Time order works well in a narrative or an expository paragraph. You may use words like *first, next,* and *finally.*

> First, we used a rope to raise the wood up into the tree. Next, our parents helped us make a frame for the floor. We nailed boards to the frame. Then the walls and roof went up. Finally, to celebrate, we had a picnic in our new tree house!

Order of Location When details are described in the order in which they are located, the description usually goes from left to right or from top to bottom. Order of location works well in a descriptive or an expository paragraph. Use words and phrases like *above, around,* and *up* to guide your readers.

> My tree's trunk is so wide around, I can't reach my arms around it! Its bark forms funny patterns as it crawls up the tree, and the tips of its branches reach for the sky.

Order of Importance News stories are often organized in the order of importance. They tell the most important news first. Persuasive or expository paragraphs are also organized in this way, with the most important detail coming first or, sometimes, last.

> Kids need a place to call their own, and a tree house is the perfect place. A tree house gives my friends and me a chance to get away from the pressures of school, homework, and little brothers or sisters.

Transition Words

Words that can be used to show location:				
above	around	between	inside	outside
across	behind	by	into	over
against	below	down	near	throughout
along	beneath	in back of	off	to the right
among	beside	in front of	on top of	under

Words that can be used to show time:				
about	during	until	yesterday	finally
after	first	meanwhile	next	then
at	second	today	soon	as soon as
before	third	tomorrow	later	when

Words that can be used to compare things (show similarities):			
in the same way	likewise	as	while
similarly	like	also	

Words that can be used to contrast things (show differences):			
on the other hand	otherwise	but	although
even though	however	still	yet

Words that can be used to emphasize a point:			
again	for this reason	in fact	so

Words that can be used to add information:			
again	for instance	and	as well
also	besides	next	along with
another	for example	finally	in addition

Words that can be used to conclude or summarize:		
as a result	finally	in conclusion
therefore	lastly	in summary

Finding Paragraphs

You know how easy it is to go on and on when you have something important to say to one of your friends: "Guess what I did? . . ." Well, the same thing can happen when you are writing. You may start out writing a simple paragraph and end up filling a whole page or two with great ideas.

Keeping Your Ideas Together

When your writing goes on and on, make sure it is organized into paragraphs before you share it. Otherwise, your readers may have trouble following your ideas. The guidelines that follow will help you find the paragraphs in your writing.

Label . . . Name . . . Find

To find the paragraphs in longer pieces of writing, keep repeating these three steps—*label, name, find*—until you come to the end of your work.

1. **Label** the first word in your paper with a paragraph sign (¶).
2. **Name** the first main idea in your writing.
3. **Find** the first sentence that is *not* about this idea.

* * * * * *

1. **Label** that sentence (#3 above) with a paragraph sign (¶).
2. **Name** the main idea of this paragraph.
3. **Find** the first sentence that is *not* about this idea.

* * * * * *

Repeat this process until you reach the end of your paper.

My favorite

Since I moved . . .

I am now in . . .

Writing [Sample]

Here is part of an autobiography by student writer Elizabeth Hartfield. As you can see, it is not divided into paragraphs.

> My name is Elizabeth Frances Hartfield. I'm going to tell you about my life starting with the day something exciting and sad happened. What happened was that I moved from my home in Springfield to a house in West Chester. I was nervous and scared. I didn't think that I would make a lot of friends, but I did. Since I moved to West Chester, I have gone to three different schools. The first one I went to was Saints Simon and Jude. I went there for first and second grade. I went to Sacred Heart Academy in Bryn Mawr for third grade, and now I go to Villa Maria Academy. I am now in fourth grade. I like to draw a lot. On April 25, 1998, I won an award for a piece of artwork that I did. My favorite activities besides art are reading and dancing. . . .

Following the Three-Step Process

Finding the paragraphs in this autobiography is easy if you follow the three-step process:

1. **Label** the first word with a paragraph sign.
   ¶ "My name is . . . "
2. **Name** the main idea in the first paragraph.
   Moved from my home in Springfield
3. **Find** the first sentence that is *not* about this idea.
   "Since I moved to West Chester, . . . "
1. **Label** that sentence with a paragraph sign.
   ¶ "Since I moved to West Chester, . . . "
2. **Name** the main idea of this paragraph.
   Different schools I've attended in West Chester
3. **Find** the first sentence that is *not* about this idea.
   (See if you can find the last paragraph!)

Writing Expository Essays

Sharing Information

Sometimes one paragraph can't hold all the facts and information you want to share. For example, the ocean is a very large subject, and one paragraph could hold only a "drop or two" of information about it. When you have a lot of ideas to present, you can write an essay.

Essay Facts

The most common type of essay is the expository essay. Like a classroom report, it contains information about a subject. But an expository essay is usually shorter than a classroom report and may also include the writer's personal thoughts.

The purpose of writing an expository essay is to inform the readers about a specific subject.

Writing an Expository Essay

You'll use the same steps to write an essay as you do to write a paragraph. Here are the "ins and outs" of the process.

Prewriting Planning Your Essay

Subject ● First choose a general subject that interests you. For example, if you are interested in the ocean, you need to narrow this general subject to a more specific topic, such as *food from the ocean*.

Audience ● Ask yourself who will read your essay. How much will your readers already know? Thinking about your audience can help you choose the right details and the best words. (Are you writing for your classmates, an e-pal, or someone else?)

Voice ● Think about your subject and your audience to determine your voice. (Do you want to sound serious, funny, or somewhere in between?)

Prewriting Gathering Details

After choosing a subject, gather details from different sources.

Explore ● Do a freewriting, listing everything you already know about your subject.

Focus ● Look over your freewriting and decide which part of your subject you want to cover.

Gather ● Gather more information if necessary. (Remember, an essay is usually three to five paragraphs long.)

Organize ● Decide which details to include in your essay and how to organize them. (**SEE** pages 47-49.)

Writing the First Draft

Each part of your essay (beginning, middle, ending) has a special purpose.

Beginning ● Your first paragraph should say something interesting or surprising about your subject to get your readers involved. It should also name the specific subject, or focus, of your essay.

Middle ● The middle should include ideas (facts, figures, examples) that support your subject. This information must be clearly presented in one or more paragraphs.

Ending ● The final paragraph summarizes the main points covered in your essay. It reminds readers of the importance of your subject and helps them remember it better.

Revising and Editing *Improving Your Essay*

The following checklist will help you as you revise and edit your first draft.

- Does my title help identify my subject?
- Do I introduce my subject in an interesting way?
- Do I have enough details in the middle of my essay?
- Should I break the information in my essay into more paragraphs?
- Does my ending remind readers of the importance of my subject?
- Do I like the sound of my words and sentences?
- Did I check for errors?

Sample   **Expository Essay**

The following expository essay gives specific information about the ocean as a food source.

Food from the Ocean
by Keesha Brooks

Beginning
The writer focuses on a narrow topic.

When you look at a globe, you will see at least four different oceans. If you look closer, you will see that these oceans are connected. There is actually one big ocean. People all over the world depend on the ocean for salt and different kinds of food.

Salt is a mineral. It comes from the rocks in the ocean. As the waves, tides, and currents beat on the rocks, salt goes into the water. The salt that is in the ocean is the same kind of salt you put on your popcorn and french fries.

Middle
Basic facts are used to support the subject.

The salty water of the ocean is home to lots of fish. Some of the best fish for food are cod, tuna, shark, and sea bass. Crustaceans like crab, lobster, and shrimp are also favorite seafoods.

Did you know that you have probably eaten seaweed? Different kinds of ice cream and hot fudge have seaweed in them. It makes them smooth. Some people also eat seaweed as a vegetable. It can be served with rice or in stir-fried foods.

Ending
The main points are summarized.

Even if you've never seen an ocean, the ocean has come to you. Maybe you tasted it on a bowl of popcorn, as a fish dinner, or in the topping of a hot fudge sundae.

Using Comparison and Contrast

One of the most common types of expository essays is the comparison and contrast essay. To write this kind of essay, you need to make a plan and gather details just as you do for an expository essay. (**SEE** page 91.) You also need to use a graphic organizer to pull your ideas together. A Venn diagram works well for this purpose. (**SEE** pages 48 and 335.)

You can organize your details in a simple chart like the one below. (This chart was used to organize the details in the essay on the next page.) List facts about topic A on one side of the line, and facts about topic B on the other. Then circle the details that are similar on both sides, and check the differences.

A LAKE SUPERIOR	B GREAT SALT LAKE
(big lake)	(big lake)
✔ freshwater lake	✔ salt lake
✔ 350 miles long by 160 miles wide	✔ 75 miles long by 40 miles wide
✔ deep, averages 1,290 feet deep	✔ shallow, averages 20 feet deep
✔ great fishing	✔ too salty for fish
(has islands)	(has islands)
✔ bordered by woods and cliffs	✔ bordered by desert and mountains
✔ partly in Canada	✔ 8 times saltier than ocean

Sample Comparison and Contrast Essay

The following expository essay compares and contrasts two lakes.

Floating or Fishing?
by Jason Burke

Beginning

The writer shares an interesting idea.

I have lived by two of the biggest lakes in the world. After living in Duluth by Lake Superior, I moved to Salt Lake City. Both the Great Salt Lake and Lake Superior are big lakes that seem more like oceans. Other than that, they are complete opposites.

Lake Superior is the largest freshwater lake in the world. It is 350 miles long and 160 miles wide. The Great Salt Lake is the biggest saltwater lake in the Western Hemisphere. Its water can be eight times saltier than ocean water.

Middle

Linking words show comparisons and contrasts.

Besides their difference in size, these lakes are very different in other ways. Lake Superior is deep (over 1,000 feet in many places) and fresh. On the other hand, the Great Salt Lake is shallow and is so salty that you can float in it without sinking! No fish can live in the Great Salt Lake; however, Lake Superior has lots of good fishing.

These two lakes are located in very different environments. Lake Superior is partly in Canada, and it is surrounded by forests and rocky cliffs. Mountains and desert surround the Great Salt Lake.

Ending

A final comparison makes readers think.

After living by both lakes, I don't know if I could pick one that I like better. When I float in the Great Salt Lake, I feel like I am in the ocean. But I miss fishing in Lake Superior and seeing the huge freighters go by. To me each lake is different and unique.

Writing Persuasive Essays

Sharing an Opinion

Everyone has opinions, and most people like to share them. Let's say that you think your school's winter vacation should be longer, and you want to share this opinion with your parents and school principal. They probably won't agree with your opinion unless you can persuade them with very good reasons. A good reason might be that students learn more if they have two weeks off in January. A less convincing reason might be that students want more time to relax.

Being Persuasive

One good way to share an opinion is to write a persuasive essay. Your goal is to convince someone to agree with you. The best way to do this is by supporting your opinion with facts and details.

When you carefully organize your thoughts into a persuasive essay, you make your opinion more convincing to your readers.

Writing a Persuasive Essay

Prewriting Planning Your Essay

Choose a Subject ● Select a subject for your essay that you feel strongly about. It is much easier to persuade readers when you write about an opinion that you really believe in.

Subject: Focus on a specific subject, one that's not too general. For example, it would be easier to write about a subject like "clean up Rainbow Beach" than it would be to write about "clean up our oceans."

Audience: Think about your audience. Choose a subject that will interest them. For example, "save our swimming pool" might be more interesting to your classmates than "save our town hall."

Think of an Argument ● Whatever your subject is, it should have two sides. If people read your opinion, they should be able to say, "Yes, I agree," or "No, I don't agree."

The same general subject of an expository (informative) essay could be used as the subject of a persuasive essay.

Expository Essay	Persuasive Essay
Mining in the Ocean	**Why We Should Mine the Ocean**
Animals of Coastal Waterways	**Save the Manatees**
Dangerous City Water Supplies	**Clean Up Our City's Waterways**

Prewriting Gathering and Organizing Details

List Details ● List details about the subject of your essay. Then collect any additional information that you need.

Manatees are – weed eaters and they unclog rivers
– gentle creatures
– endangered animals

People can – stop littering
– stop speeding in boats
– write letters to lawmakers

Outline ● After gathering facts and details, select two or three main points that best support your opinion. Next, write an outline to organize your information.

Sample Topic Outline

I. Manatees worth saving
   A. Help keep rivers clean
   B. Eat 150 pounds of weeds each day
   C. Give people pleasure
II. People destroying manatees
   A. Kill two-thirds of manatees
   B. Injure by shooting and with boats
   C. Cause deaths by littering waterways
III. People saving manatees
   A. Stop littering
   B. Obey boating speed limits
   C. Write lawmakers

Writing the First Draft

Many persuasive essays are three to five paragraphs long.

Beginning ● The first paragraph should introduce your subject and state your opinion.

Middle ● Your main ideas belong in the middle of the essay. Each main idea and its supporting details go in a separate paragraph. So, if you have two main ideas, the middle of your essay will have two paragraphs. Use your list or outline as a guide. (**SEE** page 96.) In most persuasive essays, you will put your strongest idea first. (Sometimes you put it last.)

Ending ● The last paragraph of your essay should restate your opinion and the facts that support it.

Revising Improving Your Writing

Review your first draft using the following questions. Then ask someone else to review your essay.

- ■ Does my opening paragraph introduce my subject and clearly state my opinion?
- ■ Do my middle paragraphs support my opinion?
- ■ Does each main idea have its own paragraph?
- ■ Do I give my most important idea first? (or last?)
- ■ Does the ending restate my opinion?
- ■ Does the title help identify my essay's subject?

Editing and Proofreading

Check for Careless Errors ● Make the necessary changes and improvements in your first draft. Then check it for spelling, grammar, and punctuation errors. Make a final copy before sharing your writing.

Sample **Persuasive Essay**

Marah Mehta of Orange City, Florida, asks her readers to help save the manatees. She supports her opinion with persuasive facts.

Beginning

The writer introduces her subject and states her opinion.

Middle

Supporting ideas are in two separate paragraphs.

Ending

The writer's opinion and main ideas are restated.

Help Save Our Manatees
by Marah Mehta

Manatees are giant marine mammals that live in the water around Florida. They are worth saving because only about 1,900 of these lovable animals remain.

By eating lots of water plants, manatees help clear rivers for boaters and fishers. A 1,000-pound manatee eats 150 pounds of river-clogging weeds in one day! Many people just enjoy watching these graceful creatures swim peacefully along in Florida's coastal waterways.

People cause more than two-thirds of all manatee deaths. Some people have shot manatees, and that's illegal. Often manatees are seriously injured or killed when boats run over them. Manatees also die from swallowing fishhooks, old fishing line, and garbage that litters the waterways.

Only people can save the manatee. It is easy. People can help save manatees by not littering the waterways. They can obey boating speed limits and slow down in manatee areas. And anyone can write a letter, send an e-mail, or make a phone call to lawmakers, asking for laws to help save the manatee.

Sample Persuasive Essay Using Humor

Sometimes the use of humor can help make a strong point.

Talent Show and Tell
by Corby Lester

Beginning

The writer introduces the subject with a question and states his opinion.

Wouldn't it be fun to look forward to Monday every week? I think our class should have a Monday Morning Talent Show. That would be one way to put our teacher and ourselves in a good mood for the rest of the week.

All the class comedians could try out their latest jokes. Do you know why the chicken didn't cross the road? He was chicken, of course! We could have a laugh meter based on how long everyone laughed. No booing allowed.

Middle

There is a paragraph for each type of talent: jokes, music, and hobbies.

Lots of kids are in band, but only a few get a chance to play a solo. Our Monday morning talent show would give us a chance to toot our own horns!

My seashell collection of turkey wings, lightning whelks, and shark's eyes would open some eyes. Then there's April's insect collection. You *may* get to see her giant June bugs! All our hobbies would be fun to share.

Ending

The final paragraph summarizes the points and ends by restating the opinion.

A talent show would let us discover things about our classmates. And if we shared a few jokes, talents, and hobbies, we could start each week off with a laugh.

Descriptive Writing

Describing in Detail

Part of becoming a good writer is being able to describe things well. You need to make your subject come to life for your audience. You can do this by using concrete nouns, vivid verbs, and clear, colorful modifiers. You can also include sensory details—how your subject looks, feels, tastes, smells, and sounds.

And that's just the beginning. When you write descriptions, you might compare your subject to others or you might share a story about your subject. This chapter includes many helpful guidelines, tips, and models for writing descriptions.

People write descriptions for many reasons. In school, you will write descriptions of plants for science, descriptions of famous people for history, and descriptions of countries for geography.

Writing a Descriptive Essay

Prewriting Planning Your Essay

Subject • Select a subject that can work for a descriptive essay. For example, describing your entire neighborhood would be too much to cover in a short essay; instead, select a subject that focuses on one person, place, thing, or event in your neighborhood. (**SEE** page 39 for ideas.)

Audience • You also need to think about who your audience will be for your description. Will the subject you choose interest your audience?

Voice • Think about your audience and why you're writing this description. Is it to help your audience understand your subject better? Is it to make them think seriously about it? Or is it simply to make them smile or laugh?

Prewriting Gathering Details

After you have selected a general subject, you need to gather as many details about it as possible.

Explore • Do a freewriting, listing everything that comes to mind about your subject.

Focus • Review your freewriting and decide which specific part of this subject to write about.

Gather • Gather more information about your subject: size, shape, color, sounds, and so on. Also, gather details about how your subject is like (or not like) other people, places, things, or events.

Organize • Decide which details you want to use in your essay and how you want to organize them. (**SEE** pages 48-49.)

Writing the First Draft

Beginning ● To get your reader's attention, you need to write a first paragraph that says something interesting or surprising about your subject. It should also name the main idea, or focus, of your writing.

Middle ● Write your description as freely and naturally as you can. Follow your outline or graphic organizer, but don't be afraid to add something new as you go along. The middle of your writing should include lots of specific details.

Note You can use as many paragraphs as you need to make your description complete (or as many as your teacher requires).

Ending ● The final paragraph should summarize your writing or somehow bring it to an effective end. You might write about why your subject is important or what you think your subject will be like in the future.

Revising and Editing Improving Your Essay

The questions below will help you revise and edit your first draft. (Remember, you can ask someone else to read and react to your writing.)

- Does my opening paragraph introduce my subject and get my reader's attention?
- Do I have enough details in the middle of my writing to make my subject clear and interesting to my reader?
- Did I compare my subject to similar subjects? (**SEE** *metaphor* and *simile,* pages 126 and 127.)
- Are my paragraphs clear and well organized?
- Does my essay end with a summary or end with an interesting point?
- Did I check for spelling and grammar errors?

Describing a Person

Writing about another person is often called biographical writing. (A *biography* is the story of another person's life.)

Choose a Subject ● Write about someone you know well, or someone you would like to know well.

Gather Details ● You can gather details in a number of ways. *List* details that describe your subject. *Remember* important things he or she has done. *Compare* your subject to others. *Share* a story that helps describe your subject. *Explain* why your subject is important.

Student

Beginning

The writer introduces the subject.

Middle

The writer gives specific examples.

Ending

The writer tells us how important his dad is.

Someone Who Cares

My dad is a very special person. Like many dads (and moms), he is very busy. But he still finds time to spend with me.

My dad helps me all the time. He helps me with my math homework and gives me tips about pitching. If I need to go somewhere, he always gives me a ride.

At least once a year, my dad and I take a trip together. Last summer, we took a trip through four states. We got to talk to each other for hours. My dad told me he made the same trip with his friends when he was younger. Now, it was just the two of us.

I wish everyone could have a friend like my dad. We all need someone to share good things and problems with. My dad is the best.

Describing a Place

Writing about a place can be part descriptive writing and part narrative writing.

Choose a Subject ● Write about a place that has played an important role in your life. It can be anything from a house you once lived in to a camp you went to one summer.

Gather Details ● If possible, visit this place and *describe* what you see, hear, smell, and feel. (**SEE** "5 Senses Organizer" on page 334.) If you can't visit the place again, *recall* personal experiences related to it. Also *compare* it to other places.

Student Sample

Beginning
The writer uses a creative way to start her description.

Middle
The writer adds many details.

Ending
The ending brings the city and country together.

Camp Knollwood

When I arrived at Camp Knollwood, I felt like I was in the story "The City Mouse and the Country Mouse." I was the city mouse going to the country for two weeks. I couldn't believe my eyes or nose when the bus pulled into camp. Everything was green. The camp was in the middle of a forest of evergreen trees. The trees were very tall and smelled like Christmas.

Over by the evergreens were many tents. The tents were small, blue, and floppy. Each tent had two beds and two orange crates for two campers. The beds were pretty lumpy, and they smelled like soap. The orange crates didn't hold much, so we put some things under our beds.

The food at camp was very different. We had lots of cookouts. My favorite things were bug juice, s'mores, pocket stew, outdoor spaghetti, and fruit kabobs. Everything tasted great.

After two weeks, I was happy to get back to the city. My bed wasn't lumpy, and I had a real dresser for my clothes. But I missed the camp food, so I taught my family how to make s'mores and fruit kabobs.

Describing an Object

When you write about an object, tell your readers how it looks, how it works, and why this object is special to you.

Choose a Subject ● Write about an object that you know well. You may have a special stuffed animal, a favorite baseball glove, or a useful gadget of some type.

Gather Details ● *List* details that describe the size, shape, and color of your object. *Recall* an interesting story (anecdote) related to the object. *Compare* it to other objects. *Ask* yourself why this object is (or was) important to you.

Student

Beginning
The writer gives some background information.

Middle
She shares details about the object.

Ending
The writer tells what things are like now.

Good Night, Night-Light

When I was little, I was scared of the dark. I imagined green monsters and alligators coming out of closets and out from under my bed.

Then I got a night-light, and that changed everything. My night-light was not like most night-lights. It had a blue lightbulb in it that lit up a jumping dolphin. It also would go on by itself when it got dark.

After I got my night-light, I started seeing dolphins instead of alligators! Through the years, I enjoyed having that little light next to my bed.

Now I am older, and I can say good-bye to my night-light. But when I was little, my night-light sure came through for me.

Narrative Writing

Telling a Story

What is the first thing you do when something exciting or interesting happens to you? If you're like most people, you look for a friend to share it with. This is something you probably enjoy doing and find easy to do.

Writing About an Experience

But writing about an experience is not quite as easy as telling about it, especially when that experience has just happened. You want to talk about it, not write about it. Writing is better suited for experiences that have happened in the past. With past experiences you are able to sit back, think about them, and then put your thoughts into writing.

> Telling stories and sharing experiences about yourself is fun. It's also fun to make up stories about fictional characters.

Writing a Narrative Essay

When you write a narrative essay, you give your version of a story you want to share.

Prewriting Planning Your Essay

Subject ● When you are selecting a subject, make a list of people (include yourself). Then think of something interesting or unusual that happened to someone on your list. Be sure your story entertains the readers or makes them think.

Audience ● Think about who will read your narrative. Knowing your audience helps you choose the best details and words.

Voice ● Ask yourself what you want your narrative to sound like. Do you want it to sound serious? funny? suspenseful?

Prewriting Gathering Details

After choosing a subject, decide what information you want to include in your essay.

Explore ● Do another freewriting about your specific subject. This time, write about everything you might want to include in your narrative. Include the setting for the story and details about the problem or goal of your main subject.

Focus ● Read your freewriting and decide which details you can use in your narrative essay and which ones you can't.

Organize ● Sometimes stories include answers to the 5 W's—*Who? What? Where? When? Why?* about your subject. See if this would help you organize your narrative.

 **Note** ● Narrative writing can be true or fictional. The examples in this chapter are all based on true stories.

Writing the First Draft

All good narratives have a beginning, a middle, and an ending.

Beginning ● Decide how you want to start your narrative. You can start with background details, a description of a scene, or right in the middle of some action.

Middle ● Write the middle of your narrative as freely and naturally as you can. Try to imagine that you are telling someone your story or sharing your experience with a friend. Follow your plan, but be ready to add details as you think of them.

Ending ● Like anything else you write, your narrative needs to come to a believable ending.

Revising and Editing *Improving Your Writing*

The following questions will help you review and edit your first draft. (Remember, it's a good idea to ask someone else to read your writing and suggest what changes you might make.)

- Does my beginning get my reader's attention?
- Did I tell my story or experience in a clear, colorful way?
- Did I include plenty of specific details so that my story seems real?
- Do I like the way my words and sentences sound?
- Does my ending bring everything together in an interesting way?
- Did I check for all spelling, capitalization, and grammar errors?

Note When you are writing about a personal narrative, talk about it first, write about it later.

Writing About a Memory

If you write a narrative about yourself, it is called *autobiographical writing*. If you write about someone else, it is called *biographical writing*. (**SEE** pages 154 and 155.)

Choose a Subject ● Write about some time in the past that you remember well. Think about when something happy, sad, or exciting happened to you or another person.

Gather Details ● List details that answer *who? what? where? when?* and *why?* about the experience. Then think of the different ways this experience has changed or touched you.

Student

Beginning

The writer begins with a hint of what's to come.

Middle

The writer describes her first day camping.

Ending

The mystery shared in the first paragraph is solved.

Lost in the Woods

When my Aunt Martha took me camping, we had our backpacks filled to the brim. But we kept thinking we had forgotten something.

The first night camping was fun, but a little scary. We were in a big, dark woods, and there were lots of animal noises. I was glad when morning came.

After breakfast, we went for a hike. In the woods, we spotted three woodpeckers, and we heard an owl. After walking for a long time, we felt a few drops of rain, and decided to head back to camp. But we didn't know which way to go.

For a while, we felt like we were walking in circles. Then we heard a familiar noise. It was the sound of a truck. We followed the sound and ended up on the road leading to the campground.

We had walked in a circle, and there we were back at our campsite safe and wet. We found the ponchos in camp, but we left the compass at home. Those were the two things we needed the most!

Writing About an Event

When you write about an event, try to put your reader right in the center of the action! Focus on one exciting part instead of trying to tell about everything.

Choose a Subject ● Write about any recent event, or an event you plan to attend. For example, you may have attended a hockey game, watched a parade, or gone to a wedding.

Gather Details ● Write down all of the details related to your subject. Include sights, sounds, and smells. Also try to answer the 5 W's (*Who? What? When? Where?* and *Why?*) related to it. Then describe why this event is worth sharing.

Student

Beginning
The writer thinks about her idol.

Middle
She tells the autograph story.

Ending
The writer adds a surprise.

The Unforgettable Autograph

I couldn't imagine really getting her autograph. What would it be like? I felt faint. She is my idol because she plays tennis so well. As she gets older, she will surely play even better.

While I was walking toward the practice courts, in my head I was hoping I would at least see her play. I was sure my sister was thinking the same thing. Then, suddenly, there she was, Venus Williams, wearing her tennis jacket and listening to headphones. My sister and I ran over to her as fast as horses to a finish line. I stared at her with butterflies in my stomach. She actually signed my paper.

As we made our way to our seats, I kept staring at her signature. I felt like nothing else mattered. Then later, while I was watching her play, I thought she winked at me! It was probably just my imagination.

Checklist for Essays

Use this checklist when you write and revise essays.

✔ **Purpose**

___ Do I have a clear purpose in mind?

✔ **Audience**

___ Did I think about who my audience is and what they might enjoy reading?

✔ **Voice**

___ Does my writing really sound like me?

✔ **Beginning**

___ Does my first paragraph introduce my subject in a clear, interesting way?

✔ **Middle**

___ Did I include all the important facts and details about my subject?

___ Did I organize my thoughts in the best possible order?

___ Did I use specific nouns, vivid verbs, and colorful modifiers?

___ Will my readers understand and appreciate what I'm trying to say in my essay?

✔ **Ending**

___ Does my last paragraph bring my writing to a natural ending?

___ Will my readers think, smile, laugh, or respond in some way?

Improving Your Writing Skills

Writing Basic Sentences

Control Your Ideas!

Let's say Mike's VCR goes bonkers—right in the middle of a good video. He tries everything, but the picture keeps jumping up and down like it has a bad case of hiccups. Finally, Mike gives up and turns off the machine.

Your readers may end up doing the same thing if your sentences are out of control. If they can't follow your ideas, they'll stop reading. That is why it is so important to use complete sentences. The guidelines in this chapter will help you write clear, correct sentences that contain easy-to-follow ideas.

Always check your writing for sentence errors. This may be your most important job when you edit and proofread your work.

Sentence Review

Sentences are groups of words that express complete thoughts. Your job as a writer is to share interesting ideas in a logical, clear way. The best way to do that is to write complete sentences.

The Basic Parts of a Sentence

Sentences have two basic parts—the subject and the verb.

Subject • The subject usually tells us who or what is doing something.

Mike invites Veit to his house.

Verb • The verb (also called the predicate) expresses action or links the subject to another part of the sentence.

Mike invites Veit to his house. (action verb)

They are wild about adventure movies. (linking verb)

Additional Words • Most sentences also contain additional words that describe or complete the thought.

Mike invites Veit to his house.

Compound Subjects and Verbs • A sentence may include more than one subject or more than one verb.

Mike and Veit watch videos. (two subjects)

The VCR sometimes goes bonkers and ruins the fun. (two verbs)

Compound Sentence • Two sentences may be connected with a conjunction *(and, but, or, so)*.

Mike fixes the tracking, and Veit cheers!

> **Note** You can find out more about sentences in the "Understanding Sentences" section. (**SEE** pages 412-416.)

Sentence Errors

Sentence Fragment • A sentence fragment is a group of words that only looks like a sentence. It does not express a complete thought because important information is missing.

Incorrect: **Thinks roller coasters are cool.**
(The subject is missing.)

Correct: **Martina thinks roller coasters are cool.**

Incorrect: **Not my favorite type of ride.**
(The subject and verb are both missing.)

Correct: **Roller coasters are not my favorite type of ride.**

Run-On Sentence • A run-on sentence happens when two sentences are joined without punctuation or a connecting word.

Incorrect: **The evening was warm and it was time to catch fireflies.** (Punctuation is needed.)

Correct: **The evening was warm. It was time to catch fireflies.** (A period has been added, and a letter has been capitalized.)

Correct: **The evening was warm, and it was time to catch fireflies.** (A comma and the conjunction *and* have been added.)

Rambling Sentence • A rambling sentence occurs when you put too many short sentences together with the word *and*.

Incorrect: **I went skating down at the pond and three kids from my school were there and we fell on our fannies again and again and we laughed so much our stomachs hurt!** (Too many *and*'s are used.)

Correct: **I went skating down at the pond, and three kids from my school were there. We fell on our fannies again and again. We laughed so much our stomachs hurt!**

Sentence Agreement

Make sure that the subjects and verbs in your sentences agree with each other. If you use a singular subject, use a singular verb; if you use a plural subject, use a plural verb.

One Subject • Most basic sentences have one subject followed by the verb. When they are right next to each other, it is easy to check for subject-verb agreement.

> **Amy wants to go bowling.**
>
> (*Amy* and *wants* agree because they are both singular.)
>
> **Her parents want to go bowling, too.**
>
> (*Parents* and *want* agree because they are both plural.)

Compound Subjects Connected by "And" • If a sentence contains a compound subject connected by *and,* it needs a plural verb.

> **Harry and Emil spend time playing tennis.**
>
> **Sarah and Maria join them.**

Compound Subjects Connected by "Or" • If a sentence contains a compound subject connected by *or,* the verb must agree with the subject nearer to it.

> **Either the cat or the dog pounces on me each morning.**
>
> (A singular verb, *pounces,* is needed because *dog* is singular.)
>
> **Anna or her brothers feed the pets each evening.**
>
> (A plural verb, *feed,* is needed because *brothers* is plural.)

Helpful Hint: Sometimes the subject will not come before the verb. This happens in sentences beginning with the word *there* (There are two dogs) and in questions (Is this dog yours?).

Sentence Problems

Double Subjects ● Do not use a pronoun immediately after the subject. The result is usually a double subject.

Incorrect: **Some cats they eat all the time.**
(The pronoun *they* should be omitted.)
Correct: **Some cats eat all the time.**

Pronoun-Antecedent Agreement ● Make sure the pronouns in your sentences agree with the words they replace, which are called *antecedents.*

Incorrect: **If Carlo and his friends each eat three double cheeseburgers, he will be overstuffed.**
(The pronoun *he* is singular. The antecedents—Carlo and his friends—are plural.)
Correct: **If Carlo and his friends each eat three double cheeseburgers, they will be overstuffed.**
(Now the pronoun and its antecedents agree; they are plural.)

Double Negatives ● Do not use two negative words, like *never* and *no* or *not* and *no,* in the same sentence.

Incorrect: **Never give no one a note during class.**
Correct: **Never give anyone a note during class.**
Incorrect: **I didn't have no mistakes in my paragraph.**
Correct: **I didn't have any mistakes in my paragraph.**

Confusing "Of" for "Have" ● Do not use *of* in a sentence when you really mean *have.* (When *have* is said quickly, it sometimes sounds like *of.*)

Incorrect: **We should of brought an umbrella.**
Correct: **We should have brought an umbrella.**

Combining Sentences

One Plus One Equals One

Sentence combining is making one smoother, more detailed sentence out of two or more shorter sentences. For instance, take a look at the following sentences:

My dog loves to run fast.
He loves to jump fences.
He loves to chase rabbits.

These sentences are okay, but all of these ideas can be combined into one smooth-reading sentence, which is even better.

My dog loves to run fast, jump fences, and chase rabbits.

The guidelines in this chapter will help you learn how to combine sentences. Sentence combining can help you improve your writing style.

Always check your writing for too many short or choppy-sounding sentences. Then start combining!

My dog loves to run fast

chase rabbits

Combining with Key Words

Use a key word. Ideas included in short sentences can be combined by moving a key word from one sentence to the other.

Short Sentences: **Kelly's necklace sparkles. It is beaded.**
Combined with an Adjective:
      Kelly's beaded necklace sparkles.

Short Sentences: **I am going to a sleepover. I'm going tomorrow.**
Combined with an Adverb:
      Tomorrow I am going to a sleepover.

Use a series of words or phrases. Ideas included in short sentences can be combined into one sentence using a series of words or phrases.

Short Sentences: **The gym teacher is strict.**
      The gym teacher is organized.
      The gym teacher is fair.
Combined with a Series of Words:
      The gym teacher is strict, organized, and fair.

Note All of the words or phrases in a series should be *parallel*—stated in the same way. Otherwise, the sentence will be unbalanced.

Incorrect: **This dog is friendly, playful, and he is pretty smart, too.** (The modifiers in this series are not parallel.)

Correct: **This dog is friendly, playful, and smart.** (Now all the words in the series—*friendly, playful, smart*—are single-word adjectives. They are parallel.)

Combining with Phrases

Use phrases. Ideas from short sentences can be combined into one sentence using phrases. (**SEE** page 414.)

Short Sentences: **Our cat curls up.**
He curls up on top of my homework.

Combined with a Prepositional Phrase:
Our cat curls up on top of my homework.

Short Sentences: **Mrs. Keller makes the best cookies on the block.**
Mrs. Keller is our next-door neighbor.

Combined with an Appositive Phrase:
Mrs. Keller, our next-door neighbor, **makes the best cookies on the block.**

Use compound subjects and/or compound verbs. A compound subject is two or more subjects connected by a conjunction. A compound verb is two or more verbs connected by a conjunction.

Short Sentences: **Tory danced around the room.**
Mary danced around the room, too.

Combined with a Compound Subject:
Tory and **Mary danced around the room.**

Short Sentences: **Jon skated onto the pond.**
He made a perfect figure eight.

Combined with a Compound Verb:
Jon skated **onto the pond and** made **a perfect figure eight.**

Combining with Longer Sentences

Use compound sentences. A compound sentence is made up of two or more simple sentences joined together. The conjunctions *and, but, or, nor, for, so,* and *yet* are used to connect the simple sentences. (Place a comma before the conjunction.)

Simple Sentences: **My puppy has hair hanging over her eyes.**
She looks just like a dust mop.

Combined with "And":

**My puppy has hair hanging over her eyes,
and she looks just like a dust mop.**

Simple Sentences: **Our dog likes to eat shoes.**
He won't touch my brother's smelly slippers.

Combined with "But":

**Our dog likes to eat shoes, but he won't
touch my brother's smelly slippers.**

Use complex sentences. A complex sentence is made up of two ideas connected by a subordinating conjunction (*because, when, since, after, before,* etc.) or by a relative pronoun (*who, whose, which,* and *that*).

Short Sentences: **My friend shares his lunch with me.**
He doesn't like what his dad packs.

Combined with "Because":

**My friend shares his lunch with me because
he doesn't like what his dad packs.**

Short Sentences: **Very cold weather closed school for a day.**
The cold weather came down from Canada.

Combined with "Which":

**Very cold weather, which came down from
Canada, closed school for a day.**

Writing with Style

Learning by Doing

Style is personal. You may do a certain stunt that sends you and your skateboard skyward. That's part of your own special style. You may love pepperoni on your pizza. That's also part of your style. You may wear your hair short, or long, or half-and-half. That's your style, too. What's *in style* for you, depends on you.

The Way You Write

As a young writer, you have your own way of expressing thoughts and feelings on paper. This is your writing style, and it will develop naturally as you continue to write. You can also strengthen your style by using the suggestions in this chapter.

> "Writing isn't just words on paper anymore. It's me."
>
> **—MEREDITH DEMPSEY, STUDENT**

Developing a Sense of Style

Your writing style will grow strong and healthy if you follow this advice:

- **Practice often.**
  Keep a daily journal. This is one of the best ways to develop your writing style.

- **Try different forms.**
  Explore different forms of writing. Try poems and plays; write news stories and character sketches. Each form of writing can help you develop your style.

- **Write about ideas that are important to you.**
  If you write about subjects that you care about, you will soon have a style of your own.

- **Use your voice.**
  Write with words you know and understand—words that sound like you.

- **Change writing that doesn't work.**
  If you don't feel good about your writing, fix it. Your handbook is full of ideas to help you do this. (**SEE** pages 55-59, 60-63, and 64-67.)

- **Learn about traits of effective writing.**
  Certain traits ought to be part of your writing style. (**SEE** pages 18-23.)

- **Use writing techniques.**
  The writing techniques listed on pages 124-127 will help you become a writer with style.

Express Yourself Here's an activity to help you strengthen your writing style. List five sentences from your writing. Then try to make each sentence better by changing the order of the words, by using a more lively verb or specific noun, or by adding a detail.

Using Writing Techniques

Writing techniques are specific ways you can improve your style. Try some of them each time you write.

Anecdote An anecdote is a brief story used to make a point. Here's an anecdote student writer Charles Vodak included in one of his stories.

> Sample: **To get me to keep my room clean, my mom always tells this story about her sister Ann. Ann was very messy. One day she was cleaning her closet, and she found some kittens in there. And guess what? She didn't even have a cat!**

Try this: Use anecdotes in your writing when a little story can get your point across to your readers.

Colorful Adjectives Colorful adjectives are lively words that describe nouns or pronouns.

> Sample of a not-so-good adjective:
> **Mom made some good spaghetti sauce.**
>
> Sample of colorful adjectives:
> **Mom made some delicious, spicy spaghetti sauce.**

Try this: If you're writing about food, think of words that make your mouth water when you say them.

Comparison A comparison is a description of things that are similar. Comparisons can be used throughout a long piece of writing. (**SEE** pages 92-93. Also see *simile* on page 127.)

> Sample: **Those little butterflies look like flying flowers.**

Try this: Use comparisons to make your writing clearer or more colorful. A well-written comparison paints a picture with words.

Details Details are specific facts, examples, and words used to support a main idea and add color to your writing.

> **Sample without details:**
> **My cousin is nice.**
>
> **With details:**
> **My cousin Lu loves to write friendly notes to her classmates.**

Try this: When you are writing, use details that are specific and clear. Try to stay away from words like *good, is,* and *nice* because they are not specific and clear.

Dialogue Dialogue is talking on paper.

> **Sample:** **"Could you help me find the train station?" asked the traveler.**
> **"I'd be happy to," said the young man, "but I'm a lost traveler just like you."**

Try this: Add dialogue to your stories and reports (perhaps from an interview). It adds energy to your writing and makes your style memorable. (**SEE** page 215.)

Elaboration To elaborate is to give more details. (See *details* above.)

Exaggeration When you exaggerate in your writing, you create characters or scenes that stretch the truth.

> **Sample:** **The giraffe peeked over the clouds and spotted the missing balloon.**

Try this: Think of an animal and its characteristics. (The sample above uses a giraffe and its characteristic of being tall.) Then stretch or exaggerate these natural features, especially in tall tales or children's stories.

Idiom An idiom is a word used in a way that is different from its usual or dictionary meaning.

> **Sample: Maha and Jake ironed out their problems.**
> (In this sentence, *ironed out* means "solved.")

Try this: Use idioms once in a while to make your writing sound realistic. Idioms fit better in stories than in reports.

Metaphor A metaphor is a figure of speech that compares two different things without using the word *like* or *as*.

> **Sample: That skater in the red jersey is a real roadrunner.**

Try this: Think of two things that have something in common, such as their color, size, shape, or behavior. Here are some examples: a speed skater and a roadrunner, blue eyes and the ocean, springtime air and a baby's breath.

Personification Personification is a figure of speech in which an idea, object, or animal is given the characteristics of a person.

> **Sample: The stubborn rock refused to move.**

Try this: Use personification to add life to your writing. You already have used it if you've ever said "The wind howled" or "My computer just told me to cancel that command."

Sensory Details Sensory details are details that help a reader see, feel, smell, taste, or hear a subject.

> **Sample:** **The soft, black-eared kitten purred quietly as I cuddled her in my arms.**

Try this: Use your senses to find words that will add sound, feeling, and color to your writing.

Simile A simile is a figure of speech that compares two things and uses the word *like* or *as*.

> **Sample:** **A cold lemonade is as refreshing as a dip in a pool.**

Try this: Use similes to add word pictures to your poems, stories, and descriptive writing.

Specific Nouns A specific noun is a word that names a certain person, place, thing, or idea. In the chart below, **A** nouns are very general, **B** nouns are more specific, and **C** nouns are very specific.

	person	place	thing	idea
A	boy	outdoors	toy	celebration
B	nephew	park	puppet	party
C	Rich Kurczak	Vilas Park	Pinocchio	birthday party

Try this: To make your writing as clear as possible, use very specific **C** nouns whenever you can.

Vivid Verbs A vivid verb is a powerful word that gives the reader a clear picture of the action.

> **Sample:** **The children wiggled and bounced in their seats.**

Try this: To make your writing come to life, use vivid verbs.

Modeling the Masters

Young artists can learn a lot about art by studying the work of famous painters. You can learn a lot about writing by studying the work of your favorite authors. When you come across sentences that you especially like, try following the author's pattern. This process is called "modeling."

Guidelines for Modeling

- Find a sentence (or short passage) that you especially like.
- Select a subject for your writing.
- Follow the author's pattern as you write about your own subject.
- Build your sentence one small section at a time.

One Writer's Experience

Modeling Roald Dahl

Kate enjoys Roald Dahl's stories, so every once in a while she tries to write like him. Here is a sentence from Dahl's book *Danny the Champion of the World:*

Grown-ups are complicated creatures, full of quirks and secrets.

Here is Kate's sentence about her own subject, but modeled after Dahl's writing:

Cats are peculiar pets, full of laziness and craziness.

Kate might have written, "Some cats can be really nutty. They can be sleeping on the couch one minute and flying around the room the next minute." By modeling, she can use fewer words to share the same ideas in a powerful way. She has discovered how to "model a master."

Understanding Writing Terms

This list covers terms that writers use when they are talking about their writing.

Arrangement • The way details are organized in writing. (**SEE** pages 19 and 84 for more information.)

Audience • People who read or hear what you have written.

Body • The main part of the writing that comes between the opening and closing ideas. The body of a piece of writing contains the specific details that support or develop the main idea.

Brainstorming • Freely sharing ideas in groups in order to collect a variety of thoughts on a subject.

Cliche • A familiar word or phrase that has been used so much that it is no longer a good way of saying something, such as *good as gold* or *bright as the sun.*

Closing/Concluding Sentence • The sentence that sums up the main point being made in a paragraph.

Composition • A piece of writing similar to an essay.

Description • Writing that helps a reader see a subject clearly with specific details and colorful modifiers.

Diction • The kind of language a writer decides to use. In a story about everyday life, a writer may use informal, ordinary language. In a business letter, a writer will probably use formal, proper language.

Editing • Checking a piece of writing to make sure it contains complete, smooth-reading sentences; strong, colorful words; and correct spelling, grammar, and punctuation.

Expository Writing • Writing that explains, such as a report or research paper. (Sometimes called *informational writing.*)

Figure of Speech ● A special way of describing a subject by comparing it to something else. (**SEE** *metaphor, personification,* and *simile* on pages 126-127.)

First Draft ● The first complete writing about a subject.

Focus/Main Idea ● The specific part of a subject a writer chooses to concentrate on. For example, a piece written about Abraham Lincoln could focus on his education.

Form ● The shape of writing—a poem, an essay, a novel, a play, and so on. (**SEE** pages 40-43.)

Freewriting ● Writing quickly to discover new ideas.

Grammar ● The rules and guidelines of language that you follow in order to be correct in your writing and speaking.

Journal ● A daily record of thoughts, feelings, and ideas.

Modifier ● A word or group of words that describes another word or idea. (**SEE** pages 430-433.)

Narration ● Telling a story or recalling an experience.

Objective ● Writing that includes facts, but no opinions or personal feelings.

Parallelism ● A series or repetition of words or phrases that are written in the same way: *Josie scratched her head, bit her nails, and shrugged her shoulders.*

Person ● The angle from which a story is told.

 First person: I; we
 Second person: you; you
 Third person: he, she, it; they

Personal Narrative ● Writing that tells a story from the writer's life.

Persuasion • Writing that is meant to change the way a reader thinks or acts.

Prewriting • Planning a writing project. *Selecting a subject* and *gathering details* are prewriting activities.

Process • A way of doing something that involves several steps; the writing process includes *prewriting, writing the first draft, revising, editing and proofreading,* and *publishing.*

Proofreading • Checking a final draft for spelling, grammar, and punctuation errors.

Prose • Writing or speaking that uses regular sentences.

Pun • A word or phrase used in a way that gives it a funny twist: That story about rabbits is a real *hare raiser.*

Purpose • The main reason for writing a certain piece.

Revising • Changing writing to make its meaning clear, usually by adding, cutting, or moving around the ideas and details.

Slang • Informal words and phrases used by friends when they talk to each other. "Chill out" and "cool" are slang terms.

Style • The way a writer puts words, phrases, and sentences together.

Subjective • Writing that includes opinions and personal feelings.

Supporting Details • Specific details used to develop a subject or bring a story to life.

Theme • The central idea or message in a piece of writing.

Topic • The specific subject of a piece of writing.

Topic Sentence • The sentence that contains the main idea of a paragraph. (**SEE** pages 76-77.)

Transitions • Words that help tie ideas together in essays, paragraphs, and sentences. (**SEE** page 85.)

Voice • The way a writer expresses ideas. The most effective, believable writing is written in an honest, natural voice.

Personal Writing

Writing in Journals

What a Day!

Your team won the kickball match during recess. You finally got all the words correct on your spelling test. Your best friend is coming over after school, and your dad is taking you to the movies. Days like this are so special that you want to remember each moment.

How can you be sure to remember every detail of your awesome day? Try writing about it.

Capture Your Memories

After your wonderful day is over, pull out your personal journal. It's probably the best place to record these kinds of events. Remember to tell what happened, as well as how it made you feel. If you capture your memories in your journal, they will always be there to remind you of past experiences and feelings.

Why Write in a Personal Journal?

There are many reasons to write in a journal. You can . . .

■ take notes about interesting things you see and hear,
■ collect ideas for stories, poems, and reports,
■ practice writing on your own,
■ deal with your bad days, and
■ relive all of your good times.

Here's how to get started . . .

1 **Gather the right tools.**

You need pens or pencils and a notebook, or a computer.

2 **Find a special time and place to write.**

Get up early each day and write while it is quiet in your house. Write at a regular time during school. Or find a cozy chair right after dinner and see how that works.

3 **Write every day.**

Write freely, exploring your thoughts and feelings as they come to mind. Don't worry about what you say or how you say it. Just keep writing for as long as you can (at least 5 to 10 minutes at a time).

4 **Write about what is important to you.**

Write about something that is bothering you or something you want to remember. Write about what you did last weekend or something silly you saw. Write about one thing and then, later, go on to something else.

5 **Keep track of your writing.**

Put the date on the top of the page each time you write. Read through your journal from time to time. Underline ideas you find interesting and ideas that you would like to write more about in the future.

A Closer Look at Journal Writing

Journal writing works best when you reflect on, or really think about, your experiences and learn from them. When you do this, your writing becomes lively—and full of surprises.

Reflect

Thinking and writing in the following ways will help you explore your experiences.

Ask questions. As you write, ask yourself some questions: *What was fun or interesting about this experience? How do I feel about it now? Why do I feel this way?* Then look for some answers.

Wonder. Also think about what you have learned from an experience. *Compare* it to other experiences you've had. *Wonder* about what you could have done differently, or *predict* what you might do in the future.

Express Yourself Read the sample journal writing on page 136, and you will see that this student was writing and thinking (reflecting) about her garden.

Push Yourself

If you push yourself in your writing, you are sure to make some discoveries.

Keep it going. When you start a new journal entry, pick up right where you left off in your last one. When you find an idea that surprises you, try to say more about it. When you think that you have said all that you can about a certain subject, keep going for at least a few more lines.

Make connections. For a challenge, try to make connections between ideas that seem really different. You can also make connections between your ideas and the news, movies, or songs.

Kinds of Journals

If you enjoy exploring your thoughts in a personal journal, try writing in one of the special journals listed below.

Electronic Journal • Your computer can be an electronic journal. It's easy to record your thoughts and reread them later.

Dialogue Journal • In a dialogue journal, you and a friend, parent, or teacher write to each other about experiences you've had and books you've read. (**SEE** the sample on page 137.)

Diary • A diary is a journal for keeping track of personal things.

Learning Log • In a learning log, you write about subjects like math, science, and social studies to help you understand them better. (**SEE** pages 354-355.)

Response Journal • When you have strong feelings about the stories and books you read, you can write about these feelings in a response journal. (**SEE** page 171 for writing ideas.)

A Special-Event Journal • You may want to write about your experiences with a sport, a new member in your family, or a special project.

Sample Journal Writing

July 5

Today was so great! I saw the first hummingbird in our garden! A few weeks ago we planted scarlet runner beans, and they have been growing up the tepee poles that we tied together. This week the red flowers blossomed. Red attracts hummingbirds. I wonder why.

We were in the backyard, and I saw something moving by the flowers. It was a tiny hummer! It was so neat. In a second, it zoomed off. I hope it comes back.

Sample Dialogue Journal

In the dialogue journal below, a teacher and a student carry on a conversation about a book.

Dear José,

    When I read your response to It's Disgusting and We Ate It!, I was flabbergasted myself. I had no idea that seaweed came in "snack" form or that it is in hot fudge! What a surprise. I enjoyed reading all the names of the types of seaweed, too. The funniest names were Cow Hair, Star Jelly, Sugar Wrack, and Sea Otter's Cabbage. Thanks for sharing!

                    Write back,
                    Ms. N.

P.S. Please give me more information on the book, so I can order it for our library.

Dear Ms. N.,

    Yes, the seaweed names are funny. My favorite one is Sea Otter's Cabbage. What's yours? The author of this book is James Solheim, and the publisher is Simon and Schuster.

    I also learned that millions of people like bird's nest soup. So my dad and I went to a local Chinese restaurant where the book said we could get some. We ordered it, and it was really great! Have you ever had bird's nest soup?

                    Please write back,
                    José

Writing Personal Narratives

Your Life Story

A true story about yourself—written by yourself—is called autobiographical writing. It would be too much to write your whole life story, but you can write a short story or a *personal narrative* about a special time in your life.

You can think of experiences in your life as different chapters. Any experience that has caused you to feel a strong emotion is a good subject for a personal narrative.

Daniel

> "It's not easy to travel back into your memory and gather details. But it's worth it. The details help you remember the very important chapters in the story of your life."
>
> **—SANDY ASHER, AUTHOR**

Sample **Personal Narrative**

Here's a true story that the author Sandy Asher wrote about a special experience in her life. When it happened, she felt scared, sad, and then happy.

Beginning

The main characters and the problem are introduced.

Middle

The story is organized according to time (describing what happens first, second, third, and so on).

Ending

A surprise rescue is described.

The Great Gerbil Escape

When my daughter Emily was nine years old, she had a pair of gerbils named Farrah and Festus. One day, Festus escaped from our bathtub!

It sounds silly to have gerbils in your tub, but it's not. The sides are too high to jump over and too slick to climb. We plugged the drain. We put in toys and sunflower seeds. The gerbils could exercise and play safely.

But one day, I accidentally left a fuzzy blue bath mat over the edge of the tub. When Emily and I came back, Festus was gone. He'd grabbed the mat and climbed out!

The only place he could have gone was down the heat vent in the wall. We knelt beside the vent. We could hear him! "Scritch-scratch. Scritch-scratch." We lowered a rope into the vent, but he didn't climb out. We stuffed in a towel, but he didn't climb that either.

And when we pulled the towel out, there was no more "Scritch-scratch." Oh, no! I thought. We've pushed him down the vent into the furnace. We've baked our gerbil!

Emily was heartbroken. I felt terrible. We put Farrah back in the cage and went downstairs. Then I noticed another heat vent in the hall, right below the one upstairs in the bathroom. And sure enough, we could hear Festus again: "Scritch-scratch. Scritch-scratch!"

Finally, Emily remembered that gerbils love to explore boxes. We took all the tissues out of a small tissue box. Emily lowered the box into the vent as far as her arm could reach. Then Festus climbed aboard and rode to safety in his own private elevator. And that's how the Great Gerbil Escape became the Great Gerbil Rescue!

Gathering Story Ideas

You can start gathering ideas for personal narratives by writing in a daily diary or journal, or by making lists of personal experiences. A good way to find ideas is to answer the following types of questions:

1 ## Who are the important people in your life?

Family members? Friends? Classmates? Neighbors? Think about the times you've shared with each one. What do you remember best? What would you just as soon forget? (**SEE** page 143 for suggestions for family stories.)

2 ## Where have you been?

Every place you visit is an adventure, whether it's the doctor's office, the principal's office, or the county fair. Think of the biggest place you've been, and the smallest. Think of comfortable places, and places that cause you to squirm. Think of special meeting places from your past.

3 ## What do you like to do?

Do you enjoy drawing or cooking or caring for animals? Do you like to play ball or just hang out? Do you like to talk on the phone or read at night when you're supposed to be asleep?

4 ## What do you not like to do?

Study? Clean your room? Baby-sit? Get up early? There are a lot of ways to answer this question, aren't there? And a lot of strong feelings are involved, too. Isn't it nice to know that even the worst times you can remember are at least good for story ideas?

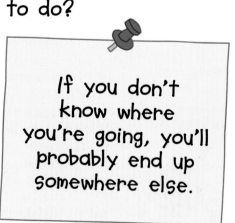

If you don't know where you're going, you'll probably end up somewhere else.

Writing Personal Narratives

Prewriting Planning Your Story

Choose a Subject ● Choosing a subject for a personal story should be easy. You want a memorable experience that happened over a short period of time. (**SEE** pages 35-39 for more help with choosing your subject.)

Helpful Hint: Try completing this sentence starter: "I remember the time . . . " Continue listing until you find a subject.

Gather Your Thoughts ● If the idea you choose is crystal clear in your mind, begin writing. If you're missing some details, try clustering or making a list before starting your draft.

Helpful Hint: After you answer the 5 W's—*Who? What? When? Where?* and *Why?*—you may be ready to write.

Writing the First Draft

Start at the Beginning ● Put yourself at the beginning of the experience ("There I stood" or "As I entered the room") and add details as they come to mind.

Revising Improving Your Story

Review Your Work ● Reading your first draft aloud may help you "hear" your writing. Have you left out any important details? Are your details in the best order? Do you sound really interested in your subject? Make any necessary changes.

Editing and Proofreading

Check for Careless Errors ● Make sure that your sentences read smoothly from start to finish. Also make sure that your words are specific and interesting. Then write a neat, final draft and proofread it.

Sample Personal Narrative

Jessica Gilbert recalls a motorcycle ride that taught her an important lesson.

Beginning
Dialogue makes the story seem real from the start.

Middle
The writer shares her thoughts and feelings.

Ending
The narrative ends on a positive note.

When I Got Burned on Dad's Motorcycle

As I was going outside, I was a little nervous because I was going to ride on my dad's motorcycle.

"Come on. Get up," said my dad cheerfully.

"Okay," I answered. But just as I was getting onto the seat, I burnt myself on one of the pipes!

"Ow!" I yelled as I started to cry.

"Are you all right?" asked my mom.

"No," I answered.

"Come here," said my mom. "Let's take a look at that burn. It's not so bad, but I don't think you should go for a ride right now."

I felt glad that my mom had said that.

"Aw, come on. It won't hurt once we get going," said my dad.

Then he picked me up and set me on the seat of the motorcycle.

"Dad, I'm not sure I want to go!" I said.

"Nonsense. It'll be fun," said my dad. And we took off.

I have to admit that during the ride, I started to laugh. My burn hardly hurt anymore. I wasn't nervous and I had a great ride.

I'm really glad my dad convinced me to get on the motorcycle. If he hadn't, I probably never would have gotten on it again. From that day on, I knew I would never give up after I got hurt. I would just get back up and try it again.

Writing Family Stories

Another kind of personal narrative you may want to write is a family story. Here are some starters to get you going.

Name Stories . . . your name first ● Write about how your first and middle names were chosen. If you don't know, go to the source. Ask a parent or guardian. There is a story behind every name. This one, the story of your name, may be the first in a whole collection of stories about the _____ family.

. . . other family names ● Now check into other family names that interest you. Are there favorite first names or middle names in your family? How about nicknames? Last names? Tell their stories.

Birth Stories ● Find out about the day you were born. Ask your parents. What was the weather like? What time of day did you arrive? What important events were going on in the world that day?

Holiday Stories ● Write about the ways your family celebrates holidays—Thanksgiving, Christmas, Hanukkah, New Year's Day, Easter. Are there any special holidays that only your family celebrates?

Recipe Stories ● Your family has favorite recipes. Write about the times, places, and people who have shared these foods with you. You may want to write up some of the recipes, too.

Heirloom Stories ● Many families have special pieces of furniture, jewelry, or photos that have been handed down from generation to generation. These objects are called _heirlooms_. What are the stories behind your family's heirlooms? Where did they come from? Why are they valuable to your family?

Think It Over
Here are some topics to get you thinking about more family stories: spooky events, disasters, unusual relatives, rascals, pranks, and special sayings.

Friendly Notes and Letters

Keeping in Touch

Do you run to the mailbox or the computer to see if "you've got mail"? Exchanging notes, letters, and messages can make friendships stronger. Hearing from distant relatives can make them feel closer. And the best way to make sure you receive mail is to send some.

Parts of a Friendly Letter

Heading **1** The heading includes your address and the date. Write it in the upper right corner.

Salutation **2** The salutation (greeting) usually begins with the word *Dear* and is followed by the name of the person you are writing to. Place a comma after the name. Write a salutation at the left margin, two lines below the heading.

Body **3** The body of the letter contains your thoughts. Indent each paragraph and begin writing on the second line after the salutation.

Closing **4** Write the closing (*Sincerely, Yours truly,* etc.) two lines below the body of your letter. Capitalize only the first word and follow the closing with a comma.

Signature **5** Put your signature under the closing.

Sample **Friendly Letter**

1 123 Wixom Road
Wixom, MI 48386
January 8, 2000

2 Dear Grace,

3 My name is Tracy, and I am your new pen pal. I'm in the fifth grade at Wixom Elementary School in Wixom, Michigan.

I'll start by telling you about some of my hobbies. I am taking keyboard lessons because I got a keyboard for Christmas, and I think it will be fun. I'm not very good, yet, but I can play two songs. Have you ever played a keyboard?

I really like to draw, paint, and read stories. I also love to read mystery books and fiction books. My favorite mystery series is Nancy Drew. Do you like to read?

I have three people in my family: my mom, my dad, and me. My mom is in advertising, and my dad is in sales. I also have ten pets: seven fish, two parakeets, and a dog. My dog's name is Chocolate. My family and I named her that because she's all brown, like a chocolate bar. My two birds, Sammy and Tweedy, are green, blue, yellow, and black. Tweedy bites, and because of that, it's really hard to train her. Sammy is trained and can ride on my shoulder in the house.

As you probably have noticed, I love animals. I want to work with animals when I grow up, especially with whales. What do you want to do when you grow up?

4 Sincerely,

5   Tracy Randlett

P.S. Write back soon!

Writing Letters and Messages

Prewriting Planning Your Writing

Choose a Subject • Pick a friend or relative to write to.

Gather Details • Make a list of things to write about, like happenings in your life, things you like to do, or a good story.

Writing the First Draft

Beginning • Greet your reader and tell why you are writing.

Middle • Choose ideas from your list and write about them freely. Ask the reader questions, and answer any he or she may have asked you.

Ending • End politely and ask the reader to write back.

Revising Improving Your Writing

Review Your Work • Check that each paragraph develops one idea. Be sure your details are clear and interesting.

Editing and Proofreading

Check for Errors • Make sure all your sentences read smoothly. Also pay special attention to capitalization, spelling, and punctuation.

- ■ **For Letters:** Neatly type or write your letter. Center it on the page with one-inch margins. Address the envelope, add correct postage, and mail your letter. (**SEE** page 181.)
- ■ **For E-Mail:** Check the e-mail address, be sure you signed off politely, and then send your message.

> **P.S.** If you finish your letter or message and suddenly remember something you want to say, add a P.S. (postscript).

Sample E-Mail Message

E-mail is a message you write and send to someone through a computer network. If you already use e-mail, you know it's an easy way to send, receive, answer, and store messages.

Tip Some e-mail messages are more like notes to friends; others, like the one below, are more business-like. Remember to read over your message before you hit the "send" key.

Date: Fri., 21 Apr. 2000 10:52:21
From: Brenden Schulz <brschulzy@aol.com>
To: Time for Kids@www.timeforkids.com
Subject: Around the World in 20 Days

Dear Sir,

I loved your article about the two balloonists ("Around the World in 20 Days," 4/11) who never gave up. That made me wonder if I should retry what I can't do. I would like to retry the high jump, because I didn't do very well on it, and I know I can jump at least four feet.

Sincerely,

Brenden Schulz

Writing Social Notes

Sometimes you will need to write special kinds of friendly letters, like thank-you notes and invitations. These are often called **social notes.**

Parts of Social Notes

A social note begins with a salutation (Dear _____ ,). The middle of your note is usually one or two paragraphs. The paragraphs are short and to the point. "Your friend" or "Love" are common closings. Don't forget to sign your note.

Invitations • When you are inviting someone to come to a party or special event, you'll need to write an invitation. Be sure to include these items:

What:	**a party, a celebration**
When:	**the date and time**
Where:	**the place and address**
Who:	**who the party is for**
Why:	**birthday, bar mitzvah, going away**

Ask in your invitation whether or not the person will be coming to your event. Add R.S.V.P. (please respond) and your telephone number in the lower left-hand corner.

Thank-You Notes • When writing a thank-you note, be specific. If you are thanking someone for something special he or she did, explain why it was important to you. If you are thanking someone for a gift, tell why you like it and how you are using it.

> **Note** You can customize your own notes with rubber stamps, markers, stickers, special lettering, or on a computer. Be creative!

Sample Invitation

April 15, 2000

Dear Josh,

My tenth birthday is coming up, and my dad said I could have a party. He's going to take us to the zoo, and the director said we could go on a scavenger hunt.

The party will be on my birthday, April 29th. You can be dropped off at my house at 12:30 and picked up at 4:00 p.m.

My address is 3200 North Main Street. Bring a raincoat if it looks like rain. Please call me to let me know if you can come.

Anna
R.S.V.P. 555-2231

Sample Thank-You Note

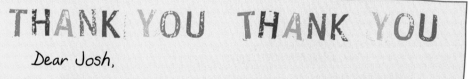
THANK YOU   THANK YOU

Dear Josh,

Thanks for coming to my party. The book and papermaking kit you gave me are great. I started reading <u>50 Simple Things Kids Can Do to Save the Earth</u>, and I'm already working on some of the ideas.

I used junk mail to make this stationery with the papermaking kit. I really had fun! Thank you very much for the presents. I really like them.

Your friend, Anna

Subject Writing

Biographical Writing

Writing About Others

Writing about someone other than yourself is called *biographical writing*. Some biographies tell the story of a person's life from birth to death. Other biographies called biographical sketches, or character sketches, present a short story or description of a person. You can write about someone you know very well, like a grandparent or a neighbor, or you can write about historical figures, like John Hancock or Sacagawea. What's important is that you share interesting information about the person.

Saving Memories

In biographical writing you can

- **save your memories of another person,**
- **discover an interesting world besides your own, and**
- **learn to understand yourself better.**

Writing a Biographical Sketch

Prewriting Planning Your Writing

Choose a Subject ● You know many people, and you could probably tell lots of things about them. Here are some ways to choose the person you will write about.

■ Think of people you know well.

■ Think of important people in your life.

■ Think of famous people you would like to write about.

Gather Your Thoughts ● The amount of information you need for this step depends on how much you already know about your subject. Here are some ideas for collecting details.

Who is your subject?	How much do you know?	Where can you get information?
mother sister	I know a lot.	Search your memory.
neighbor uncle	I know some things.	Search your memory. Interview your subject.
bus driver dentist principal	I know very little.	Interview your subject and take notes. Read information about the subject.
historical figure sports figure	I know some facts. I need more information.	Read books and magazines. Listen to interviews on radio and TV. Surf the Internet.

Writing the First Draft

Start Writing ● Try to make your biographical sketch as interesting as possible. Here are some suggestions:

- Look over the details you have gathered and choose the ones that make your subject sound very special or interesting.
- Start by introducing your subject in a special way. Tell his or her name and a memorable detail or quotation.
- In the middle, give more details about your subject. Use colorful adjectives and active verbs. You can also include a story or an anecdote about your subject. (**SEE** page 124.)
- End your biographical sketch with a thought that sums up your feelings about this person.

Revising Improving Your Writing

Review Your Work ● Look over your first draft and check the following things:

- Do your details help the reader get a picture of your subject?
- Are your paragraphs in the best possible order?
- Do you sound truly interested in your subject?

 Express Yourself Have a classmate or an adult review your writing with you. Then make any necessary changes.

Editing and Proofreading

Check for Careless Errors ● Be sure that your writing makes sense and flows well from sentence to sentence. Then check your spelling, punctuation, capitalization, and grammar to be sure they are all correct. Write a final draft of your sketch to share with others. You may want to add a picture or a drawing of your subject.

Sample **Biographical Sketch**

This character sketch is by Daly Johnson. In it, she gives details that show how well she knows her neighbor Betty. The sketch also shows that Daly is a caring listener.

My Neighbor Betty

Beginning

The writer lets you know that she is focusing on Betty's memories.

My neighbor Betty is my friend, and she's old enough to be my grandmother. Sometimes we just sit and chat, and she tells me stories about her life. She sure remembers lots of things.

Betty loves to take out her picture album and talk about the important people in her life. Her eyes light up when she talks about her Uncle Matt, a firefighter. One day she got to go to the firehouse with him. She says the best part was telling jokes with all the firefighters.

Middle

Daly shares very specific details about Betty's life.

Betty likes to wear hats. She owns woolly hats, floppy sun hats, rain hats, stocking caps, and even baseball caps. My favorite one is her blue straw hat with the big sunflower flopping down the back. She looks great in that hat.

One day I was looking out the window, and I saw bubbles floating into the air. There was Betty sitting on the steps outside her house blowing bubbles. I went out and sat with her, and we had a contest to see who could blow the biggest bubble. Guess what? Betty won!

Ending

She lets you know how important Betty is to her.

Betty is moving to a new apartment next month. She won't be my neighbor anymore, but she'll still be my friend.

Sample **Biographical Sketch**

In this biographical sketch, Sabina Mahuto writes about the Shoshone woman Sacagawea. Sabina shows how important Sacagawea was to the Lewis and Clark expedition.

Beginning

Sabina introduces her subject.

Middle

The writer gives details about Sacagawea.

Ending

Sabina tells how Sacagawea is honored today.

Sacagawea

Sacagawea was a young woman who went with Lewis and Clark on their exploration of the United States. She was a member of the Shoshone tribe. Her name means either "Bird Woman" or "Boat Launcher."

Sacagawea and her husband met Lewis and Clark in the territory that is now called North Dakota. Lewis and Clark hired her husband to go with them to talk to the tribes they met. Sacagawea went along. It turned out that she knew more languages than her husband.

Sacagawea also knew members of the tribes along the way. Her brother was the chief of a band of Shoshones in the Rocky Mountains. Sacagawea asked her brother to help Lewis and Clark. He gave them food and horses.

Sacagawea was very valuable to the Lewis and Clark expedition. She earned great respect from the explorers because of her knowledge and skill. Lewis and Clark couldn't have gotten along without her.

Today there are many things named after Sacagawea. There are parks, monuments, and even a mountain peak called Sacagawea.

Writing Newspaper Stories

Look! Up in the Sky! It's a Reporter!

Wouldn't it be cool to be Superman? You could fly, leap across the Grand Canyon, and battle super villains!

When he wasn't flying around, though, Superman had a real job. As Clark Kent, he was a reporter. Working as a reporter can be exciting, too. Reporters write about important events and talk to interesting people.

"Starting today, you can be a reporter in your own classroom, school, and community. All you need is a little curiosity, an interest in people, and, of course, a reporter's notebook! With a little energy and creativity, you can even produce your own newspaper."

—ROY PETER CLARK, AUTHOR

Three Types of Stories

Here is a list of subjects used by student writers for their classroom newspaper, the *Cougar Chronicle*. The newspaper's motto is "If a fifth grader needs to know about it, we print it." The stories fall into three types: news stories, feature stories, and opinion letters to the editor.

News Stories

- A power outage kills fish in the fifth-grade aquarium.
- Lakewood High girls are soccer champs. (**SEE** page 161.)

Feature Stories

- Meet the fastest reader in fourth grade.
- Our math teacher plays in a rock band.
- Explore the bottom of the sea. (**SEE** page 159.)

Opinion Letters to the Editor

- We should have more time for reading and more books to choose from in our classroom library.
- People should not give pets as gifts because the pets are often abandoned.
- We need to save the historical places around us. (**SEE** page 165.)

Think It Over

The more unusual the event, the more interesting the news story will be. An old joke says that when a dog bites a man, it is not news. But when a man bites a dog, that's news!

The Parts of a Reporter

A curious mind to think of story ideas

Eyes to see interesting details →

A nose for news →

A mouth to ask the right questions →

← Ears to listen for great quotations

A heart for understanding people

Hands for writing down careful notes

Feet for following up on good stories

Interviewing

Many wonderful news stories result from interviews. During interviews, reporters talk to people about their experiences. After interviewing an oceanographer, Matt Barnes wrote what he found out.

Look Out Below
By Matt Barnes

What is it like at the bottom of the sea? "Cold, dark, mysterious, and exciting," says oceanographer Dan Anderson. "It's a whole different world."

According to Dr. Anderson, the best way to see the ocean is in a small submarine. Piloting a submarine two miles deep is like driving a car at night—slowly. A submersible's top speed is about five miles per hour. Its lights appear no brighter than flashlights in the dark water. The water temperature is only 6° C (43° F), so scientists wear wet suits for warmth.

Weird-looking creatures with built-in lights swim in the ocean depths. Dr. Anderson says he often turns off the sub's lights to enjoy this under-water light show. The ocean floor has mountains and valleys like the earth's surface. One mountain range is 4,000 miles long! On each dive to the deep sea, there are new animals, natural resources, or shipwrecks to explore.

Tips for Interviewing

- Write a list of questions to ask during the interview. (Be sure the questions require more than "yes" or "no" for an answer.)
- Listen carefully so you hear exactly what the person says.
- When you take notes, politely say, "I want to write that down." The person will stop talking so you can write.
- Ask the person to spell any words that you are unsure of.
- Remember that the meaning is more important than the exact words, unless you are writing down an exact quotation.

Parts of a Newspaper Story

Headline ① The headline is the title of a newspaper story.
Lakewood Girls Win Soccer Championship!

Byline ② The byline tells who wrote the news story.
By Anna Flanagan

Lead ③ The lead introduces the story and gives the most important news:
"The girls of Lakewood High School made history yesterday. They became the first team from West Florida to win a state soccer championship. They beat Rockledge High by a score of 1-0."

Caption ④ A caption explains a photo or an illustration that accompanies a story.

Quotation ⑤ A good quotation gives the story a personal feeling:
"The girls played great," said Coach Bill Carter. "I'll always remember this team."

Body ⑥ The body of the story answers questions and adds more details for the reader.
How many games did the team win this season? Who played well?

Ending ⑦ The ending gives the reader something to remember:
"Eight members of our soccer team will return next year. I am ready for the season to start right now."

Sample **News Story**

Cougar Chronicle

1 Lakewood Girls Win Soccer Championship!

2 By Anna Flanagan

3 The girls of Lakewood High School made history yesterday. They became the first team from West Florida to win a state soccer championship. They beat Rockledge High by a score of 1-0.

4 Sue James scores the single goal for Lakewood in the final minutes of the game.

5 "The girls played great," said Coach Bill Carter. "I'll always remember this team. In my eyes they are all stars."

6 Ever since Sue James broke the team record by scoring five goals against Central, no one could stop Lakewood. Sue and her teammates Rose Munz and Colleen Kelly played such good defense that only one goal was scored against them in their last three games.

They have set a new record for their high school, ending the season with a record of 7 wins and 0 losses.

7 Coach Carter smiled as he said, "Eight members of our soccer team will return next year. I am ready for the season to start right now."

Writing a News Story

Planning Your News Story

Choose a Subject ● Write about a person or an event that is important, interesting, or unusual—something that people will want to read about. If you are stuck for ideas, see what real reporters write about. You'll find newspapers from around the world on the Internet.

Gather Details ● Collect information through personal observations, interviews, and research. Start by answering the 5 W's and H—*Who? What? Where? When? Why?* and *How?*

Writing the First Draft

Write the Lead, or First Paragraph ● In a news story, begin with the most important idea or fact. In a feature story, start with an especially interesting detail.

Write the Main Part of the Story ● Write about the most important information first and then add details. Write an ending that leaves your reader something to think about.

Revising Improving Your News Story

Review Your Work ● Make sure you have included all the important facts and details in your story and that you have presented them in the best order.

Editing and Proofreading

Check for Careless Errors ● Check your writing for word choice, correctness, and the best sentence order. In addition, pay close attention to the spelling of names! Have someone else check your work, too. Then write the final copy of your story.

Writing a Lead

The beginning of a news story is called the **lead** because it leads the reader into the rest of the story. A lead can be one sentence or a short paragraph.

Express Yourself Review Matt Barnes's lead for "Look Out Below" on page 159. How does he lead readers into his story?

There are different ways to write a lead. You can ask a question, make a surprising comparison, be suspenseful, write a colorful description, or use a quotation.

Student Samples

Here are some leads written by student reporters. See if they make you want to keep reading. Then imagine what the rest of each story is about.

Question: What is the new animal sensation in Ms. Romaro's science class? (news story)

Quotation: "It was a great victory, one we'll never forget!" exclaimed Coach Jones. (news story)

Surprise: The World's Greatest Singing Hot-Dog Salesman lives in our town. His name is Tommy Walton, a 58-year-old man with the heart and soul of a teenager. (feature story)

Description: Picture the most beautiful sunset you've ever seen. Now picture that same sunset over a new nuclear power plant. (feature story)

Suspense: Students joke about the school cafeteria serving mystery meals. What we found on our plates last week was no joke. Here's the scoop about one mystery meal. (news story)

Writing a Letter to the Editor

When you feel strongly about something and want to share your feelings with others, you can write a letter to the editor.

Prewriting Planning Your Writing

Choose a Subject ● Write about an issue that you feel strongly about—one that will interest other people, too.

Gather Details ● Answer the 5 W's—*Who? What? Where? When?* and *Why?* Also tell how you feel about the issue.

Writing the First Draft

Beginning ● In an editorial, the opening paragraph should explain the situation. First give the facts; then state your opinion as clearly as possible.

Middle ● The body of your letter should give background information that supports your opinion. Then share details that will help readers understand the issue. You want them to agree with you.

Ending ● End with a statement supporting your opinion.

Revising Improving Your Writing

Review Your Letter ● Make sure that your letter includes enough facts and details to fully explain and support your idea or opinion. Present your information in the best possible order.

Editing and Proofreading

Check for Careless Errors ● Check any dates, names, or other details for accuracy. Also have someone check your letter for errors. Make corrections and then write or type a neat final copy.

Sample Letter to the Editor

1566 Telegraph Road
Enfield, CT 06082
October 15, 2000

Editor
The Journal Inquirer
555 Middle Road
Enfield, CT 06082

Dear Editor:

At Nathan Hale School, the school board has just approved a plan to build new playground equipment. However, the tree by the gym would have to be cut down. If that old oak is cut down, a piece of history will disappear, too.

That tree was here when Nathan Hale lived here. He supposedly carved his initials in it. Even if he didn't, the tree always reminds me of our Revolutionary War hero.

My dad knows about these things, and I had him look at the plans. He said the playground could be moved 15 feet west. It might not be as convenient, but I would like to save this tree and a piece of our history.

Yours truly,

Heidi Bailey
Heidi Bailey

HEIDI BAILEY
1566 TELEGRAPH ROAD
ENFIELD CT 06082

LETTERS TO THE EDITOR
THE JOURNAL INQUIRER
555 MIDDLE ROAD
ENFIELD CT 06082

Writing Book Reviews

Sharing Your Views

The students at McPherson School really enjoy sharing their thoughts and feelings in book reviews. Their classroom is loaded with books to choose from. And after reading each other's reviews, the students always know which books they want to read next.

Becoming an Expert

The students also enjoy this form of writing because it gives them a chance to write about subjects that really interest them. For example, two students named Devon and Christa are both crazy about sports. When they read good sports stories, they *want* to write about them. And when other students want to read sports stories, they turn to Devon and Christa (and their reviews) for suggestions.

In a book review, you share your understanding of and opinion about a book you have read.

Sample Book Review

In the following model, student Anne Krogman reviews the book *Shipwreck at the Bottom of the World*. After a short introduction, Anne answers three basic questions about the book.

What is the book about?

What do I like about this book?

What is the book's theme or message?

Shipwreck at the Bottom of the World

Shipwreck at the Bottom of the World by Jennifer Armstrong is the most exciting book I've ever read. It describes one of the most amazing adventures in history.

In 1914, 28 explorers try to cross Antarctica. They never get there. Their ship becomes trapped by ice 100 miles from their destination. The explorers are stranded for almost two years near Antarctica. In Antarctica the temperature can get to -100° Fahrenheit. Ernest Shackleton, the group's leader, sails 800 miles in a 20-foot boat to look for help.

I loved reading the details of this adventure. With 40 photos from the actual explorers, I felt like I was there with them. I don't like ice and cold, but I had to keep reading to find out what these explorers did to survive.

The author describes how brave these explorers were. As I read this book, I wondered if I could have been that brave. The author shows how different people can work together as a team. She also tells how important being a good leader is. The book is great from start to finish.

Note Never tell readers everything that happens in your book or all of your reasons for liking it. Say just enough to help them decide for themselves if they want to read it.

Writing a Book Review

Prewriting Planning Your Book Review

Choose a Subject ● You may review any type of book—a mystery, an adventure story, a book about your favorite sports figure, a book of poems, and so on. Just make sure that you enjoyed the book or at least have strong feelings about it.

Gather Your Thoughts ● Your book review should answer three basic questions: *What is the book about? What do I like about the book? What is the book's theme or message?* (The "Collection Sheet" on the next page will help you gather information for your review.)

Writing the First Draft

Share Your Thoughts ● In the first paragraph of your book review, give the book's title, the author's name, and a general idea of what the book is about. Then answer the three basic questions in separate paragraphs. (**SEE** pages 167 and 169.)

Revising Improving Your Book Review

Make It Clear ● Check your first draft for ideas that seem unclear or out of order. Also be sure that you haven't said too much, or too little. (Saying too much is a common problem. You don't want to give the whole book away.)

Editing and Proofreading

Check It Out ● Make sure your review reads clearly from start to finish. Check for capitalization, punctuation, and spelling errors. (Remember that book titles should be underlined or italicized.) Then write a neat final draft and proofread it.

Collection Sheet

The ideas listed below will help you answer three basic review questions about your book, whether it's fiction or nonfiction.

1. What is the book about?

Fiction: What happens in the story? (A book review should highlight a few events rather than tell the whole story.)

Nonfiction: What is the basic subject of this book? Is there one part that seems really important?

2. What do I like about the book?

Fiction: Does the book start in an exciting or interesting way? Does it contain a lot of action or suspense? Does the main character show courage or strength? Is the ending a surprise?

Nonfiction: Does the book contain interesting, easy-to-follow information? Does the book include some good diagrams or colorful illustrations?

3. What is the book's theme or message?

Fiction: What message about life is the author sharing? (Here is a sample message: It's not easy to stand up for your rights.) What details or events in the story helped you discover the theme?

Nonfiction: Why do you think the author wrote this book? What basic information or message does the author want to share?

Express Yourself Once your review is ready, share it with your class, or with kids everywhere by posting it on the Internet. (**SEE** page 269.)

Sample Book Review Brochure

Another way to write a book review is to make a brochure. Book review brochures use words and pictures to invite others to read the book.

On the Cover

Invite others to read the book. (Draw pictures or find photos related to the subject.) →

Inside the Brochure

Use details about the story to persuade others to read the book. ↘

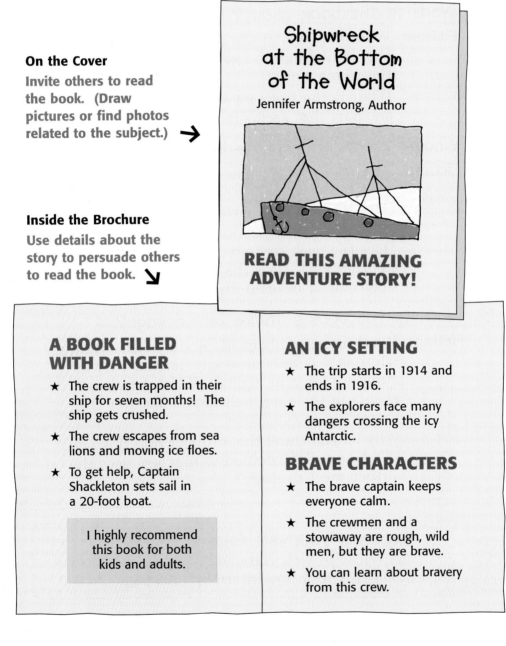

Shipwreck at the Bottom of the World

Jennifer Armstrong, Author

READ THIS AMAZING ADVENTURE STORY!

A BOOK FILLED WITH DANGER

★ The crew is trapped in their ship for seven months! The ship gets crushed.

★ The crew escapes from sea lions and moving ice floes.

★ To get help, Captain Shackleton sets sail in a 20-foot boat.

I highly recommend this book for both kids and adults.

AN ICY SETTING

★ The trip starts in 1914 and ends in 1916.

★ The explorers face many dangers crossing the icy Antarctic.

BRAVE CHARACTERS

★ The brave captain keeps everyone calm.

★ The crewmen and a stowaway are rough, wild men, but they are brave.

★ You can learn about bravery from this crew.

Writing in a Response Journal

There are many ways to think about and respond to what you read. One of the best ways is to keep a journal. In your journal, you may write about the main character, you may try to guess what will happen next in the story, or you may relate some part of the story to your own life. The choice is yours.

How to Respond

Try to write in your journal at least three times for every book you read. For longer books, make it four or five times. Some of the ideas in your journal will help you write book reviews. The following questions will help you respond as you read.

First Feelings

What did you like best about the first few chapters? How do you feel about the characters?

On Your Way

Are the events in the story clear? Do you still feel the same way about the characters? What do you think will happen next?

The Second Half

What seems to be important now? Is the book still interesting? How do you think it will end?

Summing Up

How do you feel about the ending? Has the main character changed? How does the book relate to your own life? What do you like most about the book? What do you like least? Why?

 Express Yourself Here are some more ideas: Write a poem about the book, draw a picture from the story, write a new ending, or put together a brochure. (**SEE** page 170.)

How-To Writing

Eating Dirt

Eating real dirt would be yucky, but the dirt you make following these directions tastes yummy. First, make a small package of instant chocolate pudding in a bowl. Then crush a bag of chocolate sandwich cookies. Dump most of the crushed cookies into the thick, muddy pudding. Next, if you like, pour the "dirt" into a washed out, BRAND-NEW flowerpot. Slide in some gummy worms and gummy bugs. Then put the rest of the crushed cookies on top of the dirt as a layer of topsoil. Put it in the refrigerator for one hour. Finally, dig in! If you don't like dirt, try sand. Use vanilla pudding and vanilla wafers.

Explaining Things

These directions for "Eating Dirt" may sound like a joke, but if you follow them carefully, you'll make a great dessert. There are many times when you have to give directions or explain things, like

- **how to make something,**
- **how to get someplace,**
- **how to do something, or**
- **how something works.**

Writing an Explanation

Prewriting Planning Your How-To Writing

Choose a Subject ● Think of things you know how to do: bake a cake, build a birdhouse, or do skateboarding tricks. You could also write about something you are interested in, such as how early pioneers crossed the plains or how to save endangered animals. You could tell how something works— how the body digests food or how a space shuttle flies.

Gather Details ● If you need more details before you write, do the "how-to" activity yourself, watch someone else do it, read about it, or surf the Internet.

Writing the First Draft

Explain It Clearly ● Begin with a topic sentence or title that names your subject. Explain how to carry out your activity from start to finish, listing each step. (Explanations don't have to be boring, so have fun!)

Helpful Hint: Use linking words like *first, second, next,* and *then* to help readers move from one step to the next.

Revising Improving Your Writing

Test It Out ● Carefully read your first draft to make sure the directions are clear and complete. Then have someone else read your explanation to look for any missing points.

Editing and Proofreading

Check It Out ● Be sure your revised draft reads smoothly and is free of careless errors. Make a neat final copy and proofread it before sharing it.

 Sample **How-To Writing**

How to get someplace. In the following model, Hillary Bachman provides directions for the driver of a stretch limo that took Hillary and her friends on a special birthday ride.

Birthday Ride

For my birthday ride, I want to go from my house to Billy's Restaurant in La Crosse following this route. First, drive north four blocks until you reach Montgomery Street. Then take a left. Continue past the senior high and take the second left after you pass the school. This road will take you in a big loop. After you pass the senior high again, turn right and drive past Lawrence Lawson Elementary School. Then take the second left. Drive until you reach Water Street and take a right. This will take you through downtown and past Tim's house (please honk). Turn right after you cross the bridge. This highway (16) will take us directly to Billy's. Thank you!

How something works. In the following paragraph, Lauren Kitchell explains how the digestive system works.

Digestion

The digestive system is really a process. It starts as soon as you put food in your mouth. The food gets chewed up by the teeth. Then the salivary glands make a digestive juice called saliva. The saliva covers the chewed-up food, and the food goes down the esophagus, to the stomach. Next, the food in the stomach gets churned up and covered with some more digestive juices. After the stomach does its job, the liver and pancreas add digestive juices for use in the small intestine. From the small intestine the digested food passes into the bloodstream. The wastes of the food go into the large intestine. Finally, the waste is stored in the large intestine and goes out of the body.

How to make something. Here are Kimberly Tso's steps for following a real recipe.

My Favorite Food

This is how my grandma makes fried bread. First, she puts some flour in a bowl. She puts baking soda and salt with the flour. She gets some warm water. She puts in a little bit of water at a time while mixing the flour to make a dough. She kneads or mixes the dough to make it soft. Then she covers it with a cloth. She lets it set for 5 minutes. She puts a pan with grease in it on the stove. She waits until the grease gets hot. By that time the dough is ready. Finally, she starts making fried bread. She fries pieces of dough until they are golden brown and delicious.

How to do something. Ben Koplin uses a list to present his explanation of how people can get involved in a cause.

Save Our Wilderness

People can enjoy the wilderness and still preserve it for others. Here are 10 simple rules for campers and hikers to follow:

1. Pack out whatever you pack in. Don't leave anything except footprints in the wilderness.
2. Hike on marked trails to lessen damage to plants.
3. Camp at least 20 feet away from water or trails.
4. Respect all creatures you meet, even snakes and spiders.
5. Carefully burn or bury any leftover food.
6. Don't wash dishes or yourself in rivers or lakes.
7. Make campfires only in a fire pit or a stone ring.
8. Look, touch, and smell but don't bring home any souvenirs.
9. Don't feed the wildlife.
10. Don't talk LOUD or make other loud noises.

Business Writing

When You Mean Business

A very common form of writing used in the business world is the business letter. You will want to write business letters when

- **you need information**
  (a letter of request),
- **you have a problem with a service or a product**
  (a letter of complaint), **or**
- **you need to react to a situation in your city or school**
  (a letter to an editor or official).

Other common forms of business writing include memos and e-mail messages. You will learn about the special format for the business letter and the memo in this chapter. (**SEE** pages 146-147 for information about e-mail messages.)

Writing a Business Letter

Prewriting Planning Your Letter

Choose a Subject ● Think about the reason for writing your letter. Decide what you want your reader to know or do.

Gather Details ● Gather information for your letter by making a list of important details.

Writing the First Draft

Follow the Format ● Follow the format for a business letter on pages 178-179.

Beginning ● Introduce your subject and your reason for writing.

Middle ● Explain any important facts and details in short paragraphs. Be polite and positive. Remember to use words that treat people fairly. Use *mail carrier,* not *mailman;* use *salesperson,* not *salesman.*

Ending ● Explain what you want your reader to do and then end politely.

Revising Improving Your Letter

Review Your Work ● Be sure you answered any questions your reader may have. Check to see that your letter reads smoothly.

Editing and Proofreading

Check for Errors ● Check for errors in capitalization, spelling, and punctuation. Double-check your facts and the spellings of names and places. Be certain you used the correct business-letter format.

Parts of a Business Letter

Heading ① The heading includes the sender's address and the date. Begin an inch from the top of the page at the left margin.

Inside Address ② The inside address includes the name and address of the person or company you are writing to. Place it at the left margin, four to seven spaces below the heading. If the person has a special title, such as *park ranger,* add it after his or her name. (Use a comma first.)

Mr. David Shore, Park Ranger

Salutation ③ The salutation (greeting) should begin on the second line below the inside address. Always use a colon at the end of the salutation.

■ If you know the person's name, write this:

Dear Mr. Shore:

■ If you don't know the name, use clear, fair language:

Dear Park Ranger:	**Dear Sir or Madam:**
Dear Yellowstone Park:	**Greetings:**

Body ④ The body is the main part of the letter. Begin this part two lines below the salutation. Do not indent. Double-space between paragraphs.

Closing ⑤ Write the closing at the left margin, two lines below the body. Use *Sincerely* for a business letter closing. Always place a comma after the closing.

Signature ⑥ End your letter by writing your signature beneath the closing. If you are typing your letter, skip four lines and type your full name.

Sample Letter of Request

1 4824 Park Street
Richland Center, WI 53581
January 1, 2000

2 Mr. David Shore, Park Ranger
Yellowstone National Park
Box 168
Yellowstone National Park, WY 82190

3 Dear Mr. Shore:

4 We're having a contest in my family to see who can plan the best summer vacation. I want to convince everyone that a trip to Yellowstone National Park would be better than going to New York City or even to the seashore for a week. This is not going to be easy!

I would appreciate any help you could give me. I am most interested in some up-to-date brochures with photos and maps of the park. I will also need some information about where we can stay and what we can do in the park.

Thank you for your help. Maybe I'll see you next summer.

5 Sincerely,

6 *Luke Johnson*
Luke Johnson

Sample Letter of Complaint

7534 Green Blvd.
Albany, NY 12204
March 27, 2000

Mr. Wong-Tsu, Manager
Petland
6574 Bubble Dr.
Albany, NY 12205

Dear Mr. Wong-Tsu:

Beginning
Explain the problem.

In February, our science class ordered two male gerbils from Petland. However, yesterday, one gerbil had six babies! Our class is very excited! But Mrs. King, our teacher, says that if the gerbil has another litter, we will have to get rid of all of them.

Middle
Suggest a solution.

Mr. Wong-Tsu, we'd like to trade gerbils. Could we return the babies and the female? Would you give us another male?

Next week, I'll call to ask if you are willing to trade. I hope you will be. Our class likes our male gerbil, Harry. We hope you can find new owners for Francine and all of her babies. Our whole class hopes you can help us keep our gerbils. Thank you very much. I look forward to talking to you next week.

Ending
Give final information.

Sincerely,

Jason Kornelis
Jason Kornelis

Folding Your Letter

When you finish your letter, fold it in three parts.

Like this:
- Fold bottom one-third up.
- Next, fold top one-third down.
- Crease the folds firmly.
- Insert into envelope.

Or like this:
- Fold letter in half.
- Next, fold into thirds.
- Crease folds firmly.
- Insert into envelope.

Addressing the Envelope

- Place the full name and complete address of the person to whom the letter is being sent about halfway down and slightly to the left of the middle of the envelope.
- Place your return address in the upper left-hand corner of the envelope and the stamp in the upper right-hand corner.

```
MR LUKE JOHNSON
4824 PARK ST
RICHLAND CENTER WI 53581
```
USA

```
            MR DAVID SHORE
            PARK RANGER
            YELLOWSTONE NATIONAL PARK
            BOX 168
            YELLOWSTONE NATIONAL PARK  WY  82190
```

Note When you address your envelope, the post office prefers that you use all capital letters, no punctuation, and the two-letter abbreviations for states. (**SEE** page 397.)

Writing a Memo

A memo is a short written message that you can share with a teacher, a parent, a coach, or a principal. Memos ask and answer questions, give instructions, or serve as reminders. You can use memos at school and at home.

Prewriting Planning Your Memo

Choose a Subject ● Focus on your topic. Why are you writing? What does your reader need to know?

Gather Details ● List important details.

Writing the First Draft

Follow the Format ● Follow the format for a memo. (**SEE** page 183.)

Beginning ● Include the date, your reader's name, your name, and the subject of your memo. At the beginning of your message, tell the main point.

Middle ● Give the important details of your message.

Ending ● Focus on any necessary action or special information you need. End politely.

Revising Improving Your Writing

Review Your Work ● Be sure that your memo is complete and clear. Have you answered any questions the reader might have? Are your details easy to follow?

Editing and Proofreading

Check for Errors ● Pay attention to spelling, capitalization, and punctuation. Are all of your heading and subject lines accurate? Are all of your sentences complete?

Sample **Memo**

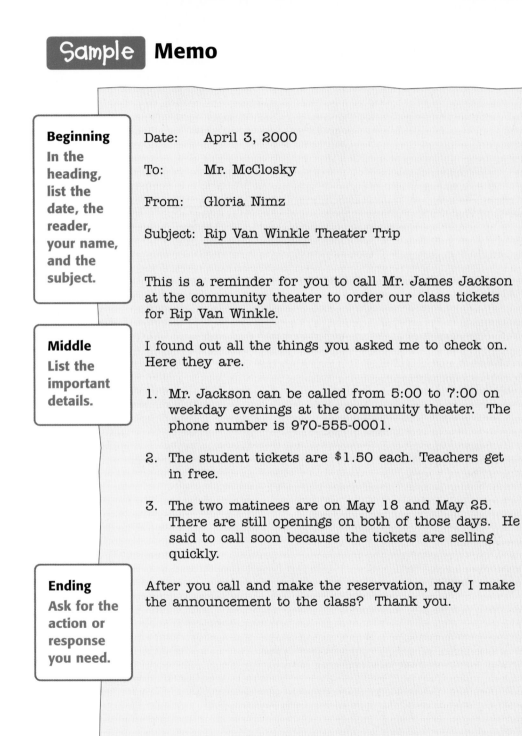

Beginning
In the heading, list the date, the reader, your name, and the subject.

Date: April 3, 2000

To: Mr. McClosky

From: Gloria Nimz

Subject: Rip Van Winkle Theater Trip

This is a reminder for you to call Mr. James Jackson at the community theater to order our class tickets for Rip Van Winkle.

Middle
List the important details.

I found out all the things you asked me to check on. Here they are.

1. Mr. Jackson can be called from 5:00 to 7:00 on weekday evenings at the community theater. The phone number is 970-555-0001.

2. The student tickets are $1.50 each. Teachers get in free.

3. The two matinees are on May 18 and May 25. There are still openings on both of those days. He said to call soon because the tickets are selling quickly.

Ending
Ask for the action or response you need.

After you call and make the reservation, may I make the announcement to the class? Thank you.

Report Writing

Writing a Summary

Learning and Remembering

Think of all the reading you are asked to do in school. Each day you are expected to read handouts, chapters, and stories. On your own, you are expected to do even more reading for special reports and projects. That's a lot of reading! And, on top of that, you are expected to understand and remember all the important ideas in what you read. One thing you can do to help you remember is write a summary.

The Big Squeeze

When you write a summary, you choose only the most important ideas from a reading selection. Then you use your own words to combine these ideas into a simple paragraph or two.

The process of writing a summary is a little like squeezing out toothpaste. You squeeze out just what you need and leave the rest in the tube.

Writing a Summary

Prewriting Planning Your Summary

Skim and List ● Learn as much as you can about a reading selection before you try to summarize it.

■ Skim it once (look at the title, headings, pictures, and so on) to get the general meaning. Then read the selection carefully.

■ List the main points on your paper. Try to figure out the main idea of the selection.

Writing the First Draft

Use Your Own Words ● Write your summary in clear and complete sentences. Use your own words, except for key words.

■ Write a first sentence that states the main idea.

■ Include only the most important information in the rest of your summary. Do not get too detailed.

■ Arrange your ideas so that they are easy to follow.

■ Add a concluding sentence, if one seems to be needed.

 **Note** The first sentence in a summary is the topic sentence. The sentences that follow must all support the topic sentence. (**SEE** page 187.)

Revising and **Editing** Improving Your Writing

Review Carefully ● Ask yourself the following questions:

■ Have I included the most important ideas?

■ Have I stated these ideas clearly and in my own words?

■ Could another person get the main idea of this selection by reading my summary?

 **Summary**

Leaves change color in autumn because they lose their green pigment. Red, orange, and yellow pigments are in the leaves, too, but they are hidden by the green. When cooler weather comes, the green chlorophyll pigment breaks down, and the other colors can be seen. Then the leaves dry up, and the wind blows them off the tree.

Original Reading Selection

Why Do Leaves Change Color?

Even though leaves may look pure green in summer, they have other colors, too. Red, orange, and yellow pigments, which protect the leaves by blocking the harmful ultraviolet rays in sunlight, are hidden by green chlorophyll. It is the chlorophyll that produces food for the tree.

In autumn, shorter days and cooler nights cause the green chlorophyll pigment in the leaves to break down and flow back into the tree. As the leaves' green color fades, the other colors begin to show themselves.

After the chlorophyll breaks down, leaves cannot make food anymore. Tubes (called xylem and phloem) that carried water to the leaf and food back to the tree become plugged. A layer of cork forms between the stems of the leaves and the tree branches.

Shortly after that, the leaves die and hang from their stems by a few strands. Cold autumn winds dry and twist the leaves until they become separated from the tree and float to the ground.

Writing Observation Reports

Using Your Senses

Do you like watching people? If you do, you will probably enjoy writing an observation report.

The writing in the box below is part of a student's observation report. The subject is a playground, and the writer has used all her senses to observe different *sights, sounds, smells,* and *feelings.* In an observation report, you simply select a location, look, listen, learn—and write.

I hear kids shouting. There is a strange scent in the air. There is a faint breeze. It is 9:35 Saturday morning, and the playground is filling up with kids. Cars keep whizzing past. Suddenly an in-line skater zooms by . . .

Writing an Observation Report

Prewriting Planning Your Observation Report

Select a Location ● Choose a place with lots of activity. Try a classroom, park, mall, local zoo, the school cafeteria, or a location you recently visited on a field trip.

Observe and Write ● In a notebook or on a laptop computer, write what you see, hear, smell, and feel at this location. Write notes quickly as you observe so you don't miss anything. Spend at least 15 minutes observing.

 Tip A camcorder or cassette recorder may be helpful for collecting observations. But check with your teacher before doing any recording.

Writing the First Draft

Prepare Your Report ● You can write your observation report in two different ways.

1. You can share all the details in the order that you observed them. In this way, your report will flow from one sight or sound to another. This is how the sample at the beginning of the chapter is written.

2. You can organize your observations around a main idea, just as you would in a descriptive paragraph. This is how the samples on pages 104 and 190 are organized.

Revising and **Editing** Improving Your Report

Check for Changes ● Review your first draft to make sure it contains your most important observations. Check that your sentences are in the best order. Each sentence should flow into the next one. Then edit your writing for any spelling, capitalization, and punctuation errors.

Sample | **Observation Report**

In this paragraph, the writer puts the main idea in the first sentence. The observations are listed in the order in which they were observed.

A Visit to Fort Laramie
By Daniel Cortez

We sit on a porch at Fort Laramie, waiting for the gate to open. The big, blue Wyoming sky stretches down to meet the grassy plains. My little brother's face and hands are smeared with chocolate. He squishes a melting candy bar into my mom's hand. She scrunches up her face and says, "Yuck." A man dressed as a mountain man walks past us carrying a long rifle. He wears a heavy buckskin jacket and a fur hat. Sweat pours down his red, sunburned face. A woman in a long green dress carries a laundry basket into a big white tent. Her dress rustles as she walks. A cannon booms and everybody jumps. "Come on, everyone," laughs my dad. "It's time for the tour."

Express Yourself Try to make your writing *show* readers what happens instead of just telling them. Dan Cortez could have told us "the man was sweating," but by writing "sweat pours down his red, sunburned face," he *shows* us instead. (**SEE** "Show, don't tell" on page 58 for more examples.)

Sample Science Observation Report

Your science teacher may ask you to write an observation report on an experiment or a project. For one of his science projects, Emery Sanford observed how mold grows on different kinds of bread. Part of his final report follows.

Observing Mold on Bread

PROCEDURE: On October 27, I brought my bread to school. I had four different kinds of bread: white bread, whole wheat bread, French bread, and pita bread. I put each piece of bread in a sandwich bag and waited a few days for the mold to grow.

OBSERVATIONS: The white bread started growing mold first. The mold was green and white. Before this, I had never seen anything other than green mold on bread. This was the first thing I learned about mold.

The whole wheat bread started by getting little white speckles on it. In four days there was mold on the bread. It got green, white, and even yellow mold. Now I had seen two new colors that I had never seen before.

The French bread got stale very quickly. It got very hard, and then it started getting moldy. The mold grew on the inside of the bread, not on the outside like the others.

My pita didn't grow mold at all. I'm not sure why. It did get hard. That's something I didn't know, that some pita bread can get stale, but not moldy.

CONCLUSIONS: I learned a lot of things during this observation. I learned that there are different colored molds, how mold grows, and what mold looks like under a microscope. And most important, I learned what kind of bread to buy if you want it to last: either pita or whole wheat.

Writing a Classroom Report

Flying Fish, Ocean Acrobats

Your teacher says, "Today, students, we're going to begin our reports on fish."

"Oh, no! Not another report," you think. "Sometimes they can be so boring." But wait a second. Your teacher is now saying this report should be on something different about fish, not the same old stuff. Maybe you've seen a "fish story" on television, in a magazine, or as part of a movie. Or maybe you have a personal story to tell.

> When you write a report, you should find a topic that you would like to know more about—a topic that you would enjoy reading about, writing about, and sharing with others.

Writing a Classroom Report

To write a good report, there are four things you must do:
(1) choose an interesting subject, (2) gather information about
the subject, (3) make a plan, and (4) write an interesting report.

Prewriting Choosing a Subject

Choose a Subject ● The first thing you have to do when you
write a report is to find a good subject. A good subject is one
that is interesting and *specific*. (*Fish* is a general subject;
saltwater fish is more specific. More about that later.) You
also have to find a subject that works well for your assignment.
To do that, you need to explore all the possibilities.

Create a Cluster (Web) or List ● You may want to use a
cluster to begin your subject search. First, put your general
subject in the middle. Then, think of questions that interest
you about the subject.

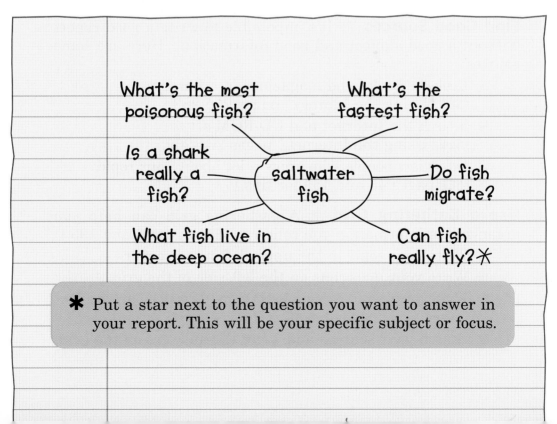

What's the most poisonous fish?

What's the fastest fish?

Is a shark really a fish?

saltwater fish

Do fish migrate?

What fish live in the deep ocean?

Can fish really fly? ✱

✱ Put a star next to the question you want to answer in
your report. This will be your specific subject or focus.

Prewriting Gathering Information

Create a List ● Once you have selected a specific subject, decide what you want to learn about it. Listing questions about your subject is one way to do this:

Flying Fish

1. How fast do they go?
2. How and why do they fly?
3. How far can they fly?
4. Has anyone seen one fly?
5. Who are their enemies?
6. How long have they been around?
7. What do they look like?

Tip Avoid asking questions that can just be answered with a simple "yes" or "no." Asking questions that begin with "how" or "why" often leads to interesting answers.

Find Good Sources ● It's impossible to write a good report without a good subject and good information. Here are some sources:

- Look for books and magazines in a library. (**SEE** "Using the Library," pages 255-263.)
- Search the Internet and CD-ROM's. (**SEE** "Using the Internet," pages 264-269.)
- Interview people who know a lot about your topic. (**SEE** pages 46 and 159 for tips.)

Use a Gathering Grid ● A gathering grid can help you organize the information you collect. (**SEE** pages 46 and 195.)

- Write your topic in the upper left-hand corner.
- Write your questions on the left side of the grid.
- Write your sources across the top. (Sources are books, interviews, magazines, the Internet, and so on.)
- Search your sources and write the answers on the grid.

Sample Gathering Grid

Sources of Information

Flying Fish	Books and Encyclopedias	Interview	Magazine Articles	Internet
1. How fast do they go?	Fly at 40 mph <u>How Fish Fly</u>, p. 2		More than 40 mph <u>Ranger Rick</u>	
2. How and why do they fly?	Tails flap 50 beats/sec. <u>How Fish Fly</u>, p. 2			Spread their pectoral fins <u>Barbados: Flying Fish</u>
3. How far can they fly?	Some glide as far as 3 football fields. <u>Flying Fish</u>, p. 42			
4. Has anyone seen one fly?		Fisherman Abe Short interview in writer's notebook	Yes, scientists did. <u>Ranger Rick</u>	
5. Who are their enemies?	Dolphins eat flying fish.			
6. How long have they been around?	Since dinosaur days <u>Yesterday, Today, & Tomorrow</u>, p. 92			
7. What do they look like?	5"–18" long <u>World Book</u>			Shaped like a herring <u>Barbados: Flying Fish</u>

Your Questions

Prewriting Gathering Information

Use Note Cards ● There can be a lot of information to write down for a report. Your grid will help you keep track of all your facts, but you may find that some of the facts just won't fit. That's when you may need to use note cards. Simply write the question across the top of a note card. List all your answers on the card. Then write the source and page references on the bottom.

> What do flying fish look like?   #7
> —5"-18" long
> —there are several kinds
> —large fins
> —two sets of fins, front and back
> —silvery color (picture)
>
> "Fish in the Air," pages 34–35

Quotations ● When you read something in a book or magazine that you want to use "word for word," copy down the quotation just as it was written. Do the same for what is said in an interview. (Remember to use quotation marks before and after a quotation.)

> #4
> Has anyone seen one fly?
> "It came sailing through the air, and before I knew it, the fish was sticking into the side of my boat. Luckily it missed me by a few inches, or I would have been hurting for sure. The next thing I knew, it wiggled itself loose and was off again."
>
> Interview with Abe Short, March 15

Note ● When you use exact words from books, magazines, and interviews, you must give credit to those sources in your report.

Prewriting Organizing Your Information

A Writing Plan ● A writing plan can help you stay organized as you write your report. Here is the five-point plan used for "Flying Fish, Ocean Acrobats."

Specific Focus: **Flying fish**
Purpose: **To report information**
Form: **Classroom report**
Audience: **Teacher and classmates**
Voice: **Serious**

An Outline ● To organize the details you have gathered, use an outline like the one below or try another graphic organizer. (**SEE** pages 48 and 333-336.)

Sample Sentence Outline

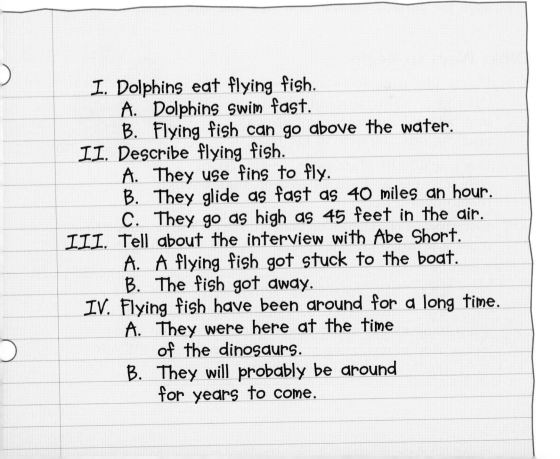

I. Dolphins eat flying fish.
   A. Dolphins swim fast.
   B. Flying fish can go above the water.
II. Describe flying fish.
   A. They use fins to fly.
   B. They glide as fast as 40 miles an hour.
   C. They go as high as 45 feet in the air.
III. Tell about the interview with Abe Short.
   A. A flying fish got stuck to the boat.
   B. The fish got away.
IV. Flying fish have been around for a long time.
   A. They were here at the time
      of the dinosaurs.
   B. They will probably be around
      for years to come.

Writing the First Draft

Once you have organized all your information, you can begin writing the first draft of your report. Here are some tips to help you make your report clear and interesting.

BEGINNING

Begin Your Report with a Hook ● Most writing needs a good hook, something that will start it off with a bang. Starting with a short story or an *anecdote* is one way to begin.

> In the ocean, two hungry dolphins pick up speed when they see a school of flying fish. Sensing danger, the flying fish swim faster and faster. Soon they are going 20 miles an hour. As the dolphins get closer, the flying fish break through the surface, spread their side fins, and take off.

Other Ways to Begin

- Use a quotation from an interview. ("It came sailing through the air, and before I knew it, the fish was sticking into the side of my boat.")

- Use a dramatic statement. (Some flying fish can soar as high as 45 feet, high enough to sail over a house!)

- Introduce a character or your subject. (You're about to meet a strange creature, one that you won't forget.)

Express Yourself When writing a report, use your own words as much as possible. It's okay to use some direct quotations from other people, but be sure to give them credit. (If you don't, it's called *plagiarism*.)

MIDDLE

Tie Your Facts Together ● Simply listing the facts you've gathered would give you a report like a shopping list: useful, but boring! Linking your facts together from beginning to end would change that list into an interesting report.

> **Flying fish are called the dragonflies of the deep. But flying fish don't have wings like dragonflies or birds. They use two sets of pectoral fins as wings to fly. Their front fins lift them out of the water, and their back fins help them soar over the surface. Their flights are actually glides.**
>
> **Because they are only gliding, the fish can't fly long distances like birds. However, they can fly as fast as 40 miles per hour, and they can glide as far as three football fields. Most flying fish glide 4 feet above the water. But some have been known to soar as high as 45 feet, high enough to sail over a house!**

Add Information As Needed ● After you've linked all your facts together, you have to decide whether you need more information. If you do, try using quotations and charts. A quotation from a real person can bring your report to life; a chart can make your report easier to understand.

> **Sometimes flying fish land in fishing boats. One fisherman, Abe Short, recalled the day a flying fish dropped right out of the sky into his boat. "It came sailing through the air, and before I knew it, the fish was sticking into the side of my boat. Luckily it missed me by a few inches, or I would have been hurting for sure. The next thing I knew, it wiggled itself loose and was off again."**

Writing the First Draft

ENDING

End with a Strong Point ● End your report with a summary of your main ideas, a strong point about your subject, or a look ahead to the future.

> **Their ability to escape enemies by taking to the air helps flying fish survive. They have been gliding since the days of the dinosaurs. Their special skill will probably keep them soaring for ages to come.**

Revising Improving Your Report

Use a Checklist ● Use the questions below as a guide for revising your report.

BEGINNING Does the opening paragraph get the reader's attention and introduce a specific subject?

MIDDLE Does each paragraph include important information? Are all of these paragraphs arranged in the best order? Should any information be added, cut, or made clearer?

ENDING Does the closing paragraph summarize the main ideas or leave the reader with something to think about?

Editing and Proofreading

Check for Accuracy ● Double-check your sources to be sure all of your facts are accurate.

Check for Errors ● Read over the revised copy of your report, looking for punctuation, spelling, capitalization, and grammar errors. Also have your teacher or a classmate check for errors.

Preparing a Bibliography

Your teacher may ask you to make a list of the materials (sources) you used to write your report. In that case, you will need to include a bibliography page at the end of your report. Follow the examples listed below.

BOOKS: Author (last name first). Title (underlined). City where the book is published: Publisher, copyright date.
> **Athenton, Pike. Fish with Wings. Miami: Marine Press, 1990.**

MAGAZINES: Author (last name first). "Article title." Title of the magazine (underlined) date (day month year): Page numbers of the article.
> **Bolton, Mary. "Fish in the Air." Marine Life 7 June 1999: 34-35.**

ENCYCLOPEDIAS: "Article title." Title of the encyclopedia (underlined). Edition or version. Other type (CD-ROM). Date published.
> **"Flying Fish." The World Book Encyclopedia. 1993 ed.**

FILMS, SLIDES, VIDEOTAPES: Title (underlined). Kind (film, videocassette). Production company, date. Time length.
> **Flying Fish and Flightless Birds—Nature's Mistakes? Video-cassette. Classroom Science Productions, 1998. 30 min.**

INTERVIEWS: Person interviewed (last name first). Type of interview. Date (day month year).
> **Short, Abe. Personal interview. 15 Jan. 2000.**

INTERNET: Author <e-mail address>. "Post title." Site title. Post date, or last update. Site sponsor. Date accessed. <Electronic address>.
> **"Barbados: Flying Fish." Barbados Tourism Encyclopedia.**
>   **Barbados Tourism Authority. 28 July 1999.**
>   **<http://www.barbados.de/flyfish.htm>.**

Note: No author, e-mail address, or post date were available.

Classroom Report

Use blue or black ink when you are writing your final copy. Write on only one side of the paper, and number each page in the upper right-hand corner, starting with page 2. (Your teacher will tell you where to write your name.)

Feb. 20, 2000

Beginning
The report begins with an action-packed story.

Flying Fish, Ocean Acrobats

In the ocean, two hungry dolphins pick up speed when they see a school of flying fish. Sensing danger, the flying fish swim faster and faster. Soon they are going 20 miles an hour. As the dolphins get closer, the flying fish break through the surface, spread their side fins, and take off.

Middle
A number of details and a drawing are included in the body.

Flying fish are called the dragonflies of the deep. But flying fish don't have wings like dragonflies or birds. They use two sets of pectoral fins as wings to fly. Their front fins lift them out of the water, and their back fins help them soar over the surface. Their flights are actually glides.

3

Bibliography

Athenton, Pike. <u>Fish with Wings</u>. Miami:
Marine Press, 1990.
Bolton, Mary. "Fish in the Air." <u>Marine Life</u>
⎯⎯ 7 June 1999: 34-35.

2

Because they are only gliding, the fish can't fly long distances like birds. However, they can fly as fast as 40 miles per hour, and they can glide as far as three football fields. Most flying fish glide 4 feet above the water. But some have been known to soar as high as 45 feet, high enough to sail over a house!

Sometimes flying fish land in fishing boats. One fisherman, Abe Short, recalled the day a flying fish dropped right out of the sky into his boat. "It came sailing through the air, and before I knew it, the fish was sticking into the side of my boat. Luckily it missed me by a few inches, or I would have been hurting for sure. The next thing I knew, it wiggled itself loose and was off again."

Their ability to escape enemies by taking to the air helps flying fish survive. They have been gliding since the days of the dinosaurs. Their special skill will probably keep them soaring for ages to come.

Middle
Quotations are added from an interview.

Ending
A final thought is added to keep the readers thinking.

Multimedia Computer Reports

A World of Sight and Sound

The word "multimedia" simply means using more than one way to communicate. A multimedia computer report includes written words, recorded sounds, and even moving pictures.

There are two basic types of multimedia reports:

- **Interactive Reports** are computer reports with "hot spots" the reader can select to see more information.
- **Multimedia Presentations** are oral reports (speeches) used with computer "slide shows."

To create a multimedia report, you need a special computer program such as Hyperstudio™ or PowerPoint™. You can also create a Web-page multimedia report on the Internet. (**SEE** page 269.)

Business people often use multimedia presentations. Encyclopedias on CD-ROM's use interactive reports to add video and sound to their texts.

Interactive Reports

An interactive report is a multimedia presentation on disk that includes the full text of your report and links from page to page.

Creating Your Report

Start with a Speech or a Written Report ● Either will do nicely. (**SEE** pages 192-203 or 311-317.)

Create a Page Design ● Create a look that will help all the pages of your report fit together.

Use a New Page for Each Main Idea ● If you outlined your speech or report, use its headings as a guide for making pages. Otherwise, consider making a new page for each paragraph. It helps to draw a plan. (**SEE** the bottom of page 207.)

Add Special Effects ● Use bullet points and tables to organize your details. (**SEE** the bottom of page 207.) Add helpful images and sounds. You can find these in your program, or you can create your own. (Be sure that each image or sound adds to your message and doesn't distract from it.)

Add Links ● Give each page a "forward" button leading to the next page and a "back" button leading to the previous page. You can also link special terms in your report to a definition page, or create buttons that play a sound, or link still pictures to video clips, and so on.

Presenting Your Report

Save your work on a floppy disk labeled with your name and the title of your report. Ask your teacher for any specific instructions about turning in your disk.

Keep in mind that anyone else who wants to view your multimedia report will need a copy of the computer program you used to create it.

Multimedia Presentations

A multimedia computer program lets you create a series of linked pages, similar to a slide show. Each click of the mouse (or press of the "Return" or "Enter" key) displays the next detail or page.

Creating Your Presentation

Decide on a Subject ● Keep in mind who your audience will be.

Prepare Your Speech ● You will find help with writing your speech on pages 311-317.

Create a Page Design ● Set up your pages so they are easy for your audience to read.

Use a New Page for Each Main Idea ● Use your speech outline as a guide for making pages. It helps to draw a plan. (**SEE** page 315.)

Present One Detail at a Time ● Make sure you know how to use the mouse to show one detail at a time. (Ask your teacher how.)

Add Pictures and Sounds ● Add visual aids, just as you would for any speech. Find samples in your program, download others from the Internet, or scan in your own.

Note Don't add distractions. Don't get carried away with too many "special effects." If a sound or visual effect doesn't help your message, don't use it.

Delivering Your Presentation

See page 316 for pointers about practicing and presenting your speech. Make sure that you also practice "when to click" for each new page or idea.

Sample **Multimedia Storyboard**

The following storyboard turns the speech on page 317 into a multimedia presentation. To view the final version, visit <www.thewritesource.com/mm4-5a.htm>.

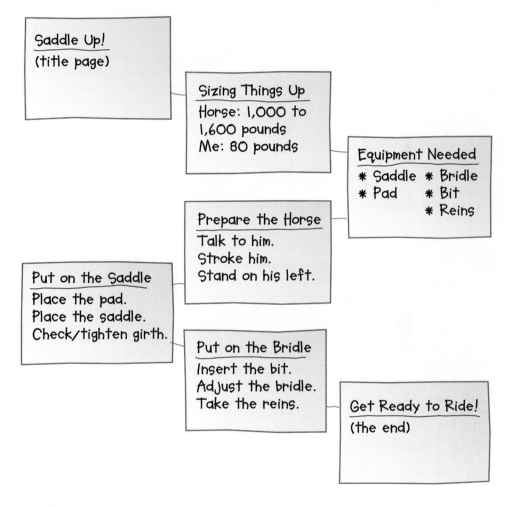

Sample **Interactive Report**

To see this subject developed as an interactive report, visit <www.thewritesource.com/mm4-5b.htm>.

Story and Play Writing

Writing Fantasies

Inventing Impossible Things

Do you ever daydream? Have you ever had an imaginary friend? Have you ever made believe you could fly, or wished you were an explorer? Have you ever invented your own private world, or pretended to be one of the characters in your favorite book? If so, you've used your imagination, and when you do that, *anything* can happen—even impossible things.

Animals That Talk?

Anytime you write stories, you use your imagination; but this is especially true with one special kind of story. It's called *fantasy,* and in this type of story, a spider can even save a pig. So let's begin by reading a fantasy story by a student writer.

> "When you write a story, you can imagine it any way you want, just as long as your readers believe you."
>
> **—NANCY BOND, AUTHOR**

Sample Fantasy: Final Draft

In this fantasy, a girl named Penny and her barnyard friends try to figure out why Montgomery the cat is acting so strangely.

Beginning

Details of the setting are described in the opening paragraph.

Middle

Katie uses dialogue to reveal the story's problem.

Montgomery Mews Mysteriously
by Katie Ambrogi

There was a dusty barn made of old gray wood. The nail marks showed signs of rust. An old silo stood next to the barn. It looked tired and was every bit as old as the barn.

Just then, Penny appeared in front of the barn. The animals looked up at her in surprise. Penny never came into the barnyard at this time of day! "I insist on a barnyard meeting, now!" declared Penny.

Sandy the pig stopped rolling in the mud. Mr. Winkle, otherwise known as Perry the rooster, stopped stalking the barnyard. Freedom the dog stopped lapping up week-old water. Oxford, the biggest ox you've ever seen, let out a great bellow from the barn, and everyone went inside for the meeting.

Baanie the sheep asked, "What's the matter?"

"Yeah, what's wrong?" chorused all the animals.

"Have any of you seen Montgomery?" Penny asked.

"No," chorused the animals.

"Well, neither have I, and I'm beginning to worry. She's hardly ever around," said Penny.

"Well," began Oxford, who was always a close observer, "Montgomery looked different today in a way I can't put my finger on, and she was very nice to Sandy. That's a sure sign that something is wrong."

"Mr. Winkle, do you think we should pry into the cat's business?" Freedom asked.

Middle

The characters discuss a plan to deal with their problem.

Sandy, who was listening to the conversation, stepped in and said, "No . . . but there could be something wrong with Montgomery. Not that I really care."

"Okay," began Oxford, "here's the deal. Winkle, you are the chief administrator of the spy office. We will run around, watch Montgomery closely, and report our messages to the office."

"What about me?" asked Penny.

"Penny, you record everything the spies report," Mr. Winkle said.

Just then, Montgomery slid into the barn. "Why is everyone staring at me like that? I'm fine." Montgomery quickly turned around and made her way out of the barn.

Hours later, they still had no clue as to what was wrong with Montgomery. Sandy sat at her desk and tapped her fingers. Mr. Winkle fluffed up his feathers and started to twiddle his thumbs. Penny jotted down reports, but nothing was good enough to lead them to an answer.

Then the barn door swung open a crack. Montgomery slid through it. Six pairs of eyes traveled to the door. "You know," Montgomery began, "I guess I should have told you." The animals listened in suspense.

Ending

After hours of suspense, the solution is revealed.

"You know how cats love privacy," Montgomery started again. Just then, two kittens timidly stepped in. "They were born three weeks ago," Montgomery said, her voice full of pride. She introduced the kittens. "The little one I call Mouse . . . "

So, somewhere in a barn in Vermont, there are six happy barnyard adults, two happy kittens, and one happy girl.

What Is Fantasy?

A fantasy is a story in which something impossible is accepted as real. In our sample story, animals talk, tap their fingers, and twiddle their thumbs.

Keep it real. You might ask, "If it's impossible, how can I make my readers believe it?" Usually, readers are willing to pretend with the writer, as long as the characters' actions make sense within the story.

In our sample, on pages 210-211, the animals have a mystery to solve. Although their talking, planning, and even their thumb twiddling are all pretend, or fantasy, we believe it all. The animals' actions make sense because they are needed to solve the story's problem.

Gather ideas. Ideas for fantasies can come from anywhere at any time. Most authors keep a notebook handy and write down ideas as they find them—a funny name, an unusual object, or a silly thought. Any one of these ideas can grow into a story in your imagination.

Ask "What if?" Many fantasy stories explore "what if" questions. What if animals could talk? What if a rhinoceros wanted to become a tightrope walker? The author must then think about how this could work. What would happen first, second, and so on? How would other characters react? And a story is born.

 **Note** Once you have an idea, it's time to start writing. The next two pages show how to expand upon your fantasy idea step-by-step through the writing process.

Writing a Fantasy

Prewriting Planning Your Story

Invent Characters ● Fantasy characters can be real people, talking animals, dragons, or creatures you invent yourself. (Think of a main character and maybe one or two others.)

Express Yourself What are your characters' names? What do they look like? What do they like to do? Write about them and find out.

Create a Problem to Solve ● Your main character may be searching for treasure, looking for the way back home, or trying to figure out a cat's strange behavior. (The way your main character solves his or her problem is the plot, the main part of your story.)

Find a Setting ● Fantasy can take place anywhere, anytime—in your neighborhood or in a magical place. (Use sensory details so your readers can see the setting in their minds.)

Writing the First Draft

Get Started ● You may begin your story by introducing the main character or describing the setting. Or, begin in the middle of the action—two characters arguing, a narrow escape, and so on. However you start, it must lead to the story's main problem.

Keep It Going ● As you continue, try to make the main character's life more and more difficult because of the problem. Include lots of dialogue. (**SEE** page 215.) This will keep your readers interested.

Stop When You Get to the End ● When the problem is solved, you've reached the end of your story. Sometimes writers go on and on and write too much.

Revising *Improving Your Writing*

Let It Sit ● After you've written your story, let it sit for a while. Then, when you read it again, try pretending someone else wrote it, and see what you think.

Make It Believable ● Remember that your story should be imaginary *and* believable. Ask, "Do my characters act in a way that fits the story? Do the actions make sense in the setting?"

Share Your First Draft ● Listen carefully to the questions your friends ask after reading or listening to your story. One reader may be confused by something you have said. Another may think that part of your story is unbelievable. Use their questions and comments to make your story better.

Helpful Hint: If you don't like the ending, try removing the last sentence or paragraph. See if your story still seems complete without it.

Editing and Proofreading

Edit ● After making the big changes, take a close look at the specific words and sentences in your story. Have you picked the best words to describe the setting, characters, and action? Are your sentences interesting and clear? Have you used enough dialogue and punctuated it correctly?

Proofread ● Check over the final draft of your story for errors in spelling, grammar, capitalization, and punctuation before sharing it.

Express Yourself Writing and reading fantasies can be enjoyable. Here are some favorite authors of fantasy for young people: Joanna Cole, Roald Dahl, Kenneth Graham, Margaret Mahy, Cynthia Rylant, and C. S. Lewis.

Writing Dialogue

Dialogue is one of a story writer's most important tools. A well-written conversation between characters can draw readers directly into the action.

Without Dialogue

> **Oxford suggested setting up a spy office. Winkle was the chief administrator. The others followed Montgomery and reported back to the office. Penny wrote everything down.**

With Dialogue

> **"Okay," began Oxford, "here's the deal. Winkle, you are the chief administrator of the spy office. We will run around, watch Montgomery closely, and report our messages to the office."**
>
> **"What about me?" asked Penny.**
>
> **"Penny, you record everything the spies report," Mr. Winkle said.**

With dialogue, we see and hear the characters in action. We learn not only *what* they do but *why* they do it. Without dialogue, the characters aren't nearly as interesting.

Punctuating Dialogue

Notice how the dialogue in the story "Montgomery Mews Mysteriously" is punctuated. The following rules make it clear who's talking, so readers don't get confused.

- The speaker's words are in quotation marks.
- The speaker's words are often identified by terms like *said* and *asked.*
- Each new speaker begins a new paragraph.
- Commas and periods go inside the quotation marks.

Writing Tall Tales

Ride That Mosquito!

A tall tale is not just any story. It is an incredible story, about an incredible character, doing incredible things! Tall tales are filled with humor and exaggeration. They are often based on legends about real people, such as Annie Oakley, Johnny Appleseed, and Daniel Boone.

Daniel Boone told of smacking a mosquito with the flat of his hatchet "to calm it down a bit." Then he put a saddle on that mosquito and rode it.

Tall tales are stories about awesome people and places and unusual things. When you read them, someone across town might hear you laughing!

Sample Tall Tale

Beginning
Musky Mike
is introduced.

Middle
A problem is
introduced,
and the hero
battles a
powerful foe.

Ending
Mike uses his
strength and
craftiness to
tame Old
Gus.

Musky Mike's Big Catch

The north woods are full of fishing stories and tall tales about Musky Mike. Why, he once caught a 40-foot musky with his bare hands. And he drained a lake with a straw to find his lucky hat. I didn't believe these stories until one day I rode my bike to Pike Lake and met Musky Mike.

Pike Lake was home to Old Gus, the biggest musky in the north woods. Old Gus was said to have swallowed a boatload of fishermen and spit them to another lake. On the pier stood Musky Mike himself. As I cast out my blue spinner smeared with peanut butter, I heard Mike chuckle. "If you're going after Old Gus, you'll need one of these," he said, holding up a boat anchor.

Suddenly, the biggest fish I ever saw jumped clear out of the water. It was Old Gus, and he was licking the peanut butter off my lure. "You got my lucky hat wet, Old Gus," Mike said and tossed the anchor into his open mouth. Old Gus took off, towing Mike behind him like a water-skier.

I never saw such a commotion. Mike and Old Gus started wrestling. Mike pinned Gus's fins. Then Gus smacked Mike with his huge tail. After five hours, the battle was over. Mike walked out of the lake, pulling an exhausted Gus behind him. Mike unhooked the anchor, and the monster musky slowly swam off. "No one will believe this, Mike. Why did you let him go?"

"I always catch and release, son," Mike said.

Writing a Tall Tale

Planning Your Story

You can write your own tall tale by following each of these guidelines:

Create a Hero ● The main character, or hero, of a tall tale is always stronger, braver, or smarter than a normal person. Use exaggeration when you describe your hero. This character may be

. . . as strong as 10 giants.

. . . able to think faster than a computer.

Choose a Powerful Opponent ● Think of a powerful foe or force for your hero to fight against. This foe may be

. . . a mosquito so big it needs a runway to land.

. . . a wind so strong that it can move mountains.

. . . a bad guy so bad that even Superman is afraid of him.

Show the Bravery of Your Hero ● To escape from or tame an opponent, your hero may

. . . outwrestle a giant fish.

. . . throw a lasso around a runaway cyclone.

A Tall Cast of Characters

Knowing something about three famous tall-tale heroes may help you plan your own story:

■ Sally Ann Thunder Ann Whirlwind Crockett uses her bowie knife as a toothpick and skins a bear faster than an alligator swallows a fish.

■ Mighty medicine man Glooskap squeezes a water monster whose warts are as big as mountains until the creature is reduced to a mere bullfrog.

■ Pecos Bill ties rattlesnakes together and invents the clothesline.

Writing Your Story

Tall tales are meant to be fun and entertaining, so include plenty of exaggeration and humor. If you use dialogue, have your hero say silly, boastful things.

Tip Tall tales were often passed from generation to generation. As you write, think of yourself as a storyteller surrounded by eager listeners. Your job is to tell a good story.

Start Out Creatively ● Introduce the main character in a creative way. (In the sample, the author introduces Musky Mike by telling a couple of quick background stories.) Also remember to share exaggerated details about the foe, or opposing force, in your tale.

Keep It Going ● Don't make things easy for your hero. Have this person overcome other obstacles before meeting the main foe. Then, when they do meet, make it a fantastic struggle.

End Your Story ● In a tall tale, the main character usually wins. Your hero should use strength, brains, or bravery to defeat the opponent. If you wish, you can also add a surprise ending.

Illustrate Your Story ● Draw a picture of the "most important" character, or illustrate your favorite scene.

Writing Realistic Stories

Amanda Comes to Life

Amanda Lowe is 10 years old. She has three big brothers who love to tease her. Her wildly curling red hair matches her fiery temper. Amanda sounds like a real person, but she isn't. She is a character in Cassie Johnson's realistic story.

What Are Realistic Stories?

Realistic stories are part real and part made-up. They usually have characters, like Amanda, who remind you of people you know. These characters have realistic problems to solve. For example, Amanda has a problem with her brothers, which is a believable problem for a 10-year-old girl. Made-up details and events add suspense or humor to the story.

Ideas for realistic stories often come from a writer's own experiences and interests. The finished products, though, are more fiction (made-up) than fact.

Writing a Realistic Story

Prewriting Planning Your Story

Before you can write your story, you need a main character who seems real, with a believable problem to solve.

Create a Character ● Choose three people you know and make a list or chart of their looks and habits. Pick details from each person's list to create a main character. The chart below is one way Cassie Johnson could have made up her character Amanda.

Name	Hair	Age	Wears	Mood	Likes	Dislikes
Su	straight black	10	glasses	stubborn	gum	swimming
Emma	short blond	9	jewelry	playful	sports	brothers
Katie	curly red	11	black shoes	fiery	TV	homework
Amanda	curly red	10	glasses	fiery	sports	brothers

Find a Real Problem ● Your character needs a problem to solve. Think of problems that you and your friends know about—problems *at school, with friends, with family,* or *in the neighborhood.* List several problems for each category. Then decide which problem you want your character to solve.

School: locker always jams, trouble with my math class
Friends: friend told my secret, friend embarrassed me
Family: my brothers bug me, sister uses my skates
Neighborhood: nowhere to ride my bike, lots of litter
Amanda's Problem: My brothers bug me.

Planning Guide

A collection sheet like the one below can help you keep track of your planning ideas. You don't need to have all five story parts planned before writing your story. You may even want to make changes to the collection sheet as you write. Check your sheet after you complete your first draft, though, to see if you included your most important ideas.

Collection Sheet

Characters:
(List the main character first. How old are your characters and what are their names? How do they look, speak, and act?)

Setting:
(Describe where and when your story takes place.)

Problem:
(What problem does the main character need to solve?)

Story Scenes:
(List some solutions to the problem that your main character could try.)

Purpose:
(Will your story be serious, surprising, scary, funny, or sad? One feeling can guide your writing.)

Express Yourself Share your story ideas with several classmates before writing your first draft. Ask them for their suggestions. Do the same thing with your first draft.

Writing the First Draft

There are many different ways to begin a story—start out with a conversation, have a character doing something, describe the setting, and so on. However you begin, make it realistic and interesting.

Start Your Story ● Here are five ways to begin a story.

Begin with action or dialogue:
"Look what they did to my in-line skates!" Amanda shouted.

Ask a question:
How did I get stuck with three big brothers?

Describe the setting:
Our small white house on Evergreen Street looks completely normal from the outside.

Begin with background information:
My three brothers taught me how to shoot baskets. Now I'm a better shooter than they realize.

Have the main character introduce himself or herself:
I'm Josh, Eric, and Matt Lowe's sister, Amanda.

Keep Your Story Going ● Don't let your character solve the problem too easily. Try two or more actions before coming up with a final solution.

Solution 1: **Throw a tantrum.**

Solution 2: **Talk to someone.**

Solution 3: **Make a plan to deal with the problem.**

End Your Story ● Give your story a realistic ending—your character may not be happy with his or her solution, someone else may have solved the problem, or the problem may still be there. However you end your story, make it believable.

Most people change as they deal with a problem, so show how your character changes by the end of the story.

Revising Improving Your Writing

Review Your Work ● Review your first draft to be sure that the characters' words and actions make sense. Also check your story's length—is it too short, or too long? If some parts seem boring, change them or take them out. If something seems to happen too quickly, add more background information.

Add Life to Your Story ● If your story needs a little zip, try adding a few details, some dialogue, or more action.

Use specific details.
What interesting sights, sounds, smells, or feelings could you describe?

Use interesting dialogue.
Dialogue shows how your characters feel. Where in the story could you have your characters talk to each other?

Use believable action.
There's nothing like a little action or suspense to keep a story exciting. What could you have your characters do?

Editing and Proofreading

Read Your Story ● After making changes in your story, have a friend read it back to you out loud. Is it smooth and clear from start to finish?

Check for Careless Errors ● Finally, check for spelling, punctuation, and grammar errors. Make a neat final copy of your story and proofread it before sharing it with your classmates. If you have time, divide the story into parts, illustrate the pages, and bind them into a book. (**SEE** page 73.)

Sample Realistic Story

You have seen how Cassie Johnson created parts of her story. Now read "Amanda Stands Tall" and see how all the parts fit together.

Beginning

Amanda introduces herself and her problem.

Middle

Amanda tries several solutions.

Ending

Amanda finally solves her problem.

Amanda Stands Tall

I'm Josh, Eric, and Matt Lowe's sister, Amanda. It's tough to have three big brothers. The day they took the rollers off my in-line skates to build their go-cart, I was steamed.

When I told my dad what happened, he grounded my brothers for two days. Then they didn't bug me for one whole week! That's when I found the rubber spiders in my shoes.

Well, I had to think of a way to stop their teasing once and for all. No one except my friend Anya knew how good I was at shooting baskets. So, I said, "Who wants to play a game of HORSE?"

"I do!" Josh, Eric, and Matt all yelled at once.

I said, "Okay, if I win, you have to stop teasing me forever."

The game started. Matt and Josh got out quickly. It was showdown time with Eric. The game was tied at HORS. I dribbled to the basket with my right hand, spun, and shot with my left hand. Eric was right-handed. I knew he'd have trouble. He drove to the basket, spun, and shot. The ball went in . . . and then spun out.

"Yes!" I yelled. "I win. And if you back out of our deal, here's a surprise." Just then Anya came out of her hiding spot with the video camera. "If you guys give me any trouble, I'll show this tape to the world!"

Writing Stories from History

Long Ago and Faraway . . .

- ■ *Would you like to roam the Wild West?*
- ■ *Would you like to meet Abraham Lincoln?*
- ■ *Would you like to walk on the moon?*

By writing a historical story, you can do any of these things. A historical story is a time machine that takes you wherever you want to go. Some stories retell historical events the way they happened. Other stories ask *what if* and tell what could have happened.

A historical story is part fact and part fiction. But all parts should be believable.

Writing a Historical Story

Prewriting Planning Your Story

Get Historical ● A historical story brings a time, a person, or an event to life. You may write about a real person . . . or create a character who takes part in a real event. Think of an interesting time in history and go there in your mind. *Who would you be? What would you be doing? Would you change history?* As you consider these questions, ideas for your story will start to form.

List Ideas ● Make a list of *times, places, events,* or *people* from history that you would like to write about. (**SEE** the historical time line on pages 478-487.) Here are some ideas:

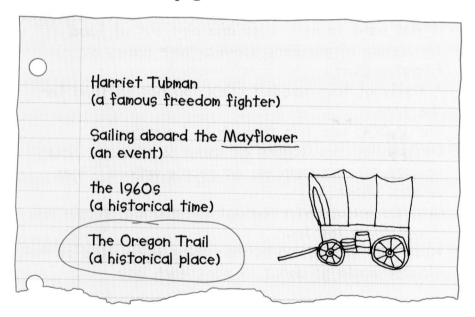

Harriet Tubman
(a famous freedom fighter)

Sailing aboard the <u>Mayflower</u>
(an event)

the 1960s
(a historical time)

The Oregon Trail
(a historical place)

Choose a Subject ● Look over your list and circle the idea that interests you the most. This idea will be the starting point for your story. Write freely for 3-5 minutes about your subject. Write down everything you know about your subject. This will show you what you still need to find out.

Gather Facts ● To begin, look for facts about your subject in your history book. Then check other reference books, search the Internet, or watch a video. Ask your teacher or librarian for help. Carefully write down any important facts or figures you discover.

The facts below were collected for a story about the Oregon Trail. Facts give you background information and interesting details for your story. (Remember, though, you don't need to use every fact in your story.)

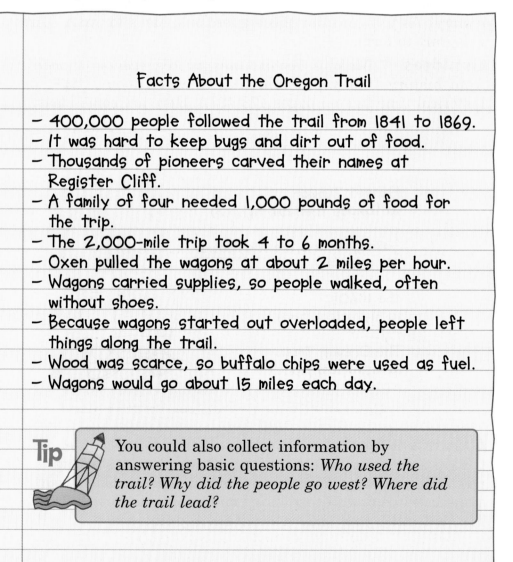

Facts About the Oregon Trail

- 400,000 people followed the trail from 1841 to 1869.
- It was hard to keep bugs and dirt out of food.
- Thousands of pioneers carved their names at Register Cliff.
- A family of four needed 1,000 pounds of food for the trip.
- The 2,000-mile trip took 4 to 6 months.
- Oxen pulled the wagons at about 2 miles per hour.
- Wagons carried supplies, so people walked, often without shoes.
- Because wagons started out overloaded, people left things along the trail.
- Wood was scarce, so buffalo chips were used as fuel.
- Wagons would go about 15 miles each day.

Tip You could also collect information by answering basic questions: *Who used the trail? Why did the people go west? Where did the trail lead?*

Identify Your Story Elements ● After collecting facts, plan the basic elements of your story. Identify the characters, the setting, and the action. A collection sheet like the one below can help you keep track of all these elements. Use your sheet as you write, but feel free to make changes as your story develops.

Collection Sheet

Characters:

(Decide how each character will look, speak, and act. Keep the time period of your story in mind!)

Setting:

(Describe the time and place of your story. Keep the setting historically accurate.)

Main Action:

(What action or event will your character participate in? The details in this part may or may not be true, but they must be believable. The main action usually includes a problem to be solved.)

Story Scenes:

(What things will your character be doing in this story: eating, hunting, hiding?)

Form:

(Decide on a form—you may use the basic story form or try something different, like diary entries or a series of letters.)

Writing the First Draft

Begin Your Story ● Get readers interested by introducing your characters and the historical event right away. Begin with dialogue, action, or a lively description. Here's how Rashon, a student writer, began his story:

> As the bright sun rose above the prairie, there were wagons everywhere. My hands shook as I helped Pa yoke the oxen. Ma packed away the last of the dishes, food, and supplies. Pa asked if everybody was ready. Just then we heard a gunshot. It was the signal to begin our journey.
>
> Pa cracked the reins, and the wagon lurched forward. Our 2000-mile journey had begun.
>
> "Oregon, here we come!" I shouted and started walking.

Keep Your Story Going ● Once you begin the main action, keep your characters moving toward the end of the event. Add background facts where they fit. Here's a scene from the middle of Rashon's story:

> "Don't climb up so high, Jessie," Eliza warned.
>
> "I'm going to carve my name in Register Cliff," I replied.
>
> "Do it down here with all the other names," Eliza pleaded.
>
> "I could, but it wouldn't be as much fun," I told her. Just then a rock gave out beneath me. I began sliding. Eliza screamed. I grabbed a branch and hung on tight. I reached for another rock and pulled myself up on the cliff. I lay there for a minute and then stood up.
>
> When I looked back over the trail, I could see the Platte River below and majestic mountains stretching for miles in the distance. I took out my knife and carved my name in the sandstone cliff, higher than anyone else.

End Your Story ● Don't drag your story out. End it soon after the main action is completed. Remember that every story does not have to have a happy ending.

Here's how Rashon ended his story:

> **It was November. We had walked across the prairie and struggled over the mountains. Now we were finally in Oregon, but our journey wasn't over. We built a raft to float us down the Columbia River to our new home. The river looked scary, but at least we didn't have to walk anymore. We all huddled in the center of the raft.**
>
> **After we shoved off, the raft was soon crashing through whirlpools and rapids. White water swirled around us. My pa rested on his oars, and the swift currents carried us along. Finally, the roaring river slowed down, and our raft floated to a canoe landing. We had finally arrived at our new home!**

Revising and Editing Improving Your Story

Use the questions below as a guide for revising and editing your story.

- Is your story based on historical fact?
- Do the characters' words and actions make sense for that historical time? (George Washington wouldn't look at a wristwatch and say, "Like, let's get to the mall, dudes.")
- Does the story build interest? (The main character should complete some action or solve a problem in the story.)
- Do your sentences read smoothly? (Have a friend read your story to you.)
- Is your final draft neat and as error free as you can make it?

Writing Plays

Using Your Senses

Do you enjoy pretending—imagining you're someone you're not, making up conversations, and solving unusual problems? If so, try writing a play. You'll need some characters, a problem for them to solve, and a little imagination.

Ideas for plays can come from real life, and from your imagination. Think about what happens to you and to other people every day. These experiences are good starting places for plays. You can also use ideas from stories, books, or TV shows.

A play tells a story through dialogue. As the characters talk, the story moves forward. When you write a play, you bring your interests, experiences, and imagination to life.

Act 1

A play begins by introducing the main characters and setting up a problem for them to solve. In the sample below, Dave and Jessica are in trouble, and they need a way out.

What Will We Tell Mom and Dad?

Characters: DAVE, 12 years old   JESSICA, 11 years old
DAD, their father   MOM, their mother
Setting: The living room of a cabin near a river

ACT 1

(The room is empty. Suddenly, JESSICA bursts through the door closely followed by DAVE.)

DAVE: *(pushing her)* It's all your fault!

JESSICA: *(pushing him back)* It's not! You're the one who couldn't wait till Mom and Dad got home from the store. You just had to go fishing the minute we got to this cabin. I should never have let you talk me into it.

DAVE: I just wanted to surprise them with a fish for dinner. And anyway, you're the one who borrowed Dad's new fishing rod.

JESSICA: Yeh, but I'm not the one who broke it, am I?

MOM: *(calling from offstage)* Jessica? Dave? Come help with these groceries.

DAVE: Oh, no! They're home! What are we going to do?

JESSICA: We'll just have to tell them we broke . . .

DAVE: *(interrupting her)* Tell them? Are you kidding? This vacation will be over before it's even begun. All we have to do is keep Dad's mind off fishing.

JESSICA: But how?

Writing a Play

Prewriting Planning Your Play

Find the Main Parts ● You'll need at least two characters, a problem, and a place (the setting) for the action. Your characters can be based on people you know. The problem and action in your play can be based on actual events that made you laugh or cry. Your setting may be a familiar place. You may also use your dreams and imagination to give you ideas.

Gather Details ● Use a collection sheet or checklist to help you plan the details of your play. But don't make your plan too complicated. Sometimes your characters can take over and almost "write" the play for you!

Collection Sheet

Main Characters #1 and #2:
(Give each character a name and an age that fits. Briefly describe how your characters look and act.)

Other Characters:
(Identify and describe any other characters in your play.)

Setting:
(Describe the place—or places—where your play happens. If it's important, also tell when the play takes place.)

Problem or Goal:
(State the problem or goal facing the main characters.)

Action:
(Describe your characters' actions as they try to solve their problem or achieve their goal.)

Solution:
(Have your characters solve the problem.)

Writing the First Draft

Set Up the Play ● Before you begin writing your play, you must let the reader know the title of the play, the names of the characters, and the setting in which the play takes place. (**SEE** page 233.)

Start the Play ● For the opening dialogue, you can have the characters describe the scene they are in or have them discuss the problem or goal of the play. Each time a person talks, you must write the name of that person, followed by a colon.

Solve the Problem ● In the middle of the play, have the characters work at solving the problem or reaching their goal. This is where most of the action takes place. It is the talking and actions of the characters that make the play move ahead. In the sample that begins on page 233, Dave and Jessica plan all sorts of fun activities to keep their dad from fishing.

Note ● To create excitement, and maybe a little fun, your main characters can disagree about how to solve the problem.

End the Play ● End your play by showing how the main characters solve their problem or reach their goal. You may also choose to have your characters fail at their solutions, just as sometimes happens in real life.

Be certain your ending is believable. Unless Dave and Jessica are millionaires, they shouldn't hop into a private jet, fly to the factory, and buy their dad a new fishing rod!

Revising Improving Your Writing

Read Aloud ● Read your first draft aloud. Decide if the play moves along smoothly and clearly from beginning to end. See if any parts should be cut out or if anything needs to be added. Pay attention to each line. Put a check next to any lines that you want to rewrite.

Write Dialogue ● Dialogue is what your characters say to each other. You want them to sound like real people talking. Listen to how your family, friends, and other people talk, and use the words they use. Which of these lines sounds more real?

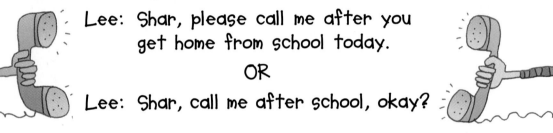

> Lee: Shar, please call me after you
>   get home from school today.
>
>   OR
>
> Lee: Shar, call me after school, okay?

Make a Point ● Plays often share a message or make a point about life. This message is carried through the characters' actions and words. By the end of *What Will We Tell Mom and Dad?*, the audience learns, along with Dave and Jessica, that it is best to tell the truth. Check to see that the point of your play comes through clearly.

Tip Ask several classmates to read your play out loud. Listen carefully to find any dialogue or actions that need changing.

Editing and Proofreading

Check Your Writing ● Look your writing over for spelling, capitalization, and grammar errors. Then write a neat final draft of your play, following the form of the sample on page 233. Proofread the final draft again before sharing it.

Act 2

In the first scene of this play on page 233, Dave and Jessica break their father's new fishing rod. They don't want him to find out. Here, in act 2, student writer Faith Brawley continues the action and adds a little suspense.

ACT 2

(The family has just finished dinner and is chatting in the living room.)

MOM: So, what did you guys do while we went grocery shopping?

JESSICA: *(in a shaky voice)* Well, we . . . um . . .

DAVE: *(interrupting JESSICA)* We played a game of cards.

JESSICA: *(glaring at DAVE)* We also went to the beach. I pushed Dave in the water. I thought he could use a cooling off.

DAD: Oh, that reminds me. Do you guys want to go fishing tomorrow, or would you rather go on a nature walk?

DAVE & JESSICA: *(at the same time)* NATURE WALK!

DAD: Okay, that settles that. We'll go on a nature walk.

MOM: *(yawning)* It's getting kind of late.

JESSICA & DAVE: *(leaving the living room)* Okay, Mom, we'll see you tomorrow.

JESSICA: That was a close one!

DAVE: You're telling me!

JESSICA: *(feeling horrible)* You know, I can't keep this a secret any longer. I'm going to tell Dad!

DAVE: *(in a panic)* You can't tell him. He'll be very upset. Remember, he hasn't had a vacation in three years.

JESSICA: I suppose so . . .

 **Note** To improve your playwriting, read plays and act in plays. Most importantly, watch and listen to the people around you.

Poetry Writing

Writing Poems

Words on High Wind

Poems are different from other kinds of writing. They have a special shape and sound. And, if you read enough of them, you'll get better and better at understanding poems. You'll even make friends with some of them. Here's how:

- Read the poem to yourself several times.
- Read the poem aloud; listen to what it says.
- Read it with feeling to friends or classmates.
- Talk or write about the poem.
- Copy the poem in a special notebook.

Words

Words! said the earth.
And the cloud
bumping into the hilltop
said back, Words!
And the words
were born
on a high wind
at the tail end of June,
when the sun brights
the sky so hard
no one can stop laughing.

—Anne-Marie Oomen

What Makes Poetry Special?

Poetry is different from prose (the regular writing you do). Here are some things that make poetry special.

1 Poetry looks different. It's easy to recognize poems. They are written in lines and stanzas (groups of lines). Some poems are short enough to fit on the inside of greeting cards, and some poems go on for many pages. Here is a one-stanza, eight-line poem.

My Ancestor
I look in the mirror
    And what do I see?
  I see an image of someone
That looks a little like me.
    Could it be the face
      Or maybe the hair?
  I know who it is now:
It's my great-great-grandma Claire.

— Phil Ryan

2 Poetry speaks to the mind as well as to the heart. You can like a poem for what it says (that's the mind part), and you can like a poem for how it makes you feel (that's the heart part). It's the "heart part" that really separates poetry from other forms of writing.

3 Poetry says a lot in a few words. Poets create word pictures using details about the sights, sounds, smells, tastes, and physical feelings connected with a subject.

I was standing on the street when . . .
The rusty old black station wagon (sight)
grunted rack-a-bump-she-bang, (sound)
and heated up my cool spot of air, (physical feeling)
and spewed oily smoke (smell)
all over my mustard-covered foot-long hot dog. (sight)

— Anne-Marie Oomen

Poetry says things in special ways. Poets sometimes create special word pictures by making comparisons. They may write a *metaphor* or a *simile,* like "I climbed slow as an old fly." Can you figure out which two things are being compared in the following examples?

Rain
Rain Rain
Wet Little Chicken Pox
On the Window . . .
— Cassie Hoek

A gentle wind at night is
my wispy grandmother.
— Tim Capewell

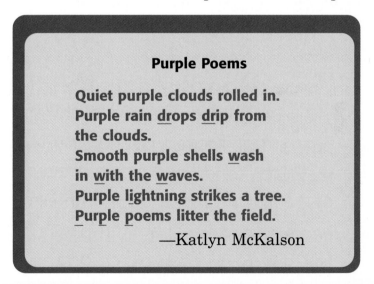 **Poetry pleases the ear.** Poets carefully arrange words until their poems sound just right. Sometimes they use words that rhyme. Sometimes they repeat certain vowel and consonant sounds to make their poems sound pleasing. Notice how this works in the poem called "Purple Poems."

Purple Poems

Quiet purple clouds rolled in.
Purple rain drops drip from
the clouds.
Smooth purple shells wash
in with the waves.
Purple lightning strikes a tree.
Purple poems litter the field.

—Katlyn McKalson

Think It Over You will find pleasing sounds, sensory details, similes, and metaphors in regular writing, too. They just stand out more in poetry.

Writing a Free-Verse Poem

The following guidelines will help you write a free-verse poem. Free-verse poetry does not follow a specific form, and it usually does not rhyme.

Prewriting Planning Your Poem

Choose a Subject ● Write your poem about a subject that truly interests you. This could be a special room, a friend, a favorite animal, music, and so on.

Gather Your Thoughts ● Freewriting about your subject can be a good way to begin. Here is Anne-Marie's freewriting about an old dog she once knew.

I knew an old alley dog. My stepmom said to never touch him. But once I tossed him half my butter sandwich, and he danced around. And once I climbed down our fire escape, and he crept up next to me. We sat near each other and watched the sunset on the brick wall. We stayed there until it was dark.

Writing the First Draft

Create a Poem ● The next step is to turn your freewriting into a poem. Begin by copying down the words, making line breaks where you hear pauses in the sentences. As you do this, you can also change some of the words or move them around.

Add New Words ● This is a good time to add new words and phrases as you develop your poem. Here is how Anne-Marie used her freewriting to create a poem.

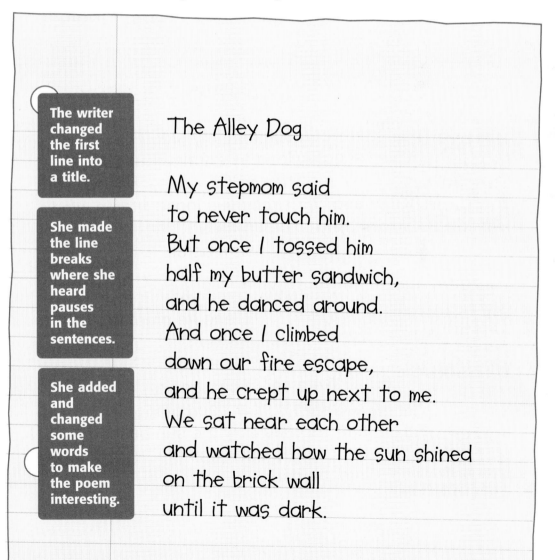

The writer changed the first line into a title.

She made the line breaks where she heard pauses in the sentences.

She added and changed some words to make the poem interesting.

The Alley Dog

My stepmom said
to never touch him.
But once I tossed him
half my butter sandwich,
and he danced around.
And once I climbed
down our fire escape,
and he crept up next to me.
We sat near each other
and watched how the sun shined
on the brick wall
until it was dark.

Revising Improving Your Poem

Now you can turn your basic poem into a very special poem by doing some revising.

Add Word Pictures ● Ask yourself what words you can add to brighten your poem. Try using word pictures like similes, metaphors, and personification. (**SEE** "The Sounds of Poetry" on page 245.)

Create a Shape ● Think about writing the words in ways that make them look and sound like the topic of your poem.

Anne-Marie moved words and added similes.

She wrote her words in the shape of a fire escape.

She also used personification.

The Alley Dog

Never touch him! my stepmom
shouted loud as a train. But once
I tossed him half my butter sandwich,
and he danced like loose litter in wind.
  And once I climbed
             slow as an
                  old fly
     down our fire escape,
         and he crept up,
         stop
         and go
  like a car in bad traffic,
and we sat near each other,
and watched how the sun pushed
the cracked brick wall
into the dark.

Editing and Proofreading

- **Make sure that your poem is complete.** Does it give your reader a vivid picture of your subject?
- **Check the line breaks.** Do they add special meaning, sound, or rhythm to your poem?
- **Make sure your poem reads well.** Do you stumble over certain words or lines in the poem? If so, change them.
- **Write a final copy of your poem,** making all of the corrections. Then proofread it carefully before sharing it.

The Sounds of Poetry

Here are some special writing devices used in poetry.

Alliteration ● The repetition of beginning consonant sounds in words like _dance, dare,_ and _drop._

Assonance ● The repetition of vowel sounds in words like _rain, makes, pavement,_ and _wavy._

End Rhyme ● The rhyming of words at the ends of two or more lines of poetry.

Metaphor ● A comparison without using the words _like_ or _as._ _The full moon is a shiny balloon._

Onomatopoeia ● The use of words that sound like the noise they name, as in _buzz, thump,_ and _snap._

Personification ● A comparison in which something that is not human is described with human qualities. _The sunflowers smiled at us._

Repetition ● The repeating of a word or phrase to add rhythm or emphasis. _The wind hissed, hissed down the alley._

Rhythm ● The pattern of sounds and beats that helps poetry flow from one idea to the next.

Simile ● A comparison using the words _like_ or _as._ _Granny's house looks like a dollhouse._

Traditional Poetry

Traditional poetry has been around for a long time.

Ballad ● Ballad poems tell a story. The ballad is written in four-line stanzas. Often the second and fourth lines rhyme. (Here is the first stanza of "Ballad of Skull Rock.")

> We miners long ago did find
> the skull rock on the <u>lake</u>.
> The silver lay in open veins,
> all shining for the <u>take</u>.

Cinquain ● Cinquain poems are five lines long with a certain number of syllables or words in each. There are many ways to write cinquain poems. Here is a pattern and an example of a syllable cinquain.

Pattern for Cinquain

Line 1: Title
Line 2: Description or example of the title
Line 3: Action about the title
Line 4: Feeling about the title
Line 5: Synonym for the title

Syllable Cinquain

Line 1: Seashells (2 syllables)
Line 2: Cockles and clams (4 syllables)
Line 3: Collecting on beaches (6 syllables)
Line 4: Waiting for me to pick them up (8 syllables)
Line 5: Treasures. (2 syllables)

Couplet ● A couplet is a two-line verse form that usually rhymes and expresses one thought.

> Back and forth the dancer <u>whirled</u>,
> A butterfly with wings <u>unfurled</u>.

Free Verse ● Free verse is poetry that does not include patterned rhyme or rhythm. (**SEE** the sample on page 244.)

Haiku ● Haiku is a three-line poem about nature. The first line is five syllables; the second, seven; the third, five.

Sun shines on sidewalks,	(5 syllables)
weeds grow sideways in small cracks,	(7 syllables)
ants take treasures home.	(5 syllables)

Limerick ● A limerick is a funny verse in five lines. Lines one, two, and five rhyme, as do lines three and four. Lines one, two, and five have three stressed syllables; lines three and four have two stressed syllables.

There once was a chef named Maurice
Who always used way too much grease.
His chicken was fine;
His fries were divine,
But his dinners could make me obese.

Lyric ● A lyric is a song-like poem that uses sensory details. Add a tune and it can become a song.

Up! Up! Bright kites fly, oooh,
   maroon, and yellow, and easy blue
      over the evening park.
I like to think they pull me, too,
   up into that blue, that easy blue,
      far away from the dark.

Quatrain ● A quatrain is a four-line stanza. In this sample, the first two lines rhyme, and the last two lines rhyme. (In some quatrains, the first and third and the second and fourth lines rhyme.)

The buses in cities are hot
And I have to ride them a lot.
But sometimes I get a good seat
And guess who is happy? My feet!

Playful Poetry

Poets have fun inventing new forms of poetry. Here are some invented forms to try.

Alphabet Poetry ● An alphabet poem uses a part of the alphabet to create a list poem.

> **D**elightful
> **E**vergreen
> **F**orever
> **G**reen

Concrete Poetry ● Concrete poetry takes on a special shape that expresses the poem's meaning or feeling.

> The way to school is d$_{own}$
>
> W I D E streets
> FULL OF **BIG** PEOPLE!!!

Definition Poetry ● Definition poetry tells the meaning of a word or an idea creatively.

> **FRIENDSHIP** ☾
> Friendship is like the moon and stars,
> hanging around together,
> walking across the Milky Way.

Five W's Poetry ● A 5 W's poem answers *Who? What? Where? When?* and *Why?*

> I (*Who?*)
> Love to skate (*What?*)
> Along Venice Beach (*Where?*)
> In the middle of the day (*When?*)
> Because people are friendly and get out of your way. (*Why?*)

List Poetry ● A list can be a poem. Often the title says what the list is about.

WHAT'S IN THE BOX UNDER MY BED?
eight marbles and a shoestring
a shiny bubblegum ring
two valuable baseball cards
some chocolate candy bars
the letter my friend wrote . . .

Name Poetry ● A name poem, or acrostic poem, uses the letters of a name or a word to begin each line in the poem.

Friendly   Calm eyes
Remarkable   Outgoing
Energetic   Open
Dude   Laid-back

Telephone-Number Poetry ● You can "find" a poem in your phone number. Each number can represent either syllables or whole words. Let's say your phone number is 362-4814. The first line of your poem will have three syllables (or words), the second will have six, the third will have two, and so on. Here's an example:

Our cat starts   (3 syllables)
his mornings on my lap   (6 syllables)
before   (2 syllables)
stalking stuffed mice   (4 syllables)
or dashing downstairs to explore.   (8 syllables)
He   (1 syllable)
likes things the same.   (4 syllables)

Terse Verse ● Terse verse is short and humorous—two words that rhyme and have the same number of syllables. The title is the subject.

Joke Books   Lemonade   Candy
  Smile   Pink   Sweet
  File   Drink   Treat

Writing Riddles

Exercising Your Mind

Question: **Why is the letter _e_ like a question mark?**

Answer: **It's found at the end of every riddle.** (Get it?)

Why do so many people enjoy asking and hearing riddles? Maybe it's because there's a laugh at the end of most riddles—along with a surprise. Can you "crack" the following riddle?

Riddle: **Inside an ivory container is a clear crystal. Inside the crystal is a heart of gold. What is it?** (See answer below.)

When you're ready to write your own riddle, start with a "Crack Up" or "What Am I" riddle.

> Writing riddles is a form of mental exercise. Because they usually contain puns (wordplay jokes), riddles develop your language skills. They are also fun and encourage you to use your imagination.

Answer: An egg

"Crack Up" Riddles

Riddle: **Why is it hard to find a home for a gloomy whale?**
Answer: **No one wants a pet that size (sighs).**

Riddle: **Where's the best place to buy a part for a clock?**
Answer: **A secondhand shop (second hand).**

In each of the "crack up" riddles above, the answer contains a pun (a word that sounds like a word with another meaning). In the first riddle, "size" and "sighs" have the same pronunciation, but different meanings and spellings. The fun part is that both words make sense in the answer. The same thing is true in the second riddle: a "secondhand" shop is a place to buy things and a "second hand" is a clock part.

Writing a "Crack Up" Riddle

 Brainstorm for words that sound alike.
Example: peace (noun)   piece (noun)
(Your words should be the same part of speech.)

2 Pick a pair of words and think of a sentence (or a phrase) in which either word makes sense.
He just wants a little peace (a little piece).

3 Ask yourself questions.
Who might want a little peace?
(someone around a lot of noise)
Who might want a little piece?
(a kid being served something yucky)

 Create a riddle question with this pattern:
Why is a _____ like a _____ ?

Riddle: **Why is a teacher with noisy students like a boy being served spinach pie?**
Answer: **Both just want a little peace (piece).**

"What Am I" Riddles

"What Am I" riddles have been around for a long time. In this type of riddle, you try to guess what object or idea is being described. Here are three different ways to write them.

Use metaphors. You can describe the appearance of an object as if it were something else. Doing this creates a comparison called a *metaphor*. In the riddle below, the shell of an egg is compared to an ivory container, the white of the egg is a clear crystal, and the yolk is a heart of gold.

> **Inside an ivory container
> is a clear crystal.
> Inside the crystal
> is a heart of gold.**

Use personification. You can describe an idea or an object as if it were a living thing. (This is called *personification*.) In the riddle below, a shout is described as if it could fly. Normally we think of wings as belonging to living things.

> **I have no wings, but I can cross the widest
> street without touching the ground.
> What am I?**

Use surprise endings. You can use your imagination to combine details that sound ordinary but take an unexpected funny twist in the end.

> **What is gray, has big ears, and squeaks?
> (It sounds like a mouse. But it could be
> an elephant wearing new shoes!)**

Writing a "What Am I" Riddle

1 **List some everyday objects and ideas (nouns).**

List: flower, night, bookshelf, joy, football, skateboard, radio, computer

2 **Choose one noun and describe it.**

Choose: night *(the answer to your riddle)*
Describe: dark, quiet, soft, comes slowly every day, can be scary, not human

3 **Compare your noun to something different (metaphor) or describe it as a living thing (personification).**

Compare: Look at the list of descriptive words for ideas. You could describe the night as if it were a black cat. Both are dark and quiet.

4 **Write your riddle.**

Write: **I'm dark and quiet. I sneak slowly and silently into your house every day. What am I?**

Express Yourself Try exercising your mind by creating a "What Am I" rhyming riddle. Here's an example:

**The more times you use me,
the shorter I'll grow.
The more I do my work,
the less yours will show.
What am I?**

Answer: *An eraser*

Finding Information

Using the Library

Ask the Experts!

Suppose you are asked to write a report about whales. You might use your own experience or talk to people you know. However, if you've never been to an ocean, or if the people you know have never seen a whale, there is another way to learn about your subject. You can do research about whales, read reports of whale watchers, explore CD-ROM's, and much more, in the library.

Searching for Information

Every library has a card catalog or a computer catalog. A card catalog lists all the books in the library. The information is written on paper cards that are kept in file drawers. Today, many libraries have a computer catalog. All the information is kept in a computer program. Either way, the catalog is the place to begin your search for information.

Catalog Entries

Whether your library uses cards or a computer, there are three kinds of catalog entries:

1. Title entries begin with the book's title. When a title begins with *A, An,* or *The,* the entry is filed under the next word in the title.

Trapped in Tar

2. Author entries begin with the name of the book's author. The author's last name is listed first.

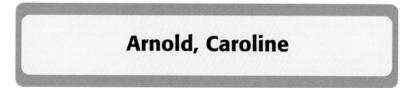

Arnold, Caroline

3. Subject entries begin with the subject of the book.

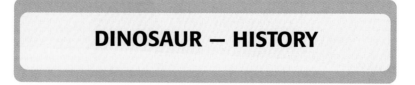

DINOSAUR — HISTORY

Using a Card Catalog

If you use a card catalog, you can find information on the same book in three ways:

1. If you know the book's **title,** look up the title card.

2. If you know the book's **author,** look up the author card. (There may be more than one card with that author's name at the top.)

3. Finally, if you know only the **subject** you want to learn about, look up the subject card.

Sample Catalog Cards

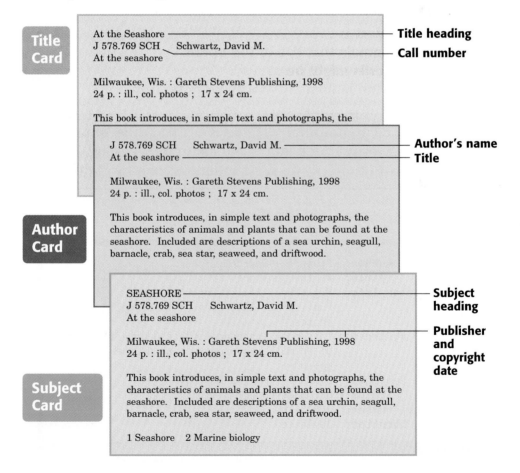

Title Card

At the Seashore —————— **Title heading**
J 578.769 SCH ⎫ Schwartz, David M. ————— **Call number**
At the seashore

Milwaukee, Wis. : Gareth Stevens Publishing, 1998
24 p. : ill., col. photos ; 17 x 24 cm.

This book introduces, in simple text and photographs, the

Author Card

J 578.769 SCH   Schwartz, David M. ——————— **Author's name**
At the seashore ————————————————— **Title**

Milwaukee, Wis. : Gareth Stevens Publishing, 1998
24 p. : ill., col. photos ; 17 x 24 cm.

This book introduces, in simple text and photographs, the
characteristics of animals and plants that can be found at the
seashore. Included are descriptions of a sea urchin, seagull,
barnacle, crab, sea star, seaweed, and driftwood.

Subject Card

SEASHORE ————————————————— **Subject heading**
J 578.769 SCH   Schwartz, David M.
At the seashore

Milwaukee, Wis. : Gareth Stevens Publishing, 1998   — **Publisher and copyright date**
24 p. : ill., col. photos ; 17 x 24 cm.

This book introduces, in simple text and photographs, the
characteristics of animals and plants that can be found at the
seashore. Included are descriptions of a sea urchin, seagull,
barnacle, crab, sea star, seaweed, and driftwood.

1 Seashore   2 Marine biology

Using a Computer Catalog

In a computer catalog, you can find information on the same book in three ways:

1. If you know the book's **title,** enter the title.

2. If you know the book's **author,** enter the author's name. (When the library has more than one book by the same author, there will be more than one entry.)

3. Finally, if you know only the **subject** you want to learn about, enter the subject or a keyword. (A *keyword* is a word that is related to the subject.)

Using Keywords

If your subject is . . .
mammals that live in the ocean,
your keywords might be . . .
marine mammals, whales, or porpoises.

 **Note** Every computer catalog is a little different. The first time you use a computer catalog, either check the instructions or ask for help.

Sample Computer Catalog Entry

Author:	Schwartz, David M.
Title:	At the seashore
Publication Info:	Milwaukee, Wis. : Gareth Stevens Publishing, 1998 24 p. : ill., col. photos.
Abstract:	This book introduces the characteristics of animals and plants found at the seashore.
Subjects:	Seashore, Marine biology
Status:	Not checked out
Call number:	J 578.769 SCH
Location:	Juvenile

Finding Books

Nonfiction Books • Nonfiction books are arranged on the library shelves according to call numbers. Every nonfiction book has its own call number.

■ **Some call numbers contain decimals.**
The call number 973.19 is a smaller number than 973.2. That's because 973.2 is actually 973.20, but the zero isn't written. The number 973.19 will be on the shelf before 973.2.

■ **Some call numbers include letters.**
The number 973.19D will be on the shelf before 973.19E.

Call numbers are usually based on the **Dewey decimal classification system.** In this system, all information is divided into 10 main classes.

The Ten Classes of the Dewey Decimal System

000 General Topics	**500 Pure Science**
100 Philosophy	**600 Technology (Applied Science)**
200 Religion	**700 The Arts, Recreation**
300 The Social Sciences	**800 Literature**
400 Language	**900 Geography and History**

Biographies • Every biography book is arranged according to the last name of the person written about. These books are shelved in alphabetical order under the call number 921. This number and the last name of the book's subject appear on the book's spine. (A biography about astronaut John Glenn would have **921 GLENN** on its spine.)

Fiction Books • Fiction books are arranged alphabetically according to the first three letters of the author's last name. These books are located in a separate section in the library.

Using Encyclopedias

An encyclopedia is a set of books (or a CD) with articles on every topic you can imagine. These topics are arranged alphabetically. Each article gives information about the topic.

Tips for Using Encyclopedias

● At the end of an article, you may find a list of related topics. Look them up to learn more about your topic.

● The index is usually in the back of the last volume, or in a separate volume. It lists all the places in the encyclopedia where you will find more information about your topic.

● Using the index may change how you decide to write about your subject. You might, for example, get a new idea from a Colonial-days story about whales or from a present-day story about Greenpeace's efforts to save whales.

Sample Encyclopedia Index

Here are some index entries for the topic *whale,* taken from the *World Book Encyclopedia Index.*

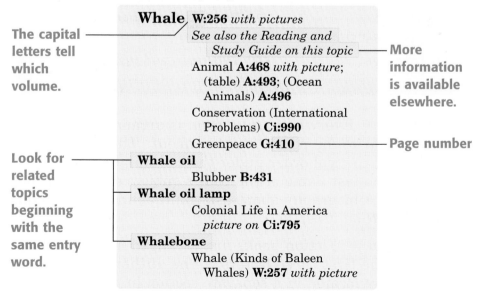

The capital letters tell which volume.

Whale W:256 *with pictures*
    See also the Reading and
      Study Guide on this topic —— More information is available elsewhere.
    Animal **A:468** *with picture;*
    (table) **A:493**; (Ocean Animals) **A:496**
    Conservation (International Problems) **Ci:990**
    Greenpeace **G:410** —— Page number

Look for related topics beginning with the same entry word.

Whale oil
    Blubber **B:431**
Whale oil lamp
    Colonial Life in America *picture on* **Ci:795**
Whalebone
    Whale (Kinds of Baleen Whales) **W:257** *with picture*

Other Reference Books

Here are just a few of the other reference books that you will find in many libraries.

- *Circling the Globe* is a guide to the culture, history, and geography of countries around the world.

- *The Dorling Kindersley Science Encyclopedia* explains the principles of science in a lively way, with more than 2,500 color photos and illustrations.

- *ESPN Information Please Sports Almanac* is a resource of sports facts, year by year and sport by sport.

- *Explorers and Discoverers* is a four-volume set focusing on 171 men and women who have made significant contributions to human knowledge, from ancient times to the present.

- *Eyewitness Books* is a series of books covering geography, history, and science topics; each book contains excellent color photographs.

- *Guinness Book of Records* lists records of all kinds, from nature to technology.

- *The Larousse Desk Reference* provides answers to thousands of everyday questions about science, art, culture, history, and geography, with more than 2,000 color illustrations.

- *Webster's New Geographical Dictionary* lists important geographical and historical information about the world's most famous places.

- *The World Almanac and Book of Facts* contains facts and statistics about entertainment, sports, business, politics, history, religion, education, and social programs.

Understanding the Parts of Nonfiction Books

When you use a nonfiction book to find information, you should know the *parts* of the book and how they can help you use that book. Below, you will find a short description of each part of a nonfiction book.

- The **title page** is usually the first page with printing on it. It mentions the title of the book, the author's name, the publisher's name, and the city where the book was published.

- The **copyright page** comes next. It gives the year the book was published. This can be important because information in an old book may no longer be accurate.

- The **preface, foreword, introduction,** or **acknowledgement** comes before the table of contents and tells what the book is about. It may also explain why the book was written.

- The **table of contents** shows the divisions of the book. It gives the names and page numbers of the sections and chapters.

- The **body** is the main part of the book.

- The **appendix** has "extra" information, such as maps, tables, and lists. (There may be more than one appendix, or none.)

- The **glossary** (if there is one) explains special words used in the book. It's like a mini-dictionary.

- The **bibliography** (if there is one) lists books or articles used by the author in writing the book. (You can use this list to find more information on the same topic.)

- The **index** is an alphabetical list of all the topics in the book. It gives the page numbers where each topic is covered. An index can help you find information on a specific topic.

Using the *Children's Magazine Guide*

The *Children's Magazine Guide* is another useful guide for finding information in the library. New issues of this guide come out every one or two months, listing the latest magazine articles on many different topics.

To use the *Magazine Guide,* simply select the issues that cover the time periods you are interested in. Then look for your subject. (The subjects are all listed in alphabetical order.)

Think It Over If you can't find your subject, think of a related topic. For example, if you are writing a report on *fossils,* you might look up *prehistoric animals.*

Reading the Guide

When you find an article you would like to read, give the magazine's title and date to the librarian. The librarian will either get it for you, or show you where you can find it.

Sample from the *Children's Magazine Guide*

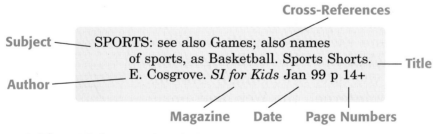

- **Subject** of the article (Subjects are listed alphabetically.)
- **Title** and **Author** of the article
- **Magazine** in which the article appears (A list of magazine abbreviations is located on the inside front cover of the guide.)
- **Date** (month, day, and year) the magazine was published
- **Page Numbers** where the article can be found in the magazine
- **Cross-References** telling where more information can be found

Using the Internet

What Is the Internet?

The Internet is a worldwide computer network. It's like a road or highway system connecting computers all around the world. The "traffic" is messages: e-mail, Web pages, money transfers, software, purchase orders, and anything else a computer can handle. On the Internet, messages travel by many different routes. If one "road" is busy or closed, the "traffic" can take an alternate route.

Using the Internet

Nowadays, you hear a lot about the Internet. Lots of people browse the World Wide Web and exchange e-mail. You have probably looked at a few Web pages, and most likely you have sent e-mail. For tips on using the Internet, the Web, and e-mail read this chapter.

The Net is getting bigger every day. It's bringing the whole world together in a brand-new way.

What Is the World Wide Web?

The Web is like a library to the world. Think of a Web *site* as a book in that library, and each Web *page* as a page in a book, with the *home page* being the title page.

Web Pages ● Like a printed page, a Web page can hold text and pictures. It can also hold animation and sounds. These pages can have hyperlinks to other Web pages. For example, "owls" on one Web page might link you to other sites, videos, sound files, or even software about "owls."

Electronic Addresses ● Each Web site has an electronic address. The electronic address for the Write Source site is **<www.thewritesource.com>**. The **www** connects your computer to the World Wide Web. The **.com** (for *commercial*) means that this is a business site. (Other common suffixes include **.net** for *network,* **.org** for *organization,* and **.gov** for *government.*)

Browser Software ● A browser is a type of program for viewing Internet sites and Web pages.

Sample **Browser Window**

Navigation buttons

Electronic address

Links

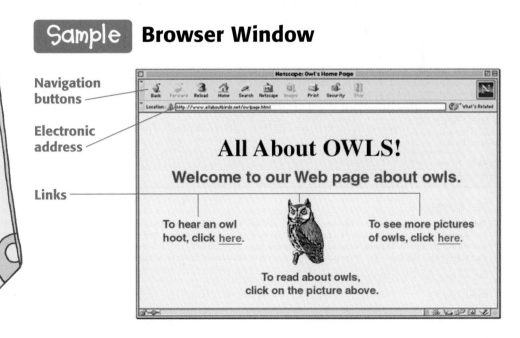

Writing On-Line

Communicating on the Internet requires good writing. Here are some pointers for doing your best on-line writing.

E-Mail

The "e" in e-mail stands for "electronic." Sending e-mail is like mailing a letter from your computer to another one across the Internet. Writing e-mail is much like writing a letter. (**SEE** pages 146-147.) You can even attach pictures and sound recordings. Here are a few things to remember:

- **Always include a subject heading.** Your reader needs to know what the message is about.
- **Don't expect an immediate answer.** Some people don't check their mail every day.
- **Don't attach huge files to your e-mail.** It may upload and download slowly.
- **Never open an attachment if you aren't sure what it is.** Your computer may get a virus!

Sample E-Mail Message with an Attachment

```
Holiday pictures                                              _□X
File  Edit  View  Tools  Message  Help
 Reply  Reply All  Forward   Print   Delete  Previous  Next  Addresses

From:     Jojoey@aol.com
Date:     Monday, Jan. 17, 2000
To:       Vlmencken@waterloo.net
Subject:  Holiday pictures
Attach:   sledding.jpg (140 KB)

Dear Grandma,

Thank you for coming to visit for the holidays. It was lots of fun seeing you. And thank
you again for the sled. I love it. Dad took a picture of me sledding down the hill behind
our house. He used a digital camera, so we have a copy on the computer. I've attached a copy
to this e-mail for you. Dad says just to click on the attachment and the picture should open.

Let me know how you like the picture.

Love, Joey
```

Bulletin Board System

BBS stands for **bulletin board system.** A BBS is a place on the Internet where you can post messages just as you might on a bulletin board at school. Other people read the message and post their replies later. Here are some ways to use a BBS:

- **Post news about your own part of the world.**
- **Give reviews of good books you have read.**
- **Share stories and poems you have written.**

Netiquette

Etiquette means "good manners." *Netiquette* is using good manners and showing respect as you write on-line. Here are a few rules of Netiquette:

Don't SHOUT.

Using all capital letters means you are SHOUTING. Instead of "shouting," you can emphasize words by typing them between asterisks (*like this*).

Be Polite.

Take care not to upset people with your words. As you write, you can always add a "smiley."
A smiley is a sideways "happy face" made of keyboard characters. :-)

Be Forgiving.

If someone says something on the Net, and you think it sounds rude or stupid, ask a question to clear it up. The person may not have meant to be rude.

Be Careful.

Never give your full name, address, or phone number over the Internet unless you first ask your parents.

Researching on the Internet

The Internet can be a great place to find information. Here's how to find your way around.

Use an Internet Address. If you know the Internet address of a site, you can type it into the address bar at the top of your browser window. Then press the "return" or "enter" key to load that page. You can visit the Write Source at the following Web address: **<thewritesource.com>.**

Use a Search Engine. Some special Web sites help you to search the Internet. They are called "search engines." To use one, type in the subject you want to learn about, then "click" its search button. The engine will give you a list of places on the Internet that tell something about your subject.

Helpful Hint: Check the Write Source Web site for a list of search engines you can use: **<thewritesource.com>.**

Save What You Find on the Internet

- Print out a paper copy of the site. Make a note of the Internet address so that you can find the site again later. If you plan to use this information in a report, try to find who the author or source of the information is. Be sure to list this source at the end of your report. (**SEE** page 201.)

- Save an electronic copy of the site on your computer or a disk. Check your browser's menu under "File" to find out how to do this. If you need to save graphics separately, check "Help" or ask an expert.

- Save the electronic address of a site you wish to visit again. Use the "bookmark" or "favorites" option on the menu bar.

Note Everything on the Net is not true or accurate. Ask an adult or check a reliable book if you are not sure about something. (**SEE** page 329.)

Publishing on the Web

Lots of students publish their work on the Web, and you can, too.

- **Submit your writing** to Web sites that display student work. (**SEE** page 72 for several publishing sites. See <thewritesource.com> for other suggested sites.)
- **Create a Web site as a class project.** Ask your teacher about this possibility.
- **Make your own Web page.** Your Internet service provider may have Web space for you to use. Ask your parents to help you explore this possibility.

Creating Your Page

If you plan to publish your own work on the Web, you must save it in a special type of computer format called HTML. Many word-processing programs let you save a regular file as HTML. Also, some Web browser programs let you make a Web page. Some multimedia programs (**SEE** pages 204-207) can save to HTML, too. Check the menu on your word processing program, browser, or multimedia program to find out how to make a Web page.

Posting Your Page

When your Web page is finished, you will need to post it on the Net. This requires a special type of program, as well as a password for the site where the page will be stored. Ask your teacher or a computer expert for help.

Advertising Your Page

Once your work is on the Web, it's time to let everyone know about it. Send e-mail to your friends and relatives, and let them know the address of your page.

Reading and Spelling Skills

Using Reading Strategies

A Plan of Action

Good readers understand and remember what they read. They read carefully and usually follow a plan. Here's a simple plan you can use:

- **Read often.**
- **Read everything:** stories, books, newspapers, magazines, Web sites . . . even cereal boxes!
- **Read smart:** use a reading strategy.

A strategy is a plan, or a way of doing something. So a reading strategy is a plan for reading. This chapter contains several strategies for understanding, remembering, and enjoying what you read.

Think and Read Strategy

Before Reading

Predict. Think about what you already know about the topic and about what you expect to find out about it.
- Ask questions about the topic.

Preview. Look over the titles, the headings, and the boldfaced or italicized words throughout the reading.
- Check the photos, maps, graphs, and diagrams.
- Review the summary at the end of the reading.

During Reading

Read. Think carefully about what you read. Stop after each section or after each page and ask yourself, "What did I just read?" Then answer in your own words.

Express Yourself Sometimes you will have to reread a section to really understand it.

Note. Take notes on the important words, phrases, or facts. Also jot down answers to any questions you may still have.

After Reading

Review. Look over the headings, boldfaced and italicized words, and illustrations again.
- Ask, "What is the main point of what I just read?"
- Ask, "What do I still not understand?"

Respond. Talk to a classmate or parent about what you've read. Talking about new ideas can make them clearer.

Write about it. Write about the reading in a journal or learning log. Try using a writing-to-learn activity. (**SEE** pages 354 and 355.)

KWL (Know, Want, Learn)

KWL is a special strategy for reading textbooks and other nonfiction books. Try it by yourself or with a partner. Set up a blank sheet of paper like the one below.

1 **Know.** Write what you know about the topic in the "K" column. This will start you thinking. Questions will begin popping into your head, which will lead you into the second column, "What do I want to learn?"

2 **Want.** Write what you want to learn in the "W" column. This will give you something to look for as you read. (Your teacher may also tell you what to look for.)

3 **Learn.** After reading, fill in the "L" column: "What did I learn?" Then check to see which questions from the "W" column you still need to answer. (You may have to find some of the answers in another source.)

Famous Walls Around the World

(K) What do I **know**?	(W) What do I **want** to learn?	(L) What did I **learn**?
1. I can think of two famous walls: Great Wall of China, the Vietnam Memorial. 2. Berlin used to have a wall.	1. How many famous walls are there? 2. How long is the Great Wall of China? 3. When was it built?	1. There are lots of famous walls! The Wailing Wall, the Berlin Wall . . . 2. The Great Wall was built more than 2,000 years ago. 3. The Berlin Wall came down in 1989.

Preview, Read, and Respond

Preview. When you read nonfiction, it's a good idea to preview the material first. Look for titles, headings, pictures, charts, and boldfaced words.

Read. Reading means more than looking at words. It means thinking, studying, and rereading when necessary.

Respond. It's important to respond to what you read. You can respond by taking notes, talking to someone about it, writing about it, or asking questions.

Preview

Kinds of baleen whales

Baleen whales have no teeth. Instead they have hundreds of thin plates in the mouth. A whale uses these plates to strain out food from the water. These plates are called baleen or whalebone and consist of the same material as human fingernails. The baleen hangs from the whale's upper jaw.

There are 10 kinds of baleen whales. Scientists divide them into three groups: (1) right whales; (2) gray whales; and (3) rorquals.

Right whales have a thick, solid body and an unusually large head. The head of most right whales makes up about a third of the total body length. Right whales swim slowly, averaging about 3 miles per hour. They feed by swimming into a mass of plankton with their mouths open. Water flows through the baleen, and the plankton becomes entangles in the baleen fibers. There are three main kind of right whales: (1) bowhead whales; (2) black right whales; (3) pygmy right whales.

Bowhead whales, also called Greenland whales, have the longest baleen of all baleen whales. They have a highly arched mouth suited to the huge baleen, which may grow as long as 13 feet. Bowhead whales are black with white areas on the tail and the tip of the lower jaw. They measure up to 60 feet long and live only in the arctic Ocean.

Black right whales usually are called simply right whales. Compare with bowhead whales, they have shorter baleen and a less highly arched mouth. They are black and some have white areas on the belly. Right whales lie in all the seas.

Rorquals are baleen whales that have long grooves on the throat and chest. These grooves may number from 10 to 100 and are 1 to 2 inches deep. They enable a rorqual to open its mouth extremely wide and gulp enormous quantities of food and water. As the whale closes its mouth, its tongue forces the water out of the mouth through the baleen, the food becomes trapped inside the baleen and is swallowed by the whale. all rorquals have a *dorsal,* or back, fin, and so they are sometimes called *finback whales.* Most of them have a long, streamlined shape and can swim faster than other whales.

There are six kinds of rorquals. They are (1) blue whales; (2) Bryde's whales; (3) fin whales; (4) humpback whales; (5) minke whales; and (6) sei whales.

Blue whales live in all the oceans but are rare. They are sometimes called *sulfur-bottom* whales because some of them have growths of tiny yellowish, or sulfur-colored plants, called *diatoms* on the belly.

Blue whales are the largest animals that ever lived. The blue whale reaches up to 100 feet (30 meters) long and can weigh over 150 tons. It has speckled blue-gray and white skin, small, thin flippers, and a large, strong tail. It can live in any ocean.

Whales   999

Read

    Blue whales are the largest animals that ever lived. The blue whale reaches up to 100 feet (30 meters) long and can weigh over 150 tons. It has speckled blue-gray and white skin; small, thin flippers; and a large, strong tail. It can live in any ocean.

    The blue whale strains food from the water using 260 to 400 thin, fringed plates called **baleen,** hanging from each side of its mouth. The whale eats primarily **krill,** a shrimplike animal. It lunges through masses of krill, taking in tons of water and food. It then closes its mouth and squirts the water out through the baleen, trapping the krill inside.

    Blue whales usually dive no deeper than about 300 feet (90 meters) because krill tend to live at shallow depths. The whales surface to breathe three to six times in rapid succession, then dive for several minutes. When surfacing, they exhale sharply through their blowholes (nostrils), producing a loud sound.

Respond

You can respond to your reading by using a web, or cluster.

Blue Whales

First, name the subject in the middle of the web.

Then, list the important details around it.

largest animal

must surface to breathe

up to 100 feet long

eat krill (shrimplike animal)

Blue Whales

Can weigh more than 150 tons

can live in any ocean

Speckled blue-gray and white, small flippers

Writing to Learn: There are many other ways to respond to reading. (**SEE** pages 354-355.)

ategy for Reading Fiction

en you read fiction, use a plot line to help you keep track
story. Most short stories, novels, and other works of
n have five parts:

1. The **exposition** describes the setting and introduces
   the main characters.
2. The **rising action** tells about the problems the
   characters face.
3. The **climax** is the highest point of action or suspense.
4. The **falling action** tells what happens after the climax.
5. The **resolution** is the ending; it tells how things finally
   turn out.

Sample Plot Line

"The Boy Who Cried Wolf"

No one believes the boy.

A wolf really
attacks the sheep.

climax

He lies again and again.

The wolf eats
the sheep.

The boy lies
about a wolf.

rising action

falling action

Sheep, meadow,
shepherd boy

The boy loses
his job and
his friends.

exposition

resolution

Elements of Fiction

Like most people, you know a good story or book when you read one. But can you put into words why you liked it? The following glossary of what "goes into" a story (the elements) will help you understand and write about what you've read.

Action • The action is everything that happens in a story.

Antagonist • An antagonist (sometimes called a villain) is a person or thing that fights against the hero.

> The wolf is the antagonist of the three little pigs.

Character • A character is a person or humanlike animal in a story.

Conflict • Conflict is the "problem" in a story. There are five basic types of conflict:

- *Person vs. Person:* Two characters in the story have a conflict, or disagreement.
- *Person vs. Society:* A character has a conflict with society or part of society—a school or the police force, for example.
- *Person vs. Himself or Herself:* A character has an inner conflict or struggle, such as whether to lie or not.
- *Person vs. Nature:* A character has a conflict with nature—a blizzard, a drought, a tornado.
- *Person vs. Fate:* A character is in conflict with something that he or she cannot control, such as an accident or a disability.

Dialogue • Dialogue is the talking characters do in a story. (**SEE** page 215.)

Mood • Mood is the feeling a reader gets from a story—happy, sad, peaceful, and so on.

Moral • A moral is a lesson the writer wants readers to learn from a story. The moral of "The Boy Who Cried Wolf" is that if you tell lies, no one will believe you, even when you tell the truth.

Narrator • The narrator is the one who tells the story. Harold the dog tells the story in *Bunnicula,* so Harold is the narrator (even though he is a dog!).

Plot • The plot is the action or series of events that make up the story.

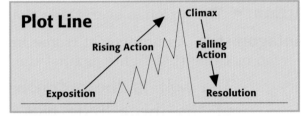

Point of View • Point of view is the angle from which a story is told.

- When the narrator tells a story about himself or herself, this is called *first-person point of view.*

  > Yes, I had been told that dragonflies could sew my mouth shut, but my friend didn't know everything.

- When the narrator tells a story about others, this is called *third-person point of view.*

  > Yes, she had been told that dragonflies could sew her mouth shut, but her friend didn't know everything.

Protagonist • The protagonist is the hero of the story.

Setting • The setting is the time and place of a story.

Theme • The theme is the main idea or message of a story. The theme of *Charlotte's Web* is the importance of friendship.

Tone • The tone is the feeling the author creates in a story. For example, the tone of a story may be serious, funny, or angry.

Types of Literature

Autobiography • An autobiography is a story the writer tells about her or his own life.

Biography • A biography is a story the writer tells about another person's life.

Comedy • A comedy is a story with a happy ending, or a story that makes readers smile or laugh.

Drama • Drama is another name for a play. *Drama* is also the term for a serious story.

Fable • A fable is a story meant to teach a lesson. A fable often has animal characters.

Fiction • Stories about made-up characters and events are called fiction.

Folktale • A folktale is a story made up and passed on by the common people.

Historical Fiction • Historical fiction is a story that is mostly fact, but partly fiction.

Myth • A myth is an old story, handed down through time, that explains something about life or nature. The characters are often gods and goddesses with supernatural powers.

Nonfiction • Stories about real people and real events are called nonfiction.

Novel • A novel is a book that tells a made-up story (fiction).

Science Fiction • A science-fiction story is based on real or made-up inventions. It is often set in the future, on other planets, or under the sea.

Tragedy • A tragedy is a story with an unhappy ending.

Reading Graphics

A Picture Is Worth . . .

Did you know that the first writing ever invented used pictures instead of words? Five thousand years ago, Egyptian children learned by "reading" a kind of picture writing called **hieroglyphics:**

K L E O P A T R A

Native American tribes also used picture writing to "talk" to other tribes that didn't speak their language. That's one useful thing about simple pictures—they mean the same thing to everybody. "Bear" is *oso* in Spanish, *ours* in French, and *honaw* in Hopi, but everybody understands . . . .

Symbols

The drawings used in picture writing are called "symbols." A **symbol** is a simple picture or drawing that stands for something else.

Picture Symbols • It's easy to tell what a symbol means when it looks just like the thing it stands for.

Signs and Symbols • Sometimes symbols stand for things that you can't really draw a picture of—like the equal sign. In this case, the symbol stands for an idea; everybody who knows basic math knows that = means "equals." Here are a few examples of signs and symbols used in different subjects. How many do you know?

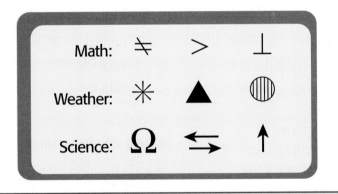

Note If you see a symbol and you don't know what it means, look in the appendix or glossary of the book you are reading. You may also look for "Signs and Symbols" in the table of contents of your dictionary.

Diagrams

Diagrams are simple pictures that usually include words (labels). Diagrams can show everything from the parts in your computer to the bones in your hand.

Cycle Diagram • A cycle diagram shows how something happens over time. It shows a series of events that happen over and over again, always leading back to the starting point.

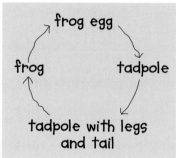

Line Diagram • A line diagram helps you see where someone or something fits into a situation (like a family tree). A line diagram can also show how things are organized into groups.

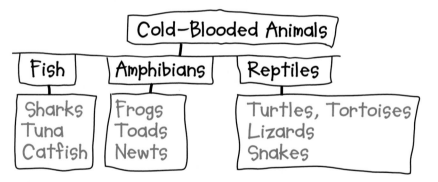

Picture Diagram • A picture diagram uses drawings to show how something is put together, how the parts relate to one another, or how the thing works.

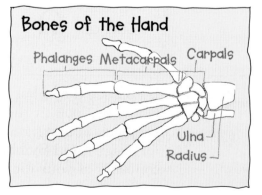

Graphs

Graphs share information about how things change over time or about how things compare to one another. They give you a picture related to the words on a page. They also help you see information "at a glance." There are different kinds of graphs for different kinds of information. There are **bar graphs, line graphs,** and **pie graphs.**

Bar Graph • A bar graph compares two or more things at one point in time—like a snapshot. The bars of the graph can go up and down or sideways. Both bar graphs below compare the number of guppies in the 4th-grade aquarium to the number in the 5th-grade aquarium at the end of the school year.

Sample **Bar Graphs**

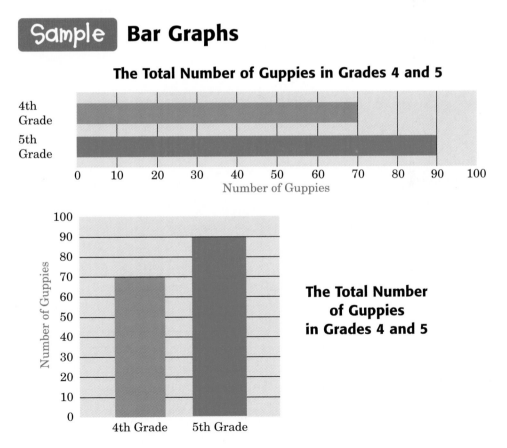

The Total Number of Guppies in Grades 4 and 5

The Total Number of Guppies in Grades 4 and 5

Line Graph • A line graph is drawn on a "grid." The horizontal (left-to-right) side of the grid shows time passing. The vertical (top-to-bottom) side shows the subject of the graph. The line drawn through the grid lets you see the subject as it passes through time.

The line graph below shows how many guppies were in the 5th-grade aquarium in each month of the school year. "Number of guppies" is the *subject* of this graph, and *time* is measured in months (September through June).

Sample **Line Graph**

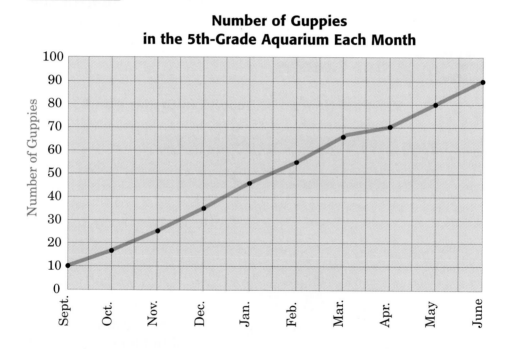

**Number of Guppies
in the 5th-Grade Aquarium Each Month**

Note Sometimes a line graph has dots or points on the line to make it easier to read. (See the graph above.) Other times, the line has no markings on it, and you must picture the points in your mind's eye.

Pie Graph • A pie graph shows how each part of something compares to the other parts and to the whole "pie." The graph below shows what part (or percentage) of the total number of guppies is contained in each grade's aquarium. For example, if there were 100 guppies in the whole school, the 5th-grade class would have 62 guppies, because 62% of 100 is 62.

Sample Pie Graph

Percentage of Guppies in Each Grade

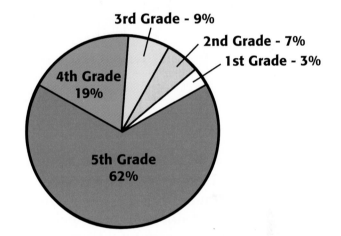

Quick Guide to Graphs

■ Every graph has a subject—just like a paragraph.
■ A **bar graph** compares things at the same time.
■ A **line graph** tells you how things change over time.
■ A **pie graph** shows how the parts of something compare to one another and to the whole.
■ Some graphs repeat information you already read somewhere on the page; other graphs tell you more about a topic.

Tables

Like diagrams and graphs, tables share information in "picture" form. **Tables** have *rows* (going across) and *columns* (going down). Rows show one kind of information, while columns show another kind of information.

Schedule • The table below is a bus schedule. The rows show days of the week; the columns show times of day. A check mark means a bus leaves on that day, at that time.

Bus Departures	8 a.m.	Noon	6 p.m.
Mon. - Fri.	✔	✔	✔
Saturday	✔	✔	
Sunday		✔	
Holidays	✔	✔	✔

Distance Table • Another common kind of table is a distance or mileage table. To read a distance table, find the place you're starting from. Then find the place you're going to in the opposite part of the table. Finally, look at the number where the row and the column meet—that's how far it is from one place to the other. For example, it is 2,912 miles from New York to Seattle.

Distance in Miles	Los Angeles	Seattle	Baltimore
Los Angeles	0	1,141	2,701
New York	2,787	2,912	197
Tampa	2,591	3,096	997

Other Kinds of Tables • Look over the many other kinds of tables in the "Student Almanac" of this handbook. (**SEE** pages 437-487.)

Conversion Table • Conversion tables help you convert (change) information from one form to another. The chart below shows you certain American measurements that have been converted to metric measurements.

AMERICAN MEASUREMENTS		METRIC
1 inch		2.54 centimeters
1 foot	12 inches	0.3048 meter
1 yard	3 feet	0.9144 meter
1 pint	2 cups	0.4732 liter
1 quart	2 pints	0.9463 liter

Custom-Made Tables • You can make your own table to show any kind of information you choose. Imagine that for your science project you need to guess the weight of certain animals or people, and then weigh them to find out how well you guessed. You could make a table like the one below.

Things I weighed	Guessed weight	Actual weight	Difference over (+) under (-)
my hamster	1 pound	7 ounces	+9 ounces
my cat	5 pounds	8 pounds	-3 pounds
my dog	50 pounds	68 pounds	-18 pounds
my friend	100 pounds	75 pounds	+25 pounds
my mom	250 pounds	118 pounds	+132 pounds
me	90 pounds	75 pounds	+15 pounds

Building Vocabulary Skills

The Tools You Need

Think of your vocabulary as the tools you need for reading, writing, and talking. The more tools you have, the more you can do with language.

Suppose your friend Sean says to you, "Jim *donated* $10 for our clubhouse, but now he says he only *lent* us the money!" If you don't know what *donated* and *lent* mean, you won't know why your friend is upset. But if *donated* and *lent* are in your "word toolbox," you'll understand: Sean thought the money was a *gift,* but Jim is telling Sean he has to *pay it back.*

> Wonderful, wild, and whimsical words wander in and out of the world of writers.

Strategies for Building Your Vocabulary

1 Read and Check.

When you are reading and you come to a word you don't know, check the surrounding words to figure out its meaning. Here are some ways to do this:

- Study the sentence containing the word, as well as the sentences that come **before and after it.**

- Search for **synonyms** (words with the same meaning).
  Because I plan to be an actor, Dad calls me a thespian.
  (A *thespian* is an "actor.")

- Search for **antonyms** (words with the opposite meaning).
  Dad says fishing is tedious, but I think it's exciting.
  (*Tedious* means "boring," the opposite of "exciting.")

- Search for **a definition** of the word.
  We saw yuccas, common desert plants, on our drive to the Grand Canyon.
  (*Yuccas* are common desert plants.)

- Search for **familiar words in a series** with the new word.
  In the South, many houses have a veranda, porch, or patio.
  (A *veranda* is a large, open porch.)

- Watch for words that have **multiple meanings.**
  He charged me 50 cents for the candy bar.
  My mom charged the battery on my go-cart.

- Watch for **idioms** (words that have different uses from their dictionary meanings).
  "I'm cutting out." (This phrase could mean "using scissors," or it could mean "leaving a place.")

- Watch for **figurative language** like similes and metaphors. (**SEE** pages 126-127.)

2 Use a Dictionary.

You can always use a dictionary to find the meaning of new words. A dictionary can also help you with the following:

Spelling • If you don't know how to spell a word, try looking it up by how it sounds.

Capital Letters • A dictionary shows if a word needs to be capitalized.

Syllable Division • A dictionary shows where you can divide a word. Heavy black dots (•) divide a word into syllables. A hyphen (-) shows that the word is hyphenated.

Accent Marks • An accent mark (´) shows which syllable should be stressed when you say a word.

Pronunciation • To remember a word and its meaning, it helps if you know how to say it. A dictionary shows each word spelled phonetically (as it sounds).

Parts of Speech • A dictionary tells what part of speech (noun, verb, etc.) a word is. Some words can be used in more than one way.

Word History • Some words have stories about where they came from or how their meanings have changed through the years. This information appears inside brackets [ ].

Synonyms and Antonyms • Synonyms (words with the same or similar meanings) are listed, and some words are used in sample sentences. Antonyms (words with opposite meanings) may be listed last.

Meaning • Some words have only one meaning. Some words have several meanings, and you will have to choose the best one.

Tip There may be a dictionary and a thesaurus on the computer you use. These helpful tools may be part of your writing program, or they may be on a CD-ROM.

Sample **Dictionary Page**

Guide words ———— **muscular/musky**

————— **Pronunciation**

mus•cu•lar (mŭs´kyə ler) *adj.* **1.** Of, relating to, or consisting of muscle: *a muscular arm.* **2.** Having strong well-developed muscles: *a muscular gymnast.* –**mus• cu•lar•i•ty** (mŭs´kyə lăr´ĭ tē) *n.* –**mus•cu•lar•ly** *adv.*

Synonyms ——— Synonyms: muscular, athletic, brawny, burly, sinewy. These adjectives all mean strong and powerfully built. *I lift weights because I want a more muscular body. The athletic young woman won all the races at the company picnic. They need brawny friends to help move that piano. The wharf was crowded with burly men waiting to unload the ship's cargo. Professional dancers are usually lean and sinewy.* **Antonym: scrawny.** ———— **Antonyms**

muscular dys•tro•phy (dĭs´trə fē) *n.* A hereditary disease in which a person's muscles gradually and irreversibly deteriorate, causing weakness and finally complete disability.

————— **Parts of speech**

Syllable division ———— **mus•cu•la•ture** (mŭs´kyə lə chŏŏr´) *n.* The system of muscles of an animal or of a body part.

muse (myōōz) *intr. v.* **mused, mus•ing, mus•es.** To consider at length; ponder; meditate: *musing over his chances in tomorrow's game.* [First written down in 1340 in Middle English and spelled *musen,* from Old French *muser,* possibly from *mus,* snout.]
❏ *These sound alike:* **muse, Muse** (goddess), **mews** (alley).

Spelling and capital letters ———— **Muse** (myōōz) *n.* **1.** In Greek mythology, one of the nine sister goddesses who preside over the arts and sciences. **2. muse. a.** A guiding spirit. **b.** A source of inspiration. [First written down in 1380 in Middle English from ———— **Word history** Greek *Mousa.*]
❏ *These sound alike:* **Muse, mews** (alley), **muse** (consider).

————— **Accent mark**

mu•se•um (myōō ze´əm) *n.* A building in which objects of artistic, historical, or scientific interest are exhibited. [First written down in 1615 in Modern English, from Greek *Mouseion,* shrine of the Muses.]

mush[1] (mŭsh) *n.* **1.** A porridge made of corn meal boiled in water or milk. **2.** A thick soft mass. **3.**

Usage label — *Informal.* Extreme sentimentality: *That movie was just a lot of mush.* [First written down in 1671 in American English, probably alteration of *mash.*]

mush[2] (mŭsh) *intr.v.* **mushed, mush•ing, mush•es.** To travel over snow with a dogsled. –*interj.* An expression used to command a team of sled dogs to start pulling or go faster. [First written down in 1862 in American English and spelled *mouche,* possibly alteration of French *marchons,* let's go!]

mush•room (mŭsh´rōōm´ *or* mŭsh´rŏŏm) *n.* **1.** Any of various types of fungus having a stalk topped by a fleshy umbrella-shaped cap. Some mushrooms are used as food, but many kinds are poisonous. **2.** Something resembling a mushroom in shape.

mushroom
/
Caption

Pronunciation key

ă	pat	oi	boy
ə	pay	ou	out
âr	care	ŏŏ	took
ä	father	ōō	boot
ĕ	pet	ŭ	cut
ē	be	ûr	urge
ĭ	pit	th	thin
ī	pie	*th*	this
îr	pier	hw	whoop
ŏ	pot	zh	vision
ō	toe	ə	about
ô	paw	N	*French* bon

3 Use a Thesaurus.

A thesaurus is a book of words and their synonyms (other words that mean the same thing). A thesaurus also lists antonyms (words that have the opposite meaning). You can use a thesaurus to build your vocabulary and improve your writing. You go to a thesaurus when you know the meaning but want or need a word.

Sample Thesaurus Entry

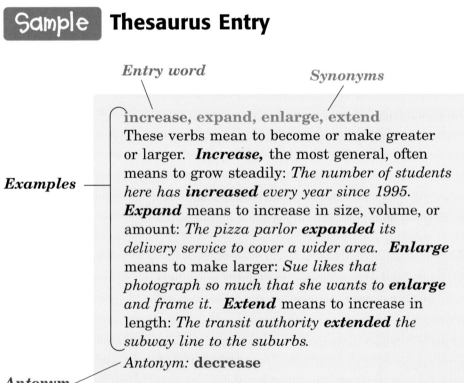

Entry word

Synonyms

Examples

increase, expand, enlarge, extend
These verbs mean to become or make greater or larger. **Increase,** the most general, often means to grow steadily: *The number of students here has **increased** every year since 1995.* **Expand** means to increase in size, volume, or amount: *The pizza parlor **expanded** its delivery service to cover a wider area.* **Enlarge** means to make larger: *Sue likes that photograph so much that she wants to **enlarge** and frame it.* **Extend** means to increase in length: *The transit authority **extended** the subway line to the suburbs.*
Antonym: **decrease**

Antonym

Choose•A•Word: A thesaurus may list words alphabetically, like a dictionary, or you may need to look up your word in the index. The sample thesaurus above was used to find the best word to fill the blank below.

■ My brother's paper route is going to ___expand___ to include the new housing development.

4 Keep a Personal Dictionary.

You can improve your vocabulary by keeping a personal dictionary. Add new words as you read or hear them.

1. **Look up each new word** in a regular dictionary to learn what it means and how to say it.
2. **Write the word** and its part of speech on a note card or in a notebook.
3. **Write the word's meaning** (or meanings).
4. **Write a sentence** using the word.
5. **List some synonyms,** too.

chuck (verb)
  1. To toss or throw
  2. To pat or tap lightly

He chucked his old ragged shirt.

synonyms: flip, fling, heave

original (adjective)
  – Something that isn't copied

Daisy wrote an original poem about bugs.

synonyms: new, imaginative, unused

Learn About Word Parts.

You can figure out the meanings of new words by learning about the three basic word parts:

- ■ **prefixes** (word beginnings),
- ■ **suffixes** (word endings), and
- ■ **roots** (word bases).

Learn the meanings of some prefixes, suffixes, and roots.

The prefix **sub** means "under."
The root **terra** means "earth."

Look for those word parts whenever you meet a new word.

The story is about a **subterranean** city.

(If you know that *sub* means "under" and *terra* means "earth," you can figure out that *subterranean* means "under the earth.")

Watch for Word Families.

Word families are groups of words that are built from the same basic word. If you know the meaning of the basic word, you can often figure out the meanings of other words in the same "family."

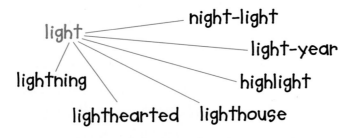

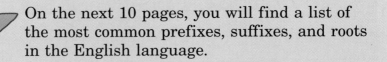

On the next 10 pages, you will find a list of the most common prefixes, suffixes, and roots in the English language.

Prefixes

Prefixes are word parts that come *before* the root or word base (*pre*=before). Prefixes can change the meaning of a word.

ambi, amphi *[both]*

ambidextrous *(skilled with both hands)*

amphibious *(living on both land and water)*

anti *[against]*

antifreeze *(a liquid that works against freezing)*

antipollutant *(designed to work against pollution)*

astro *[star]*

astronaut *(star or space traveler)*

astronomy *(study of the stars)*

auto *[self]*

autobiography *(writing about yourself)*

autonomy *(self-government)*

bi, bin *[two]*

binocular *(using both eyes)*

biweekly *(every two weeks)*

circum *[around]*

circumference *(the line that goes around a circle)*

circumnavigate *(to travel completely around)*

co *[together, with]*

coauthor *(one who writes with at least one other person)*

copilot *(one who flies with and assists the main pilot)*

ex *[out]*

exit *(the act of going out)*

expel *(drive out)*

hemi, semi *[half]*

hemisphere *(half of a sphere)*

semicircle *(half of a circle)*

hyper *[over]*

hyperactive *(overly active)*

hypersensitive *(overly sensitive)*

inter *[among, between]*

intermission *(a pause between the acts of a play)*

international *(of or between two or more nations)*

macro *[large]*

macroclimate *(general climate of a large area)*

macrocosm *(the entire world)*

mal *[badly, poorly]*

maladjusted *(poorly adjusted)*

malnutrition *(poor nutrition)*

mono *[one]*

monochrome *(one color)*

monorail *(runs on one track)*

non *[absence of, not]*

nonfat *(absence of fat)*

nonfiction *(not fiction)*

oct *[eight]*

octagon *(a shape with eight sides)*

octopus *(a sea animal having eight armlike tentacles)*

penta *[five]*

    pentagon *(a figure or building having five angles and sides)*
    pentameter *(a line of verse composed of five metrical feet)*

poly *[many]*

    polychrome *(many colors)*
    polygon *(a figure having many angles or sides)*

post *[after]*

    postscript *(a note added after the end of a letter)*
    postwar *(after a war)*

pre *[before]*

    premature *(happening before the proper time)*
    preview *(showing something before the regular showing)*

pseudo *[false]*

    pseudonym *(false name)*
    pseudopod *(false foot)*

quad *[four]*

    quadrant *(one quarter of a circle)*
    quadruple *(four times as much)*

quint *[five]*

    quintet *(group of five musicians)*
    quintuplet *(one of five children born in a single birth)*

re *[again, back]*

    return *(to come back)*
    rewrite *(to write over again)*

sub *[under]*

    submerge *(put under)*
    subsoil *(layer under the topsoil)*

trans *[across, beyond]*

    transoceanic *(crossing the ocean)*
    transplant *(to move something)*

tri *[three]*

    triangle *(a figure that has three sides and three angles)*
    tricycle *(a three-wheeled vehicle)*

un *[not]*

    uncomfortable *(not comfortable)*
    unhappy *(not happy)*

uni *[one]*

    unicycle *(a one-wheeled vehicle)*
    unique *(one of a kind)*

Numerical Prefixes

Prefix	Symbol	Equivalent	Prefix	Symbol	Equivalent
deca	*da*	tenfold	**deci**	*d*	tenth part
hecto	*h*	hundredfold	**centi**	*c*	hundredth part
kilo	*k*	thousandfold	**milli**	*m*	thousandth part
mega	*M*	millionfold	**micro**	*u*	millionth part
giga	*G*	billionfold	**nano**	*n*	billionth part
tera	*T*	trillionfold	**pico**	*p*	trillionth part

Suffixes

Suffixes are word parts that come at the end of a word. Sometimes a suffix will tell you what part of speech a word is. For example, many adverbs end in the suffix *ly*.

able *[able, can do]*
   agreeable *(willing to agree)*
   capable *(able to do something)*

ed *[past tense]*
   called *(past tense of call)*
   learned *(past tense of learn)*

er *[one who]*
   baker *(one who bakes)*
   teacher *(one who teaches)*

er *[used to compare things]*
   neater *(more neat than another)*
   tougher *(more tough than another)*

ess *[female]*
   lioness *(a female lion)*
   princess *(female royalty)*

est *[used to show superiority]*
   fastest *(most able to move rapidly)*
   hottest *(highest temperatures)*

ful *[full of]*
   careful *(full of care)*
   helpful *(full of help)*

ing *[an action or process]*
   talking *(to talk)*
   writing *(to write)*

ist *[one who]*
   artist *(one who does art)*
   chemist *(one who specializes in chemistry)*

less *[without]*
   careless *(without care)*
   hopeless *(without hope)*

ly *[in some manner]*
   bashfully *(in a bashful manner)*
   quickly *(in a quick manner)*

ment *[act of, result]*
   achievement *(result of achieving)*
   movement *(act of moving)*

ness *[state of]*
   carelessness *(state of being careless)*
   restlessness *(state of being restless)*

ology *[study, science]*
   biology *(study of living things)*
   geology *(study of the earth, rocks)*

s *[plural, more than one]*
   books *(more than one book)*
   trees *(more than one tree)*

sion, tion *[state of]*
   action *(state of doing something)*
   infection *(state of being infected)*

y *[inclined to]*
   cheery *(inclined to be cheerful)*
   itchy *(inclined to itch)*

Roots

A **root** is the main part of a word. If you know the root of a difficult word, you can most likely figure out the word's meaning. This can be very useful when learning new words in all your classes.

acid, acri *[bitter, sour]*
> **acrid** (*bitter taste or odor*)
> **antacid** (*works against acid*)

act, ag *[do, move]*
> **action** (*something that is done*)
> **agent** (*someone who acts for another*)

ali, alter *[other]*
> **alias** (*a person's other name*)
> **alternative** (*another choice*)

am, amor *[love, liking]*
> **amiable** (*friendly*)
> **amorous** (*loving*)

anni, annu, enni *[year]*
> **anniversary** (*happening at the same time every year*)
> **annually** (*yearly*)
> **centennial** (*every 100 years*)

anthrop *[man]*
> **anthropoid** (*humanlike*)
> **anthropology** (*study of human beings*)

aster *[star]*
> **aster** (*star flower*)
> **asterisk** (*starlike symbol*)

aud *[hear, listen]*
> **audible** (*can be heard*)
> **auditorium** (*a place to listen*)

bibl *[book]*
> **Bible** (*sacred book of Christianity*)
> **bibliography** (*list of books*)

bio *[life]*
> **biography** (*writing about a person's life*)
> **biology** (*study of life*)

centri *[center]*
> **centrifugal** (*moving away from the center*)
> **concentric** (*having a common center*)

chrom *[color]*
> **chromatics** (*scientific study of color*)
> **monochrome** (*one color*)

chron *[time]*
chronological *(in order of time)*
synchronize *(together in time)*

cide *[kill]*
genocide *(race killer)*
homicide *(human killer)*

cise *[cut]*
incision *(a thin, clean cut)*
precise *(cut exactly right)*

cord, cor *[heart]*
cordial *(heartfelt)*
coronary *(relating to the heart)*

corp *[body]*
corporation *(a legal body)*
corpulent *(having a large body)*

cosm *[universe, world]*
cosmos *(the universe)*
microcosm *(a small world)*

cred *[believe]*
credit *(belief, trust)*
incredible *(unbelievable)*

cycl, cyclo *[wheel, circular]*
bicycle *(a cycle with two wheels)*
cyclone *(a circular wind)*

dem *[people]*
democracy *(people rule)*
epidemic *(on or among the people)*

dent, dont *[tooth]*
denture *(false teeth)*
orthodontist *(someone who straightens teeth)*

derm *[skin]*
dermatology *(the study of skin)*
epidermis *(outer layer of skin)*

dic, dict *[say, speak]*
dictionary *(a book of words people use or say)*
predict *(to tell about something in advance)*

dynam *[power]*
dynamite *(powerful explosive)*
dynamo *(power producer)*

equi *[equal]*
equilibrium *(a state of balance; equally divided)*
equinox *(day and night of equal length)*

fac, fact *[do, make]*
factory *(a place where people make things)*
manufacture *(to make by hand)*

fer *[bear, carry]*
conifer *(a cone-bearing tree)*
ferry *(carry from place to place)*

fide *[faith, trust]*
confident *(trusting oneself)*
fidelity *(faithfulness to a person or cause)*

fin *[end]*
final *(the last or end of something)*
infinite *(having no end)*

flex *[bend]*
flexible *(able to bend)*
reflex *(bending or springing back)*

flu *[flowing]*
fluid *(flowing, waterlike substance)*
influence *(to flow in)*

forc, fort *[strong]*
force *(strength or power)*
fortify *(to make strong)*

fract, frag *[break]*
fracture *(break)*
fragment *(a piece broken from the whole)*

gastr *[stomach]*
gastric *(relating to the stomach)*
gastritis *(inflammation of the stomach)*

gen *[birth, produce]*
congenital *(existing at birth)*
genetics *(study of inborn traits)*

geo *[earth]*
geography *(study of the earth)*
geometry *(measuring the earth)*

grad *[step, go]*
gradual *(step-by-step)*
graduation *(taking the next step)*

graph *[write]*
autograph *(self-writing)*
photograph *(light-writing)*

greg *[herd, group]*
congregation *(a group that is functioning together)*
segregate *(tending to group apart)*

hab, habit *[live]*
habitat *(the place in which one lives)*
inhabit *(to live in)*

hetero *[different]*
heterogeneous *(different in birth or kind)*
heterosexual *(with interest in the opposite sex)*

homo *[same]*
homogeneous *(of same birth or kind)*
homogenize *(to blend into a uniform mixture)*

hum *[earth]*
exhume *(to take out of the earth)*
humus *(earth; dirt)*

hydr *[water]*
dehydrate *(take water out of)*
hydrophobia *(fear of water)*

ject *[throw]*
eject *(to throw out)*
project *(throw forward)*

leg *[law]*
legal *(related to the law)*
legislature *(persons who make laws)*

log, ology *[word, study]*
psychology *(mind study)*
zoology *(animal study)*

luc, lum *[light]*
lumen *(a unit of light)*
translucent *(letting light come through)*

magn *[great]*
magnificent *(great)*
magnify *(increase to a greater size)*

man *[hand]*
manicure *(to fix the hands)*
manufacture *(to make by hand)*

mania *[madness]*
kleptomania *(an abnormal tendency to steal)*
maniac *(a mad person)*

mar *[sea, pool]*
marine *(related to the sea)*
marsh *(a wet, grassy area)*

medi *[middle, between]*
mediterranean *(lying between lands)*
medium *(in the middle)*

mega *[great]*
megalopolis *(great city or an urban region)*
megaphone *(great sound)*

mem *[remember]*
memo *(a note; a reminder)*
memorial *(a remembrance of someone)*

meter *[measure]*
meter *(a unit of measure)*
voltmeter *(instrument to measure volts)*

migra *[wander]*
emigrant *(one who leaves a country)*
migrant *(someone who wanders from place to place)*

mit, miss *[send]*
emit *(send out; give off)*
missile *(an object sent flying)*

mob, mot *[move]*
mobile *(capable of moving)*
promotion *(to move forward)*

mon *[warn, remind]*
admonish *(warn)*
monument *(a reminder of a person or an event)*

morph *[form]*
amorphous *(with no form or shape)*
metamorphosis *(change of form)*

mort *[death]*
immortal *(something that never dies)*
mortuary *(a place for the dead)*

multi *[many, much]*
multicultural *(including many cultures)*
multiped *(an organism with many feet)*

nat *[to be born]*
　innate *(inborn)*
　nativity *(birth)*

neur *[nerve]*
　neuritis *(inflammation of a nerve)*
　neurologist *(a physician who treats the nervous system)*

nov *[new]*
　innovation *(something newly introduced)*
　renovate *(to make like new again)*

numer *[number]*
　enumerate *(to find out the number)*
　innumerable *(too many to count)*

omni *[all, every]*
　omnipresent *(present everywhere)*
　omnivorous *(all-eating)*

onym *[name]*
　anonymous *(without a name)*
　pseudonym *(false name)*

ortho *[straight]*
　orthodontist *(someone who straightens teeth)*
　orthodox *(straight or usual belief)*

pac *[peace]*
　Pacific Ocean *(peaceful ocean)*
　pacify *(make peace)*

path, pathy *[feeling, suffering]*
　empathy *(feeling with another)*
　telepathy *(feeling from a distance)*

patr *[father]*
　patriarch *(the father of the family)*
　patron *(special guardian or father figure)*

ped *[foot]*
　pedal *(lever for a foot)*
　pedestrian *(one who travels by foot)*

pend *[hang, weigh]*
　pendant *(a hanging object)*
　pendulum *(a weight hung by a cord)*

phil *[love]*
　Philadelphia *(city of brotherly love)*
　philosophy *(love or study of wisdom)*

phobia *[fear]*
　acrophobia *(fear of high places)*
　agoraphobia *(fear of public, open places)*

phon *[sound]*
　phonics *(related to sounds)*
　symphony *(sounds made together)*

photo *[light]*
　photograph *(light-writing)*
　photosynthesis *(action of light on chlorophyll)*

pop *[people]*
　population *(the number of people in an area)*
　populous *(full of people)*

port *[carry]*
　export *(carry out)*
　portable *(able to be carried)*

proto *[first]*
　protagonist *(the first or leading character)*
　prototype *(the first model made)*

psych *[mind, soul]*
psychiatry *(healing of the mind)*
psychology *(study of the mind)*

rupt *[break]*
interrupt *(break into)*
rupture *(break)*

sci *[know]*
conscious *(knowing or being aware of things)*
omniscient *(knowing everything)*

scope *[see, watch]*
kaleidoscope *(instrument for viewing beautiful forms)*
stethoscope *(instrument for listening to sounds in the body)*

scrib, script *[write]*
manuscript *(written by hand)*
scribble *(write quickly)*

sen *[old]*
senile *(showing the weakness of old age)*
senior *(an older person)*

sequ, secu *[follow]*
consecutive *(following in order, one after another)*
sequence *(one thing following another)*

spec *[look]*
inspect *(look at carefully)*
specimen *(an example to look at)*

sphere *[ball, orb]*
hemisphere *(half of a sphere)*
stratosphere *(the upper portion of a sphere)*

spir *[breath]*
expire *(breathe out; die)*
inspire *(breathe into; give life to)*

strict *[draw tight]*
boa constrictor *(snake that constricts its prey)*
constrict *(draw tightly together)*

tact, tag *[touch]*
contact *(touch)*
contagious *(transmission of disease by touching)*

tele *[far]*
telephone *(far sound)*
telescope *(far look)*

tempo *[time]*
contemporary *(those who live at the same time)*
tempo *(rate of speed)*

tend, tens *[stretch, strain]*
extend *(to make longer)*
tension *(tightness caused by stretching)*

terra *[earth]*
terrain *(the surrounding earth or ground)*
terrestrial *(relating to the earth)*

therm *[heat]*
thermal *(related to heat)*
thermostat *(a device for controlling heat)*

tom *[cut]*
anatomy *(cutting apart a plant or animal to study it)*
atom *(cannot be cut or divided)*

tox *[poison]*
intoxicated *(poisoned inside)*
toxic *(poisonous)*

tract *[draw, pull]*
traction *(the act of pulling or gripping)*
tractor *(a machine for pulling)*

trib *[pay]*
contribute *(give money to)*
tribute *(pay honor to)*

turbo *[disturb]*
turbulent *(violently disturbed)*
turmoil *(very disturbed condition)*

typ *[print]*
prototype *(first print)*
typo *(a printing error)*

vac *[empty]*
vacant *(empty)*
vacuum *(a space empty or devoid of matter)*

val *[strength, worth]*
equivalent *(of equal worth)*
evaluate *(find out the worth)*

vert, vers *[turn]*
divert *(turn aside)*
reverse *(turn back)*

vid, vis *[see]*
supervise *(oversee or watch over)*
video *(what we see)*

viv *[alive, life]*
revive *(bring back to life)*
vivacious *(full of life)*

voc *[call]*
vocal *(calling with your voice)*
vocation *(a calling)*

vor *[eat greedily]*
carnivorous *(flesh-eating)*
herbivorous *(plant-eating)*

zo *[animal]*
zodiac *(circle of animals; the constellations)*
zoology *(study of animal life)*

Use Vocabulary Words Correctly

When you learn new vocabulary words, it's important to use them correctly. There are formal and informal ways to use words.

Formal Language

You use formal language when you write informational essays, research papers, and when you write business letters.
- Pay careful attention to word choice.
- Follow rules of formal grammar.
- Use a serious tone.

> **There are large cows on the streets of downtown Chicago. Each cow is actually a work of art decorated in a clever or artistic way. The cows will be auctioned to buyers around the country. The money will be given to local charities.**

Informal Language

You use informal language when you write friendly letters, personal narratives, and character sketches.
- Use everyday language.
- Follow basic rules of grammar.
- Write with a friendly tone.

> **You should see the cows roaming around downtown Chicago. They're not the real thing, but they're decorated from head to hoof. They'll soon be auctioned off for charity. Who knows, one may show up in your town!**

Becoming a Better S-p-e-l-l-e-r

A Self-Help Guide

When you write, you work hard to share your best ideas. You try to use vivid, descriptive words. So take care to also spell those words correctly.

Why? *Beecus speling erers ar harrd tu rede. And besides, people won't know how smart you really are ef yew spel lack thes.*

Here are four things you can do to become a good speller.

1 Make a Spelling Dictionary.

2 Use Strategies to Remember Spellings.

3 Learn to Proofread for Spelling.

4 Learn Some Basic Spelling Rules.

1 Make a Spelling Dictionary.

Get a notebook and label the pages with the letters of the alphabet. (Put one letter at the top of each page.) Then, each time you have to look up a word in the dictionary, write it in your own spelling dictionary, too. Whenever you can, study the words in your dictionary. You'll be spelling these words correctly in no time!

2 Use Strategies to Remember Spellings.

Use Your Senses. One of the best ways to remember spellings is to use your senses—seeing and hearing especially. Try this the next time you study for a spelling test:

- **Look at the word as you say it aloud.**
- **Write the word. Name each letter as you write it.**
- **Read the word aloud again.**
- **Check to make sure you spelled the word correctly.**
- **Cover the word and write it again. Name each letter as you write it. Check your spelling.**

Use Sayings. Memorize (or make up) a few sayings.

You have a **PAL** in your princi**PAL**.
People say **BR**rrr in Fe**BR**uary.
I always want Second**S** of de**SS**ert.
Writing pap**ER** is station**ER**y.

Use Acrostics. Make up funny sentences.

GEOGRAPHY—
Giraffes **e**at **o**ld, **g**reasy **r**ugs **a**nd **p**aint **h**ouses **y**ellow.
ARITHMETIC—**A r**at **i**n **t**he **h**ouse **m**ight **e**at **t**he **i**ce **c**ream.

Use Familiar Words. The spelling of some words makes more sense when you place them in a word family.

mu**SC**le - mu**SC**ular   ob**E**y - ob**E**dient
si**G**n - si**G**nature   t**W**in - t**W**o

3 Learn to Proofread for Spelling.

After you have revised your writing, you must check it for punctuation, grammar, and spelling errors. (We suggest that you check your spelling last.) Here are some suggestions.

Read from Bottom to Top. Start with the last line of your draft and read from bottom to top. This will force you to concentrate on each individual word.

Tip Hold an index card or a half sheet of paper right beneath the line you are studying. After checking one line, move the index card up and check the next line.

Correct the Misspellings. Cross out each misspelled word and make the correction above it. (*Remember:* Skip every other line when you write your draft; it will be much easier to make corrections.)

Circle the Puzzlers. If you are not sure about a spelling, circle it. Double-check the circled words when you have finished checking your entire paper.

Use a Spell Checker. When you write with a computer, you may use a spell checker. Just remember that a spell checker can't replace a human proofreader. It can't tell you if you've used the wrong word (for example, *by* instead of *buy*) or how to spell a name.

Ask for Help. Finally, have a friend or classmate check your corrections and look for other spelling errors in your writing.

> **Note** For more help, check out the following pages:
> **Checking Your Spelling** (pages 398-401)
> **Possessives and Plurals** (pages 385, 394-395)
> **Using the Right Word** (pages 402-411)

4 Learn Some Basic Spelling Rules.

You can avoid some spelling errors by learning a few basic rules. As you will see, most of these rules deal with adding endings to words.

Words Ending in Y ● When you write the plurals of words that end in **y,** change the **y** to **i** and add **es.**

> bully, bullies   country, countries

Except: If the word ends in a **vowel plus y,** just add **s.**

> boy, boys   monkey, monkeys

Consonant Ending ● When a one-syllable word with a short vowel needs the ending **ed, er,** or **ing,** the final consonant is usually doubled.

> bat, batted   drop, dropper   get, getting

I Before E ● For words spelled with **i** and **e** together, repeat this: "**i** before **e,** except after **c,** or when rhyming with *say,* as in *neighbor* and *weigh.*"

> believe, receive, sleigh

Except: Here are some exceptions:

> either, neither, their, height, weird, and seize

Silent E ● If a word ends with a silent **e,** drop the **e** before adding an ending (suffix) that begins with a vowel.

> use, using, usable
> believe, believing, believable

Except: Do **not** drop the **e** when the suffix begins with a consonant (*-ful, -ty, -teen*).

> nine, ninety, nineteen

Speaking, Viewing, and Listening Skills

Giving Speeches

Preparing a Speech

How do you feel when you are asked to speak in front of others? Do you get nervous and excited? Or do you enjoy sharing your feelings and ideas? Some people just naturally like speaking to groups. Others learn to enjoy having an audience.

Whichever way you feel, talking about things you know a lot about makes giving speeches easier. That's why it's important to select the right topic whenever you are asked to give a report or speech in class.

People who like "being on stage" often become teachers, actors, politicians, or lawyers. Their hearts may start pounding when they stand before an audience, but that's part of what they love about public speaking.

The Steps in the Process

No matter what type of speech you are writing, follow these nine steps from start to finish.

1 **Decide Which Kind of Speech You Will Give.**
The first question you have to ask yourself when you begin searching for a good topic is "Why am I giving this speech?" Is it to share information, to demonstrate something, or to change people's minds?

Speech to Inform

An **informational speech** gives interesting or important facts and details about a subject. You might inform your audience, for example, about a new discovery that uses recycled plastic to make roads that get fewer potholes.

Speech to Demonstrate

A **demonstration speech** shows how to do something. You might show your audience how to put a saddle and bridle on a horse, or how to make peanut-butter fudge.

Helpful Hint: A multimedia report is another way to present information. (**SEE** pages 204-207.)

Speech to Persuade

A **persuasive speech** tries to convince listeners to agree with the speaker about something. You might try to persuade your audience that there should be a law that all school buses must have seat belts.

2 Pick Your Topic Carefully.

When you are asked to prepare a speech, begin with a good topic. Ask yourself these questions:

- What do I know a lot about?
- What would I like to know more about?
- What do I enjoy doing?
- What do I like to read about?
- What do I talk about with my friends?

(**SEE** "Choosing a Subject" on pages 35-39 for more help.)

3 Narrow Your Topic.

Let's say that because you love horses, you've chosen that as the topic of your speech. First you need to narrow your topic.

Speech to Inform

For an **informational speech,** you could give information about how to take care of a horse, or you could talk about the different kinds of horses.

Speech to Demonstrate

For a **demonstration speech,** you could show your audience how to saddle and bridle a horse, or you could show them how to braid a horse's mane for a horse show.

Speech to Persuade

For a **persuasive speech,** you could try to convince your listeners that horseback riding is a good hobby, or that there should be more public riding parks.

Helpful Hint: Consider your audience when you choose a subject, just as you consider your guests when you plan a party. If you invited grandparents, would you play rap music? If you invited your friends, would you play waltzes?

Gather Information.

Begin gathering information by looking through books and magazines. Then look further.

- **Observe** and take notes on people, places, and events.
- **Talk or write** to experts in your school, family, or neighborhood.
- **Watch** videos, movies, and TV programs.
- **Search** the Internet.
- **Recall** past experiences.

Note: To get your ideas across, use drawings, photos, props, or videotapes during your speech or multimedia report.

Prepare an Exciting Introduction.

After gathering information, write the beginning of your speech. Here are some good ways to begin:

- Use a famous quotation.

   " . . . forbid that I should go to a heaven in which there are no horses." —Theodore Roosevelt

- Tell a story.

   One day two summers ago, I was riding my horse in the field near our house when suddenly . . .

- Refer to a recent incident.

   At the last Olympics, the U.S. basketball team won a gold medal. So did the U.S. horse-jumping team.

- Make a striking statement.

   Horses understand body language better than people do. The slightest twitch of your body can tell a horse to move.

- Ask an interesting question.

   Did you know that horses have a language of their own?

6 Write an Outline.

After writing your introduction, write an outline of your speech. Put your outline on note cards or on a sheet of paper. Use short phrases—just enough words to remind you of what you want to say. (It's a good idea, however, to write out your introduction and conclusion word for word.)

Sample **Note Cards**

#1

Introduction:

The average horse weighs between 1,000 and 1,600 pounds. When you consider that I weigh just a small fraction of that, it seems amazing that I can climb onto a horse and get him to take me where I want to go. One thing that helps me is knowing the personality of each horse, but I also depend on my equipment: a saddle, saddle pad, bridle, bit, and reins.

#2

Show and Tell the Following:
I. Prepare the horse for the saddle.
   A. Talk to horse.
   B. Rub under his mane.
   C. Stroke his neck.
   D. Stand left of hor
   E. Place saddle pad
      (Use diagram

#3

II. Saddle the horse.
   A. Place saddle on top of pad.
   B. Check and straighten girth.
   C. Tighten girth from left.
   D. Later, tighten a second time.

7 Write Your Speech.

You may give your speech using your outline, or you may write out your speech word for word. If you decide to write out your speech, review "Steps in the Writing Process" on pages 8-11. Also remember to do the following:

- Keep your purpose (to inform, demonstrate, or persuade) in mind and remember your audience.
- Choose the best words and write clear, interesting sentences.

8 Practice Your Delivery.

Practice your speech on at least two different days. You've heard that practice makes perfect, but how can you practice a speech? Simple. Do one or more of the following:

- Practice in a quiet place where you can listen to yourself.
- Practice in front of friends or parents. Ask for their suggestions.
- If possible, videotape or tape-record yourself. Play back the tape to see how you can improve your speech.
- Review the points in step 9 below and keep them in mind as you practice.

9 Present Your Speech.

When you are ready to give your speech, remember these points:

- Look at your audience.
- Stand up tall; don't slump, sway, or lean.
- Speak loudly—use your "outside" voice.
- Speak clearly; don't mumble or use words like *ah, dah,* or *um.*
- Speak slowly—don't rush.

The Final Speech

If you follow the steps in the process, you should end up with a speech that is interesting to your listeners. Here is a sample speech about how to saddle and bridle a horse.

Saddle Up!

The average horse weighs between 1,000 and 1,600 pounds. When you consider that I weigh just a small fraction of that, it seems amazing that I can climb onto a horse and get him to take me where I want to go. One thing that helps me is knowing the personality of each horse, but I also depend on my equipment: a saddle, saddle pad, bridle, bit, and reins.

The first step is to prepare the horse for the saddle. I talk to my horse, rub under his mane, and stroke his neck to help him relax. I always stand on the left side of my horse as I place the saddle pad just below his withers, which is the ridge between his shoulders.

Next I place the saddle on top of the pad. From the right side, I check and straighten the girth, the strap that fastens the saddle on the horse. Then I tighten the girth from the left side. Just before I mount, I will tighten it a final time.

Now I'm ready for the bridle, bit, and reins. They are all connected. I hold the bridle from the top with my right hand with my arm resting over my horse's head. Then I guide the bit into the horse's mouth with my left hand. Next I pull the bridle up over his ears and buckle it under his throat. I make sure his mane is not caught under the bridle. That would hurt, just like it hurts when something pulls your hair.

All I have to do then is collect the reins. That just means that one rein is on each side of the horse's neck, and the ends are in my hand. After I mount, I'm ready to ride!

Performing Poems

Perform It!

Some poems are meant to be read silently. Others beg to be acted out. They have special sounds that are fun to say, and they talk about actions that make you want to move or dance or shout.

When you find that kind of poem—or when you write one—have fun performing it!

Flamingo of Spring

The Flamingo of Spring
walks through winter.
The Flamingo of Spring
brightens everyone's daisies.
The Flamingo of Spring
welcomes the baby animals
to the world.
The Flamingo of Spring
stands on one leg
in a shimmering lake.
The flowers open to
a beautiful song made
by the Flamingo of
Spring.

—Melinda Castillo

Moving Poetry from Page to Stage

What do you do if you have a wonderful poem to share? You can form your own theater group and perform the poem for your class, your parents, or for a community group. Here's what you need to do: *form a team, find a poem, script the poem, score the poem,* and *perform the poem.*

1 Form a Team.

Performing alone is fine, but it is often more fun to perform poems with a team of two, three, or four members.

2 Find a Poem to Perform.

Look through your portfolio, classroom collections of student poems, and any poems published in your local or school newspaper.

Collect several poems. Collect a variety of poems (funny *and* serious). Take turns reading your poems out loud with other team members. This will help you find the best-sounding poems.

Choose the right poem. It is easiest to perform poems that have a lot of action. Poems about ideas and feelings are harder to act out. Here are some questions to ask about your poem:

- Who is the main speaker?
- Who are the other characters (people, animals, things)?
- Where and when does the poem take place?
- What happens in the poem that could be acted out?

Note There may be more characters in your poem than people on your team. If so, each person can take two or more parts and use a different voice for each character.

3 Script the Poem.

After you have selected the poem you want to perform, it's time to script the poem. Scripting a poem means dividing it into speaking parts. Let's imagine that your team has chosen to perform "I'm Glad."

> I'm Glad
>
> I'm glad the sky is painted blue,
>   And the earth is painted green,
> With such a lot of nice fresh air
>   All sandwiched in between.

You could decide to simply have each person say one line. But wait: Performing poetry is not that simple! Instead of dividing the poem by lines, try dividing it by characters: the sky, the air, the earth, and I (the narrator who tells the story).

A "Scripted" Poem Find the characters in your poem and assign them to the actors on your team. Remember, characters can be people, places, things, or animals. Here are two ways to script "I'm Glad."

Cast: **1** = Narrator   **2** = The sky   **3** = The earth   **4** = The air

Two Scripting Possibilities

All: "I'm Glad," author unknown
  1: I'm glad the sky is painted
  2: blue,
  1: And the earth is painted
  3: green,
  1: With such a lot of
  4: nice fresh air
2 & 3: All sandwiched in between.

  1: "I'm Glad," author unknown
  2: I'm glad
  3: the sky is painted blue,
All: And
  4: the earth is painted green,
All: With such a lot of
  2: nice fresh air
3 & 4: All sandwiched in between.

4 Score the Poem.

Next, you will "score" the poem. Scoring a poem means choosing feelings and actions to go with each line. Imagine that you want to score the following poem, "The 5:15."

The 5:15

The peanut sat on the railroad track.
Its heart was all aflutter.
The 5:15 came rushing by—
Toot! Toot!
Peanut Butter!

A "Scored" Poem Here is one way to score this poem, which has been scripted for three characters.

Cast: **1** = Peanut   **2** = Engineer   **3** = Bystander

Line	Emotion	Actions
1: The peanut sat on the railroad track.	*(excited)*	sit on chair
1: Its heart was all aflutter.	*(frightened)*	pat heart or bite nails
1: The 5:15 came rushing by—	*(surprised)*	raise both hands
2: Toot! Toot!	*(threatening)*	raise and lower hand as if pulling the chain of a whistle
3: Peanut Butter!	*(happy)*	pretend mouth is full of peanut butter

Express Yourself You don't need emotions and actions for every word or line. Sometimes you can simply read the poem out loud, letting the words stand on their own.

5 Perform the Poem.

After you have scripted and scored your poem, you need to practice reading and acting it out. You don't need a stage or special lights for your final performance. The front of the classroom will do just fine. (You can use simple costumes and props if you wish.)

Five Performance Tips

- **Face your audience.**
  As a rule, do not turn your back to the audience. Think of them as someone who must see and hear you at all times.

- **Introduce the poem and the poet.**
  Before your performance, stand shoulder to shoulder, facing the audience. Together, in clear, confident voices, announce the title of the poem and the poet's name. Then move quickly to your starting positions for the performance.

- **Stand and move with confidence.**
  Always stand up (or sit up) straight. Standing straight and still will help you perform with confidence.

- **Use your "outside" voice.**
  Speak loudly and clearly so everyone can hear you. Try to find a voice somewhere between soft-spoken and yelling!

- **Take a bow!** When your performance is over, pause for a moment. Take a bow. Then leave the "stage."

Now You Try It!

The following poem was written by students at Beverly Elementary School, Edmonds, Washington. It is scripted for four people. Experiment with different ways of scripting, scoring, and performing this poem. (**SEE** pages 320-322.)

The Salmon People
by students from Beverly Elementary School

1 2 3 4: I am salmon,
    1: I am fast;
    2: A fish that likes to swim in the past.
1 2 3 4: I am going somewhere!
    3: To Seattle,
    4: To the Kingdome.
1 2 3 4: To the Salmon People who live in the ocean.
    1: I have magic wings that help me fly.
    2: I can swim through a river of stars.
    3: My skin is slippery like a wet bar of soap.
    4: My scales shine like fluorescent fingernails;
1 2 3 4: Pink, orange, yellow, green, blue, and purple
  1 2: Salmon People have long gold and silver hair.
  3 4: Their skin is different colors;
1 2 3 4: Mixed together like the rainbow.
    1: I need food.
    2: I'm going on a mission
    2: To survive.
    3: To talk to the people;
    3: To help the people.
    4: Can the people help me?
1 2 3 4: Be kind to the salmon.

Improving Viewing Skills

Becoming a Smart Viewer

According to a recent survey, kids between 6 and 11 years old spend an average of 19 hours and 49 minutes a week watching television. If you're average, you spend nearly 20 hours a week taking in what's on TV.

What you see on television has an impact on

- what you know about the world.
- what you believe about people, places, and events.
- what you buy, thanks to commercials.

Because television affects you so much, you need to be a smart viewer. And that's just what this chapter can help you become.

Watching the News

1 ## Watch for completeness.

A news story must answer the 5 W's and H about an event.

WHO was involved:	Tom and Jerry, the 5th-grade gerbils,
WHAT happened:	escaped
WHEN did it happen:	last night.
WHERE did it happen:	The cage is kept on the windowsill.
WHY did it happen:	The janitor opened the window.
HOW did it happen:	The cage fell out the window, and its door opened.

2 ## Watch for correctness.

A news story should report only facts. If the reporter doesn't know all the facts yet, the story should say something like this:

> **We are getting reports that there is a fire in Yosemite National Park, but official sources have not confirmed this.**

Helpful Hint: The underlined words tell you that the report may not be correct. Watch for news updates.

3 ## Watch for balance.

A news story should tell all sides of the story.

What facts and pictures are included? Let's say there's a story about the possible need for a new school. The old school has a leaky gym roof and no computer lab. But most of the school is in good shape. A news story that only showed the leaky roof would not be balanced.

Who is interviewed? The story should include reliable people who have different views. If a reporter talked with an administrator and a community member who want a new school, and with an administrator and a community member who are against it, the story would have balance.

Watching Television Specials

A television special is a featured program that usually gives information about one subject. Here is a plan to help you learn from television specials:

Before Viewing

- Think about what you already know about the subject.
- Write down questions about the subject.

During Viewing

- Watch and listen for the answers to your questions.
- Take a few notes. Write down interesting facts and feelings.
- Watch for completeness, correctness, and balance. (**SEE** 325.)

After Viewing

- Compare notes with someone who saw the special.
- Write about the program in your learning log.

Notes from TV Special
Saturday, January 8, 2000
Lake Baykal—The Deepest Lake in Russia

It's so deep and so cold, it's got life in it that's found nowhere else in the universe! That's because it was formed 25 million years ago. Here are some animals you can find only in Lake Baykal.
  golomyanka and other kinds of fish
  Baykal seal
It's beautiful and wild—336 rivers flow into it, but only one flows out. The lake is frozen from January to May—that's a long time!

Watching for Fun

Even when it's just for fun, it's important to think about what you're watching on TV.

Is it real or staged? There are medical, crime-fighting, and family comedy shows that are based on real-life situations. But these shows may exaggerate emergencies, chase scenes, or jokes. Remember, such shows are designed to entertain you. They are not real life.

Documentaries often re-enact important historical events, like the Lewis and Clark Expedition (it happened nearly 200 years ago). They may also use actual films of tigers in China or kangaroos in Australia. Watch and listen carefully. Try to tell the difference between what is real and what is staged.

Is it fact or opinion?
A movie star on a talk show may say, "It's time for everyone to become a vegetarian." Remember that celebrities are not necessarily experts on nutrition and food. Their opinions are just that: opinions.

Is it showing stereotypes? A stereotype is a kind of prejudice. It is like saying, "If *one* _____ is a certain way, then *all* _____ are that way." Here are two examples of stereotypes:

Doberman pinschers are mean. **Boys can't draw.**

It's true, some Doberman pinschers are mean, but others are as nice as can be. And some boys can't draw, but many boys are great artists. Watch out for stereotypes in TV shows. Make sure you don't judge people (or anything else) by a stereotype.

BE AWARE: Watching Commercials

Commercials have one purpose—to get you to buy things. Here are five common selling methods:

Slice of Life • These commercials may look like home videos. The people in them are happy because they are drinking Brand X cola or wearing Brand X shoes.

BE AWARE: The people in these commercials are actors. They're being paid to look like they're having fun.

Famous Faces • These commercials use athletes and other famous people. If you want to be like a famous athlete, you'll want to eat the same fast food he or she eats, right?

BE AWARE: Famous people may not really use the products they sell on TV. They are paid to be in the ads.

Just the Facts • These commercials quote facts and figures. Let's say a commercial says, "Nine out of ten fourth graders ask for our cereal!" Where did those figures come from?

BE AWARE: The survey of fourth graders may not have been fair. The cereal company may have asked, "Which would you rather have for breakfast: peas and carrots, or our cereal?" That's a silly example, but you get the idea!

Problem-Solution • These commercials show someone with a problem. Then they show Brand X solving the problem. For example, Janet hates to do her homework. Her parents buy her a new computer with lots of software. Suddenly, Janet loves doing homework.

BE AWARE: Very few problems can be solved just by buying something.

Infomercials • These commercials look like TV shows (usually half an hour long). They give a lot of information to get you to believe their products are the best you can buy.

BE AWARE: Infomercials are just long commercials. Most of the people in them are hired to help sell the product.

Viewing Web Sites

Like television, the Web is a source of information and entertainment. Try to answer these questions:

Who publishes the Web site? The publisher may be a company, a school, a person, a club, or other group. Knowing who publishes the site can help you answer these questions:

Is the information from an expert source? Imagine that you're looking for information about tornadoes. A Web site published by the National Weather Service has information from experts you can trust. A Web site published by someone who chases tornadoes as a hobby may not be so trustworthy.

Is the information balanced or biased? Let's say you're looking for information about good eating habits. A Web site published by a respected health magazine will have balanced information. A Web site published by a snack-food company may be biased, making its products sound more healthful than they really are.

Who pays for it? Whoever pays for a site has the most to say about what is posted there. The Web site is paid for by the publisher or companies that place ads on the Web site.

How often is the site updated? Many Web sites are updated every day or every week. But some sites have information that is weeks, months, or even years out of date.

How does the information compare to other sources? When you search for information on the Web, look at more than one site, or check the information with a book or magazine. This comparison helps you check for accuracy. Be sure to give credit to any research sources you use. (**SEE** page 201.)

Improving Listening Skills

"Now Listen Carefully!"

Since this page and the next are about listening, find a partner to read them out loud—while you listen. If that isn't possible, do the next best thing: **Continue reading.**

Did you know that we spend more time listening than we do speaking, reading, and writing combined? Our ears make it possible for us to *hear*, but our minds make it possible for us to *listen*.

> Listening is more than just hearing—
> it is thinking about what we hear.

Becoming a Good Listener

Because we are human, we don't always listen. We get distracted. We daydream. We sometimes *hear* people without actually *listening* to them. So how can you become a better listener, both in and out of school? Here's a whole page of suggestions.

- **Listen with a positive attitude;** you'll learn more.
- **Listen with your eyes as well as your ears;** you'll hear more if you look at the speaker.
- **Listen for the main ideas;** you'll stay on track.
- **Listen for the speaker's tone of voice;** you'll get the true meaning.
- **Listen for specific directions;** you'll know what you're supposed to do.
- **Listen for key words (first/second, before/after);** you'll keep things in the right order.
- **Take notes or make drawings;** you'll remember things longer.
- **Think about what you hear;** you'll understand better if you relate ideas to what you already know.

Good listeners are not only popular everywhere, but after a while they get to know something.

Express Yourself After listening, write down any questions you have. Also write a summary of what you learned—to show how well you listened.

Thinking Skills

Using Graphic Organizers

Becoming a Better Thinker

Thinking is probably the most important thing you do in school. You think when you read, write, listen, and speak. In short, you are thinking whenever you are learning.

It's no surprise, then, that the better you think, the more you learn. This chapter will help you become a better thinker by showing you how to organize your thoughts and get them on paper. Use the graphic organizers to . . .

- organize your reading notes,
- plan what you will write,
- gather details for writing,
- compare and contrast,
- record what you hear, and
- show what you know.

Kinds of Graphics

Graphic organizers come in many different shapes and sizes. On these two pages you'll find some common graphic organizers and tips on when to use them.

Web Organizer •
Use a web whenever you gather facts or respond to reports, personal narratives, stories, and poems.

5 W's Organizer •
Use the 5 W's whenever you gather details for newspaper stories, personal narratives, and fictional stories.

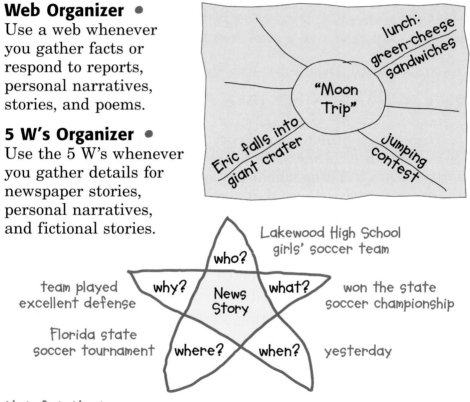

Helpful Hint: (**SEE** page 161 for a sample news story.)

5 Senses Organizer • Use it whenever you gather details for observation reports and descriptive paragraphs.

Sight	Sound	Smell	Taste	Touch
bright Ferris wheel	people laughing	popcorn	nachos with warm cheese	Carmen spilled wet, sticky cola on me

Compare-and-Contrast Organizers • The design shown below is called a Venn diagram. It can be used to organize your thoughts when you need to compare or contrast two subjects. Put the important details for one of your subjects in area **1**. Put the details for the second subject in area **2**. In area **3**, list the details the two things have in common. Now you can clearly see the similarities and differences. (Also **SEE** pages 48 and 92-93.)

Venn Diagram

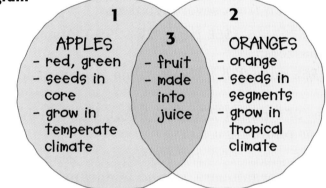

Cause-and-Effect Organizers • Each organizer used for recording cause and effect looks a little different. It all depends on how many causes and how many effects it shows. Use these organizers when you gather details for explanations. Two examples are shown below.

Many causes, one effect   **One cause, many effects**

More Graphic Organizers

There are other kinds of graphic organizers throughout your handbook. Turn to them and think about how you could use each one to help you organize your thoughts.

Outline (**SEE** pages 49, 96, and 197.) An outline helps you organize information for book reviews, expository or persuasive essays, research reports, and so on.

Gathering Grid (**SEE** pages 46 and 195.) Use a grid when you gather information from several sources.

Reading Strategies (**SEE** pages 271-279.) Pay close attention to these organizers:

>**Cluster** (**SEE** page 275.) Use it when you want to gather details.

>**Plot line** (**SEE** pages 276 and 278.) Use it when you are reading or planning a story.

Graphics (**SEE** pages 280-287.) Diagrams, graphs, and tables are all graphic organizers. Some diagrams work best for specific kinds of information:

>**Cycle diagram** (**SEE** page 282.) Use it when you read and write about science.

Time Line (**SEE** page 48 and 478-487.) A time line shows the time order in which things happened. Use it when you read and write about history.

Tips for Using Graphic Organizers

- Think about which organizer will work best for the kind of thinking or writing you are doing.

- Try several kinds of organizers. Seeing information in two or three different ways can help you learn more.

- Invent your own graphic organizer! You may think of a whole new way to organize your thoughts.

Basic Writing and Thinking Moves

This chart shows you the kinds of "thinking moves" you can use to help you gather and organize your thoughts.

OBSERVE

Watch	Listen	Taste	Feel	Smell

GATHER

Use personal experiences	Freewrite, cluster, list	Brainstorm with others	Talk to others	Read, write, draw

QUESTION

Ask *who, what, when, where, why*	Ask *how, how much*	Investigate, survey

ORGANIZE

Put in the right order	Compare, contrast	Give reasons	Group, define	For or against

IMAGINE

Create new ideas	Experiment, invent	Wonder *what if . . .*	Predict, guess

RETHINK

Re-examine (Is this the best *way*?)	Rearrange (Is this the best *order*?)	Revise (Is this the best *wording*?)	Restructure (Is this the best *form*?)

EVALUATE

Judge (Is it clear? Accurate?)	Criticize (Is it interesting?)	Persuade (Is it worthwhile?)

Thinking and Writing

Learning to Think

You go to school to learn how to read, how to write, and how to speak. But before you can do any of these things—or at least do them well— you have to learn how to think.

This chapter explains six kinds of thinking:

- **Recalling**
- **Understanding**
- **Applying**
- **Analyzing**
- **Synthesizing**
- **Evaluating**

This chapter will help you use different kinds of thinking in your writing.

Recalling

When you *recall,* you remember information you talked about in class or read about in a book.

You recall when you . . .

- write down facts and definitions,
- study information until you know it well, or
- answer basic test questions.

This test question asks you to recall.

DIRECTIONS: List in complete sentences five important facts you have learned about acid rain.

1. Acid rain is caused by pollution from cars and some electric-power plants.

2. When acid rain is still in clouds, it can blow far away from where the pollution started.

3. Acid rain kills plants and trees.

4. When acid rain falls on lakes and rivers, it kills fish.

5. The worst acid rain contains as much acid as lemon juice.

Tips for Recalling

- Listen in class and read your assignments carefully.
- Write things down. (**SEE** pages 326, 374-375.)
- Use graphic organizers to help you remember things.

Understanding

When you *know* information well enough to talk or write about it, you understand what it means.

You understand when you . . .

- can explain something,
- tell how something works, or
- restate important details.

This assignment asks you to show understanding.

> DIRECTIONS: In a short paragraph, explain acid rain.
>
> Acid rain is a kind of pollution. It starts when chemicals from cars and power plants go into the air. In the atmosphere, the chemicals mix with the tiny drops of water that make up clouds. When rain falls from the clouds, the acid chemicals are in the rain. The acid kills plants, trees, and fish.

Tips for Understanding

- Write a summary of the information in your own words.
- Review the information out loud with a friend or family member.
- Teach the information to someone else, using a drawing, a chart, or a graphic organizer.

Applying

When you *apply* information, you are able to use what you've learned.

You apply when you . . .

- use what you've learned in art, music, or sports to help you practice or perform; and when you
- use information you've learned to solve problems.

This test question asks you to apply information to your own life.

DIRECTIONS: In a letter to the director of a power plant in your area, explain what you've learned about acid rain. Ask this person to write to you about what is being done at your local power plant to prevent acid rain.

Dear Mr. Gray:

In school, I learned that electrical power plants that burn coal are a major cause of acid rain. They release chemicals that mix with clouds and can be blown far away, even to other countries, before the acid rain falls. When it falls, it can kill plants and animals.

Please write to let me know if your power plant releases these chemicals. If it does, what are you doing to stop this pollution?

Sincerely,

Tip for Applying

- In a learning log, write about what you've learned and try to apply it to your past, present, or possible future experiences.

Analyzing

When you *analyze* information, you break it down into parts.

You analyze when you . . .

- tell how things are alike or different,
- tell which parts are most important,
- put things into groups or categories, or
- give reasons for something.

This assignment asks you to analyze what you know.

> DIRECTIONS: In a paragraph, discuss the causes of acid rain.
>
> Acid rain is caused by air pollution. But not all air pollution causes acid rain. It is only caused by certain chemicals. When coal or gasoline is burned, nitrogen oxides and sulfur dioxide are some of the chemicals released into the air. They mix with the water droplets in the clouds. When the water droplets fall as rain, the acid chemicals are still there. The acid in acid rain kills trees and fish.

Tips for Analyzing

- Consider what different parts make up the whole.
- Think about how the parts work together. (**SEE** the cause-and-effect organizers on page 335.)
- Decide whether the parts could best be described in order of importance, time order, or order of location. (**SEE** page 84.)

Synthesizing

When you *synthesize,* you use what you already know to create new information.

You synthesize when you . . .

- add some new ideas to the information,
- use the information in a made-up story or other piece of creative writing, or
- predict what will happen in the future based on this information.

This assignment asks you to synthesize what you know.

> DIRECTIONS: Write a title-down paragraph about acid rain. Use the letters in the words "acid rain" to begin each sentence.
>
> Acid rain starts with air pollution.
>
> Cars are one source of air pollution that causes acid rain.
>
> Industry is another source of air pollution that causes acid rain.
>
> Damage from acid rain lasts for years.
>
> Rain that is polluted kills plants and animals.
>
> Acid snow is just as harmful as acid rain.
>
> In Canada, forests and lakes are dying from acid rain caused by pollution from the United States.
>
> Nitrogen oxides are one group of chemicals that cause acid rain.

Tip for Synthesizing

■ Be creative! Use your imagination to restate information.

Evaluating

When you *evaluate,* you judge what you have learned. You tell the value of something, how good or bad it is.

You evaluate when you . . .

- tell your opinion about something,
- tell the good points and bad points about something, or
- tell the strengths and weaknesses of something.

This assignment asks you to evaluate something.

DIRECTIONS: Evaluate the latest attempts to stop acid rain.

The latest attempts to stop acid rain are not strong enough. In most places, the main chemical in acid rain is sulfur. Sulfur forms a gas (sulfur dioxide) when it is burned at electric-power plants. Many new power plants have "scrubbers" to keep sulfur from getting into the air. That helps prevent acid rain. But, if we want to do more to prevent acid rain from getting worse, all power plants must have scrubbers.

Tip for Evaluating

■ Before you can evaluate something, you must understand it very well. Then you can form your opinion.

Guidelines for Thinking and Writing

This chart reviews the important types of thinking you will use in school assignments and tests.

Use **recalling** when you are asked to . . .
- fill in the blanks
- define terms
- list facts or words
- label parts of something

Use **understanding** when you are asked to . . .
- explain something
- summarize something
- tell how something works
- tell if something is true or false
- choose the best answer

Use **applying** when you are asked to . . .
- use information in your own life
- solve a problem

Use **analyzing** when you are asked to . . .
- compare things
- contrast things
- put things in order
- divide things into groups
- give reasons for something
- tell why something is the way it is

Use **synthesizing** when you are asked to . . .
- create something
- imagine something
- combine things
- predict something

Use **evaluating** when you are asked to . . .
- judge something
- rate something
- tell your opinion of something

Thinking Clearly

Use Your Brain!

You don't have to **be** a brain to **use** your brain. In fact, as you read this page, you are already using your brain. You are observing, comparing, analyzing, evaluating, and solving problems. Plus, you've been doing these things since you were very young, without even "thinking" about it.

Even though you've been practicing a long time, there's still more to learn about using your brain. You need to think clearly in order to . . .

- **use facts and opinions correctly,**
- **avoid fuzzy thinking,**
- **make good decisions, and**
- **solve problems.**

Why think? Thinking saves time, prevents accidents, leads to success, and helps you figure things out—that's why.

Using Facts and Opinions Correctly

A **fact** is something that is true—something that really happened. An **opinion** is something that someone believes; it may or may not be based on fact. Facts tell about the way things are; opinions tell about how a person thinks or feels.

Opinion: **Recycling paper should be required by law.**

Fact: **If paper is not recycled, trees must be cut down to make more paper.**

Fact: **We are running out of places to dump our trash, and much of our trash is paper.**

Writing an Opinion Statement

First you must decide what your opinion is; then put it into words that others will understand. Follow the simple formula below to help you write a good opinion statement.

Formula: **A specific subject (Recycling paper)**

+ your opinion (should be required by law)

**= a good opinion statement
(Recycling paper should be required by law.)**

Tip

Opinions that include very strong positive or negative words such as *all, best, every, never,* or *worst* are difficult to support.

(Recycling *all* paper should be required by law.)

Supporting Your Opinion

Use clear, specific facts to support your opinion. Readers are more likely to agree with an opinion based on facts. Notice the difference between these two statements:

Opinion Based on a Fact: **Recycling paper should be required by law, because it would save trees.**

Opinion Based on Another Personal Opinion: **Recycling paper should be required by law, because it is the right thing to do.**

Avoiding Fuzzy Thinking

When you're trying to get others to agree with you, it's important to think clearly, write clearly, and stick to the facts! There's really no room for fuzzy thinking. Here are some suggestions to help you keep your thinking clear.

Don't make statements that jump to conclusions.

"Because ozone is a gas found in smog, ozone is bad."

This statement jumps to a conclusion. It says that ozone is bad because it is part of smog, which is bad. But ozone can be good. The natural ozone in the atmosphere protects the earth from the sun's rays.

Don't make statements that compare things that aren't really like each other.

"When acid rain falls, it's like liquid fire falling on the earth."

This statement compares acid rain to something that is really much worse. The worst acid rain is about as acidic as lemon juice. That's bad for the earth, but not as bad as liquid fire!

Don't make statements that are based on feelings instead of facts.

"All big factories should be shut down because they cause air pollution."

This statement is based on feelings, and there are no facts to back it up. First, not all big factories cause air pollution. Second, there are other ways to stop air pollution besides shutting down factories.

Don't make statements that are half-truths.

> "Acid rain is 2,000 times more acidic than unpolluted rain."

This statement makes it sound like all acid rain is 2,000 times more acidic than unpolluted rain. Some is, but some is only 10 times more acidic. The statement makes part of the truth sound like the whole truth.

Don't make statements that make things seem worse— or better—than they are.

> "Americans recycle tons of paper, so we're saving trees that would have to be cut down to make new paper."

This statement makes things sound better than they are. It sounds like most paper is recycled, so only a few trees need to be cut down to make paper. But only about half of all paper is recycled. Each year, forests that took hundreds of years to grow are destroyed to make paper.

Don't make statements just because most people agree with them.

> "Acid rain is not a bad problem, because most people I talked to don't think it is."

This statement is based on the idea that if most people believe something, it must be true. But "most people" can be wrong. They may not know how bad acid rain really is.

Helpful Hint: After you have read each of the six **don't** statements, go back and read them again. Then rewrite each of the "fuzzy" examples so that they are clear. Compare answers with your classmates.

Making Good Decisions

You make decisions every day. You decide what to wear to school, where to sit at lunch, what book to read for your next report. Many of these decisions can be made quickly and easily.

Other decisions are much more difficult and take a good deal of time and thought. Here are some guidelines you can use for facing a tough decision:

1 Define your goals.
- What are you trying to figure out or accomplish?
- What decision do you have to make?

2 List your options or choices.
- What options have you already tried?
- What other things could you do?

3 Study your options.
- Think carefully about each option.
- Write down the pluses and minuses of each.

4 Rank the options.
- Put your options in order from best to worst, from easiest to most difficult, from quickest to longest, etc.
- Ask for help from someone who knows about this issue.

5 Choose the best option.
- Consider all your options carefully.
- Select the best option. (Remember, the best option for you might not be the option for someone else.)

6 Review all the steps.
- Let some time pass.
- Repeat the process to see if your thinking has changed.

Solving Problems

Just like doctors, teachers, moms, and dads, you have to solve problems every day. Some problems are small and easy to solve. Other problems are big and hard to figure out. For big problems, you need a step-by-step plan to find the best solution.

1 Identify or name the problem.
- What is the problem?

2 List what you know about the problem.
- What exactly is wrong or needs to be done?
- What caused the problem?
- Has this problem happened before?

3 Think of possible solutions.
- What could you do right now?
- What could you do a little at a time?

4 Try out the solutions.
- Imagine each solution in action.
- Imagine the result of each solution. What will happen?
- Try out different solutions if you can.

5 Choose the best solution.
- Think of what's best for others as well as for you.
- Put your plan into action.

6 Evaluate the result.
- How did things work out?
- If you had it to do over again, would you choose the same solution?

Learning Skills

Writing as a Learning Tool

Organize Your Thoughts

Learning to write is important because it helps you communicate with others—friends, teachers, relatives. But writing is good for many other things, too. It helps you figure things out and organize your thoughts. In other words, it helps you learn.

Learning Logs

One way to write and learn is to keep a learning log. A learning log is a place to gather your thoughts—to keep them from being scattered. It's similar to journal writing, but it focuses on a subject you are studying. There are some special learning-log activities that you can try after reading this chapter.

Learning logs can help you organize your thoughts and think about what you've learned.

Keeping a Learning Log

Writing in a learning log is like thinking on paper. Here are some things you might write in a learning log:

■ your thoughts and feelings about a subject or assignment,

■ questions you have about it, or

■ new vocabulary words.

Making a Learning Log:

1. **Divide a notebook into sections**—one section for each subject you will write about.

2. **Plan a time to write** in your learning log each day. Set aside more time for writing about a subject that is hard for you.

3. **Write freely** and use your own words. Start by writing the date. Then try to get all your thoughts down without stopping. You may write for 3-5 minutes, or perhaps longer.

April 21, 2000

What a crazy world! We want big factories to provide good jobs. We want lots of heat and light in our homes, and we love to ride around in our cars. But scientists say that the acid rain produced by factories, power plants, and cars may be wrecking our buildings and highways. And what's really bad is that this acid rain is also hurting our lakes, streams, and rivers. Many are just dead bodies of water. So should people give up jobs and cars? Should we . . . ?

Writing-to-Learn Activities

Here are more ideas for keeping a learning log. Try them all! Then decide which ones work best for you.

First Thoughts • Make a list of key words that come to mind after a lesson. These key words will help you focus on the most important ideas.

Stop 'n' Write • Stop whatever you are studying and write about it. This is a quick way to be sure your mind is on your work.

Nutshelling • Have you ever heard the phrase "in a nutshell"? It means "to say a lot in a few words." Try *nutshelling:* In one sentence, write the most important idea from a class discussion or a reading assignment.

Notes to the Teacher • Jot down any questions you may have about the subject and give them to your teacher. Ask your teacher to respond to your questions.

Unsent Letters • Write a letter to any person about the subject. Writing a letter will help you think about the topic in a personal way.

Graphic Organizers • Graphic organizers are a good way to organize your thoughts in a learning log. You can find out about graphic organizers on pages 334-336.

Drawing • You can draw pictures in your learning log to show what you have learned or thought about. For example, you could draw the setting or one of the characters in a story you read.

Completing Assignments

Learning Made Easier

How do you learn? Is learning easy for you? Do you sometimes wish it could be easier? Well, it can be if you first understand *how* you learn. How you learn depends on three things: **you, your teachers,** and **your texts.**

Your teachers start the learning process by introducing a unit of study. Your texts (this includes books, CD-ROM's, videos, and so on) give you the information for the unit. Your job is to read and study this material until you become the best student you can be.

Let's Get Started!

We'll help you do your job by showing you how to set goals, manage your time, and complete your assignments. It's as easy as **1 2 3!**

Setting Goals

Before you started school, you set goals for yourself all the time—like learning to ride a bike or dribble a basketball.

And you're still setting goals—like learning to play an instrument, earning money to buy something, or getting a good grade on your next test.

No one plans to fail; they just fail to plan.

Some Helpful Guidelines

1 Be realistic.

Learn to set realistic goals. Can you learn to play a guitar in a day? Of course not. Some goals can only be achieved one step at a time. For example, you might plan to do one part of a science project each day for a week. Or, if you play a sport, you might try to improve just one specific skill at a time.

2 Work toward your goals.

Continue working toward your goals—no matter what happens! If you choose to keep a journal, set aside a specific time each day to write in it. If you want to improve in a certain sport, talk to your coach, a parent, or a friend about how to do it. Then practice often.

 **Think It Over** Remember, there will be times when you won't be able to write or practice—when you are sick, for instance. Find another time to make it up.

3 Reward yourself.

Whenever you reach a goal, reward yourself in some way. Let's say you've decided to keep a daily journal. When you have written in your journal every day for two weeks, do something special, or share your success with a parent or teacher.

Managing Your Time

If you're like most students, you have a limited amount of time, and lots of things to do. The best way to make sure you get everything done is to use a planner.

Daily Planner ● In a daily planner you can list assignments you have for each day. Your planner may be a simple list.

■ **MONDAY,** _____(date)_____

English
Read page 102. Write a topic sentence.

Math
Do workbook page 16. (Test tomorrow)

Social Studies
Answer question sheet by Wednesday.

■ **TUESDAY,** _____(date)_____

English
Write a paragraph using my topic sentence.

Social Studies
Finish question sheet for tomorrow.

Science
Collect five different leaves; take to class.

Weekly Planner ● A weekly planner is a schedule of all the important things you have to do during a week.

Day	Before School	School	After School	Evening
Mon.	Make lunch for field trip	Field trip	Open gym	Study math
Tues.	Take garbage out	Math test	Do homework	Choir practice

Doing Your Assignments

Plan Ahead

- **Write down** exactly what your assignment is and when it has to be done.
- **Figure out** how much time you'll need to complete your assignment. Write down study times on your planner.
- **Get the phone numbers** of one or two students in your class. Ask if you can call them when you have a question about an assignment.
- **Gather all the materials you need** to complete your assignment: paper, pens, notebook, handouts, and so on.

Do the Work

- **Find a time** that works best for you.
- **Work in a quiet place** where you won't be interrupted.
- **Read over your assignment** so that you know exactly what to do.
- **Set goals.** How much will you get done before you take a break? How much will you get done today? Stick to your plan!
- **Keep a list of questions** to ask your teachers.

Note Remember to use reading strategies for your reading assignments. (**SEE** pages 271-279.)

Working in Groups

Making Your Group Work

What was it like the last time you worked in a group? Did your teacher ask you to work with other students in the class? Did you work with a group of kids in the neighborhood or at a club meeting? Did you have a good time? Did you accomplish something?

Getting Started

Working in a group can be fun if everyone gets along and gets the job done. In this chapter, we'll look at how you can use "people skills" to make your next group a success. You can begin by *making a plan*.

Listening, clarifying, and cooperating are often called "people skills" because they help people work and learn better in groups.

Making a Plan

Every group project should begin with a plan. The members of the group should ask themselves these questions:

■ What is our project or assignment?
■ What jobs do we need to do to complete it?
■ What job or jobs will each group member do?
■ What deadlines must we meet?

Try using an outline like the one below to help your group make its plan. Be sure everyone understands what he or she needs to do.

I. Group Plan
   A. Our project is
      (Is it to solve a problem, answer questions, research a topic?)
   B. Things we need to do
      1.
      2.
      3.
      (Add more lines if you need them.)
   C. Jobs for each group member:
      1. Name   Job
      2. Name   Job
      3. Name   Job
      (Some sample jobs: writer or recorder, researcher, artist, coordinator)
   D. This is our schedule:
      1. By this date (   ) we will have this done:

      2. By this date (   ) we will have this done:

II. Results

Skills for Listening

Listening is important when you work in groups. People can only work together if they listen to one another. Imagine a group of firefighters at a huge fire. If they didn't listen to one another, they could never cooperate well enough to put out the fire.

Just listen. Remember, listening means *thinking about* what is being said. So you can't truly listen and do something else at the same time. Don't doodle, write notes to your friends, or make animals out of paper clips while you're listening.

Listen actively. You'll have to try hard to keep your mind on what's being said. It's natural for your mind to wander. Because people can't talk as fast as you can think, your mind can race ahead and get off the track. To stay on track, do the following:

- **Look at the person who is speaking.**
  This helps you listen because your mind thinks about what your eyes see.
- **Listen for key words and phrases.**
  For example: "The only solution is . . . " or "Here's what I think we should do."
- **Write down a few notes.**
  Write down some of the main points or details that you hear.

Ask questions. If you don't understand something, ask about it. But don't interrupt the person who is speaking unless you're really lost. Wait until she or he is finished. Then ask a good, clear question, such as "Karen, you're saying we should do a report instead of making a model, because a report will be easier—right?"

Note Listening is not as easy as it sounds! To **hear,** you need only your ears. To **listen,** you need your ears and your mind.

Skills for Cooperating

Cooperating means working with others to solve a problem or reach a shared goal.

Give your ideas and opinions. It's important to let other group members know what you think. When you like someone's idea, say so! When you don't, say so. But don't say, "That's a stupid idea!" Say, "I don't think that will work *because* . . . ". (When you give your opinion, give your reasons, too.)

Be willing to change your opinions. Listen to everyone's opinions with an open mind. Remember, you are trying to reach a decision everyone agrees with.

Don't get personal. Try not to criticize or say anything too personal. And if you hear a personal comment, remind the speaker that this is a group project and everyone needs to work together.

Skills for Clarifying

Clarifying means "clearing up." If someone in the group is confused, the group can't work together toward its goal. Here's how you can help clear up confusion:

Remember your goal. Remind everybody what the group's goal is. Also suggest steps that will help you reach that goal. For example: "First let's decide whether to do a report or make a model. Then let's decide what each person's job will be."

Re-explain it. If someone doesn't understand something, ask if anyone else in the group can think of a new way to explain it.

Stay on track. If someone gets off track, say something as simple as, "I think we should get back to the main point."

Making a Group Decision

Successful groups make decisions by *consensus*. Reaching a consensus means getting everyone in the group to agree with the decision. How do you get everyone to agree? Here are some tips.

Reaching a Consensus

- Ask everyone in the group for ideas and suggestions. Listen carefully to each person's ideas.
- Discuss each idea and how it would (or wouldn't) work.
- Select the idea or ideas everyone agrees will work well.
- If you select more than one idea, try to combine them into one plan, a plan everyone can agree on.

Think It Over

Remember, to reach a consensus, everyone must agree. That doesn't mean everyone thinks the decision is the best decision; it means everyone agrees to accept the decision.

Evaluating Your Work

Well, how did your group do? The proof that your group succeeded is a successful product. Before you hand in your assignment, judge the work your group accomplished. You can do this by having everyone answer and discuss these questions:

- Does our final product meet all the requirements of the assignment?
- Did all the group members do their jobs and contribute to the final product?
- Are we proud to say that this is our product?

Helpful Hint: If you have to answer "no" to any of these questions, you may want to go back and revise your work. Then answer the questions again.

Sharing Books

One common group project is to talk about a story or novel you have all read. Below you will find some guidelines for discussing fiction.

Before You Begin

Group members should list ideas they plan to share.

The Plot

What is the most important or exciting event in the story?

What parts of the story remind you of your own life? In what way?

What other stories is this one like?

The Characters

Who are your favorite characters? Why?

How did the main character change during the story?

Overall Effect

Do you think the book has a good ending? If you were the author, how would you have ended the book?

Do you think the title fits the book?

What is the author trying to tell the reader about life?

Who else should read this book?

As You Share

In a small group (no more than six), sit facing each other.

- Listen carefully to one another and write down your reactions and questions.
- Add to what the others say about the book.
- Make sure you share your personal thoughts about the book, too.

Taking Tests

Getting Your Act Together

You're having a test? Well, it had to happen sooner or later! Taking a test is a good way for you—and your teacher—to find out what you have learned. (And what you haven't learned.) But tests don't have to be a big deal. If you follow these two simple rules, you'll do just fine: **be prepared** and **pay attention.**

Test-Taking Strategies

On the following pages, you'll find lots of strategies and hints for doing your best on tests. There are tips for taking objective tests and for writing short-answer and essay tests. There are also tips to help you remember things better. We hope they help.

> To do well on tests, you must do well in class. Starting on the first day, you must organize yourself, your time, and your work.

Preparing for the Test

Ask questions . . .
- What will be on the test? (Ask your teacher.)
- What kind of test will it be? (Multiple choice? Essay?)

Review your notes . . .
- Reread your class notes carefully. (Get any notes or materials you may have missed.)
- Rewrite your most important notes or put them on note cards.

Review your textbook . . .
- Skim your textbook. (Also review quizzes and worksheets.)
- Read difficult material out loud as you review.

Tip Use lists, diagrams, songs, or rhymes to help you organize and remember the material. (**SEE** pages 372-373.)

Taking the Test

Listen attentively . . .
- Listen carefully to your teacher. How much time will you have? Can you use notes, a dictionary, or your handbook?

Read carefully . . .
- Skim the whole test, so you know which questions will take the most time.
- Then go back and read the directions carefully. Be on the lookout for words like *always, only, all,* and *never.*
- Don't spend too much time on any one question.

Check closely . . .
- Double-check to be sure you have answered all the questions. (Check each answer if you have time.)
- Ask your teacher about any questions that still confuse you.

Responding to Writing Prompts

Sometimes test questions are like writing prompts that ask you to share what you know about a certain topic in a certain way. Here are two samples:

■ **Explain what happens in a volcanic eruption.**

■ **Describe a volcanic eruption.**

Both prompts have the same topic: a volcanic eruption. But each prompt asks you to write about the topic in a different way. The first asks you to *explain,* and the second asks you to *describe.*

1 Find the key word.

It is important to understand the key words used in test questions. Here are some common ones:

Compare/contrast • To **compare,** tell how two things are alike. To **contrast,** tell how things are different. A prompt may ask you to compare, contrast, or both. *(Compare and contrast the Arctic and the Antarctic.)*

Define • To **define** something, tell what it means, what it is, or what it does. *(Define ultraviolet light.)*

Describe • To **describe** something, tell how it looks, sounds, smells, tastes, and/or feels. *(Describe your school cafeteria.)*

Explain • To **explain** something, tell how it works, how it happens, or how to do it. *(Explain the effects of acid rain.)*

List • To **list,** give a number of facts, ideas, reasons, or other details about the topic. *(List five reasons the American Revolution began when it did.)*

Persuade • To **persuade,** give facts and reasons that would make someone agree with your opinion or position. *(Write a note that persuades your friend to help you clean your room.)*

2 Make good use of your time.

Here's how to make the best use of your time:

- Listen carefully to all directions.
- Find out how much time you have for the test.
- Think about the prompt before you begin writing.
- Pay attention to the key word.
- Make a simple plan or list for your writing.
- Once you begin, keep writing! Let your thoughts flow.

3 Focus on the key word.

The two answers below are completely different, even though they are about the same topic. The first answer *explains;* the second answer *describes.*

■ **Explain** what happens in a volcanic eruption. (The answer tells how a volcanic eruption happens.)

> The extreme heat at the center of the earth melts rock deep inside the earth. The melted rock is called magma. Magma gets mixed with gas and rises through cracks in the earth toward the surface. The hot, gas-filled magma is under great pressure. The pressure causes the gas and melted rock to blast out of the volcano.

■ **Describe** a volcanic eruption. (The answer tells how a volcanic eruption looks, sounds, and smells.)

> A volcanic eruption is an amazing sight. Huge dark clouds rise over the volcano, and hot rivers of melted rock flow down its sides. Sometimes large chunks of hot rock are blasted into the air in ear-splitting, earth-shaking explosions. Hot ash and dust settle on everything around the volcano, and a burning smell fills the air.

The Objective Test

To really shine on an objective test, keep the following hints in mind.

Multiple-Choice Test

■ Read all the choices carefully. Don't just mark the first correct choice, because there may be more than one correct answer. If there is, look for a choice such as "all of the above" or "both a and b."

Question: **Mammals are animals that**
   a. produce milk   **b.** grow hair   **c.** fly   (**d.**) both a and b

■ A question may ask you to find a mistake in one of the choices. Look to see if one of the choices is "no mistake."

Question: **Mark the sentence that needs to be corrected.**
   a. Cows and dogs are mammals.
   b. Mammals' babies are born alive.
   c. People are mammals.
   (**d.**) No mistake

■ Look for negative words like *not, never, except,* and *unless.* Watch for numbers.

Question: **The following two animals are not mammals.**
   (**a.**) shark   **b.** kangaroo   **c.** horse   (**d.**) spider

■ A question may ask you to mark the choice that matches a sample sentence. Read all the choices carefully.

Question: **Mark the sentence below in which <u>control</u> has the same meaning as in the following sentence:**

Some mammals keep the insect population under control.
   a. She tried to <u>control</u> her temper.
   b. The pilot adjusted the right <u>control</u>.
   (**c.**) The Salk vaccine helped to <u>control</u> polio outbreaks.

True/False Test

■ Read the entire question before answering. For a statement to be true, the entire statement must be true.

■ Watch for words like *all, every, always, never.* Statements with these words in them are often false.

Question: **Mark each statement below with "True" or "False."**

_____ 1. Plastic can never be recycled.

_____ 2. All plastic can be recycled.

_____ 3. Vinyl is a kind of plastic used to make tires.

Answers: All are false. 1. *Some* plastic can be recycled. 2. Not *all* plastic can be recycled. 3. The first half is true—vinyl is a kind of plastic—but it is *not* used to make tires.

Matching Test

■ Before you make any matches, read both lists quickly.

■ Check off each answer you use.

Question: **Match the product (on the left) to the recycled material that it is made from (on the right).**

_____ Asphalt   a. Motor oil

_____ Mulch for plants   b. Christmas trees

_____ Motor oil   c. Tires

Answers: (c) Asphalt, (b) Mulch, (a) Motor oil

Fill in the Blanks

■ Read each sentence completely before filling in the blank.

Question: **Fill in the blanks below with the correct answers.**

1. Paper makes up about _____ of our trash.

2. _____ and _____ can be recycled.

Answers: 1. one-third 2. plastic, glass, etc.

Remembering for Tests

In addition to knowing how to take a test, you have to remember the material you're being tested on. Here are some tips for remembering what you have learned.

Use graphic organizers. They help you organize information, and that makes the information easier to remember.

Use acronyms. Acronyms are made up of the first letters of the words in a phrase or group of words. NATO, for example, is an acronym for North Atlantic Treaty Organization. To help you remember things, you can create your own acronyms.

> **HOMES . . . H**uron, **O**ntario, **M**ichigan, **E**rie, **S**uperior
> (the Great Lakes)

> **ROY G. BIV . . . R**ed, **O**range, **Y**ellow, **G**reen, **B**lue, **I**ndigo, **V**iolet
> (the colors of the rainbow)

Use poems. Sometimes a simple (even silly) poem can help you remember things. Do you remember either of these?

> "i" before "e," except after "c," . . .

> In 1492, Columbus sailed the ocean blue.

Use songs. Sometimes a familiar song can help you remember things. You can substitute something you want to remember for the words in the song.

A B C D E F G H I

Talk to others. Here are some ways that talking will help you learn and remember information:

- Form a study group. Ask each other questions.
- Teach someone else what you need to remember.
- Say out loud what you need to remember.

Draw or visualize. Drawing or picturing something in your mind can help you remember. Here's an example of a drawing used for remembering prepositions.

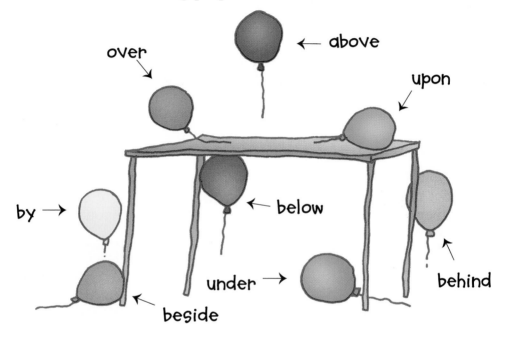

Rewrite it. There are many ways to use writing to help you learn and remember. You can begin by writing in a journal or learning log. (**SEE** pages 353-355 for more suggestions.)

Make a poster of what you need to remember and hang it where you'll see it often.

Carry note cards around and use them like flash cards anytime during the day.

Taking Good Notes

Write to Remember

If you were told to get bagels, orange juice, a dozen eggs, a gallon of milk, and a bag of popcorn at the store, you *might* remember everything. If you had a list handed to you, remembering would be a lot easier. And, if *you* wrote the list, you might not even need to look at it once you got to the store. That's how powerful writing is as a learning tool!

Don't *Just* Write

Note taking is a very important writing tool. But it's not just writing down everything you hear—it's listening carefully and writing down the important ideas in your own words. That's what being a good note taker is all about.

Being able to take good notes is a helpful skill, one you'll use more and more throughout your school years.

Guidelines for Improving Note-Taking Skills

The guidelines that follow will help you improve your note-taking skills. Read and follow each hint carefully.

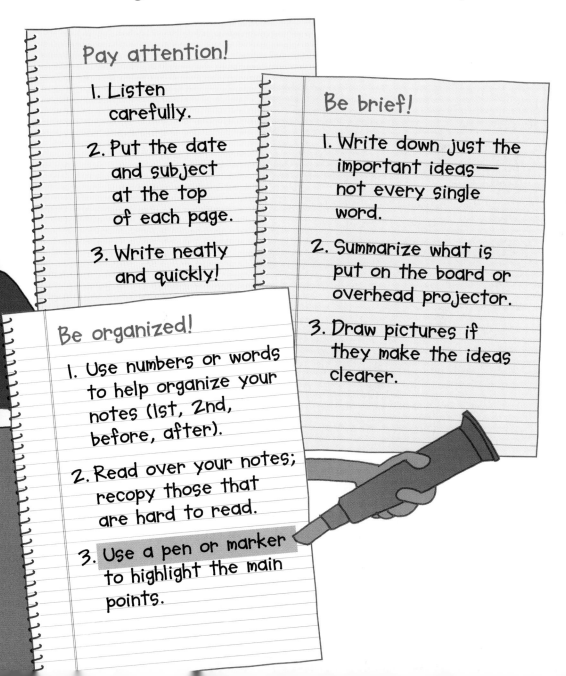

Pay attention!

1. Listen carefully.

2. Put the date and subject at the top of each page.

3. Write neatly and quickly!

Be brief!

1. Write down just the important ideas— not every single word.

2. Summarize what is put on the board or overhead projector.

3. Draw pictures if they make the ideas clearer.

Be organized!

1. Use numbers or words to help organize your notes (1st, 2nd, before, after).

2. Read over your notes; recopy those that are hard to read.

3. Use a pen or marker to highlight the main points.

Proofreader's Guide

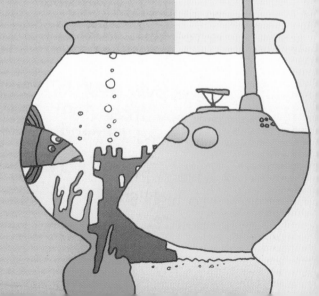

Marking Punctuation

Period

A **period** is used to end a sentence. It is also used after initials, after abbreviations, and as a decimal point.

At the End of a Sentence	Use a period to end a sentence that makes a statement, a command, or a request.
	Taro won the fishing contest. (statement)
	Take his picture. (command)
	Please pass the bait. (request)
After an Initial	Place a period after an initial in a person's name.
	Susan B. Anthony **A. A. Milne**
As a Decimal	Use a period as a decimal point and to separate dollars and cents.
	Robert is 99.9 percent sure that the bus pass costs $2.50.
After Abbreviations	Use a period after each part of an abbreviation.
	Mr. **Mrs.** **Ms.** **B.C.E.** **C.E.**
	Jr. **Dr.** **Ph.D.** **U.S.A.**
After Final Abbreviations	Use only one period when an abbreviation is the last word in a sentence.
	When Josie is nervous, she whistles, wiggles, winks, etc.

Ellipsis

An **ellipsis** (three periods) is used to show omitted words or sentences and to indicate a pause in dialogue.

Tip: When typing or writing an ellipsis, leave one space before, after, and between each period.

To Show Omitted Words	Use an ellipsis to show that one or more words have been left out of a quotation.
	Complete Quotation:
	"All I know is that something long and shiny on my line jumped. It leaped out of the water so many times. It finally got away."
	Shortened Quotation:
	"All I know is that something long and shiny . . . finally got away."
At the End of a Sentence	If the words left out are at the end of a sentence, use a period followed by three dots.
	"All I know is that something long and shiny on my line jumped. . . . It finally got away."
To Show a Pause	Use an ellipsis to indicate a pause in dialogue.
	"That's . . . incredible!" I cried.

Comma

Commas are used to keep words and ideas from running together. They tell your reader where to pause, which makes your writing easier to read.

Between Items in a Series	Place commas between words, phrases, or clauses in a series. (A *series* is three items or more in a row.) **I know someone who likes pepperoni, pineapple, and olives on her pizza.** (words) **During the summer I read mysteries, ride my bike, and play basketball.** (phrases)
In Dates and Addresses	Use commas to separate items in addresses and dates. **We are having a family picnic on July 4, 2001, at Montrose Beach.** **Mia's new address is 3344 South First Street, Atlanta, GA 30200.** *Tip:* Do not use a comma between the state and ZIP code.
To Keep Numbers Clear	Place commas between hundreds, thousands, millions, and so on. **Rodney's car has 200,000 miles on it. He's trying to sell it for $1,000.** *Tip:* Commas are not used in years: 1776, 1999, 2010.
To Set Off Interruptions	Use commas to set off a word, phrase, or clause that interrupts the main thought of a sentence. **As it turned out, however, Rodney sold the car for $250.**
To Set Off Dialogue	Set off the exact words of the speaker from the rest of the sentence with a comma. **The stranded frog replied, "I'm just waiting for the toad truck."** No comma is needed when *reporting* rather than *repeating* what a speaker said. **Talia said she missed her favorite show.**

Comma (continued)

In Direct Address	Use commas to separate a noun of direct address (the person being spoken to) from the rest of the sentence. **Please, Carla, find some new jokes.**
Between Two Independent Clauses	Use a comma between two independent clauses that are joined by coordinating conjunctions *and, but, or, nor, for, so,* and *yet.* **Aquarium workers love animals, so they rescue hurt ones.** **The team rehabilitated the sick sea lion pups, and then they released them.** *Tip:* Do not connect two independent clauses with a comma only. (**SEE** page 381 for more information about independent clauses.)
In Letter Writing	Place a comma after the salutation, or greeting, in a friendly letter and after the closing in all letters. **Dear Uncle Jim,** (greeting) **Your niece,** (closing) **Sincerely,** (closing)
To Separate Adjectives	Use commas to separate two or more adjectives that equally modify a noun. **I like the feel of cold, salty water when I go wading.** *Tip:* Use these tests to discover if adjectives modify equally: ● Switch the order of the adjectives; if the sentence is still clear, the adjectives modify equally. ● Insert *and* between the adjectives; if the sentence reads well, use a comma when *and* is omitted.
To Set Off Interjections	Use a comma to separate an interjection or a weak exclamation from the rest of the sentence. **Wow, look at that sunrise!** **Hey, we're up early!**

To Set Off Appositives	Use commas to set off appositives. An *appositive* is a word or phrase that renames the noun or pronoun before it.
	My father, a great cook, makes the best egg rolls in town. (an appositive phrase)

To Set Off Introductory Phrases and Clauses	Use a comma to separate a long phrase or clause that comes before the main part of the sentence.
	After checking my knee pads, I started off. (phrase)
	If you practice often, skating is easy. (clause)

Semicolon

The **semicolon** is sometimes used in place of a period; other times, it works like a comma.

To Join Two Independent Clauses	Use a semicolon to join two independent clauses when there is no coordinating conjunction between them.
	My aunt has a new motorboat; I wish I were big enough to drive it.
	She takes me fishing in it; however, I still don't get to drive it.
	Tip: Independent clauses can stand alone as separate sentences. (**SEE** page 414 for more information about independent clauses; **SEE** page 435 for an explanation of coordinating conjunctions.)

To Separate Groups of Words That Contain Commas	Use a semicolon to separate a series of phrases that already contain commas.
	We crossed the stream; unpacked our lunches, cameras, and journals; and finally took time to rest.
	Note: The second phrase contains commas.

Colon

A **colon** is used to introduce a list or draw attention to information that follows. Colons are also used in business letters and between the numbers expressing time.

To Introduce a List	Use a colon to introduce a list following a complete sentence. **Snorkelers need the right equipment: fins, masks, and life belts.** When introducing a list, the colon often comes after summary words like *the following* or *these things*. **Scuba divers often see the following: barracuda, eels, turtles, and jellyfish.** *Tip:* It is <u>incorrect</u> to use a colon after a verb or a preposition. **I made a salad of: lettuce, tomatoes, cucumber, and dressing.** (The colon is <u>incorrectly</u> used after the preposition *of.*) **My favorite salad toppings include: bacon, raisins, sunflower seeds, croutons.** (The colon is <u>incorrectly</u> used after the verb *include.*)
After a Salutation	Place a colon after the salutation of a business letter. **Dear Ms. Koplin: Dear Chairperson:**
Between Numbers in Time	Place a colon between the parts of a number indicating time. **The race begins at 1:30 p.m.** **I'll meet you at 12:00 noon.**
As a Formal Introduction	Use a colon to introduce an important quotation in a serious report, essay, or news story. **President Lincoln concluded the Gettysburg Address with these famous words: "that government of the people, by the people, for the people, shall not perish from the earth."**

Hyphen

A **hyphen** is used to divide a word at the end of a line. Hyphens are also used to join or create new words.

To Divide a Word	Use a hyphen to divide a word when you run out of room at the end of a line. Divide words only between syllables. (The word *en-vi-ron-ment* can be divided in three places.) **John McConnell showed concern for the environment by founding Earth Day.** *Tip:* Here are some other guidelines for hyphenating words: ● Never divide a one-syllable word: **showed, great.** ● Never divide a one-letter syllable from the rest of the word: **i-dentity.** ● Never divide contractions: **haven't, shouldn't.**
In Compound Words	Use a hyphen in certain compound words. **well-done baby-sitter off-key**
Between Numbers in Fractions	Use a hyphen between the numbers in a fraction. **One-fourth of the group gobbled seven-eighths of the cake!**
To Form an Adjective	Use a hyphen to join two or more words that work together to form a single adjective *before* a noun. **blue-green sea sister-proof closet** **big-grin smile knee-worn jeans**
To Create New Words	Use a hyphen to form new words beginning with the prefixes *self, ex, great, all,* and *half.* A hyphen is also used with suffixes such as *free* and *elect.* **self-made all-purpose fat-free** **great-aunt half-baked president-elect**
To Join Letters and Words	Use a hyphen to join a letter to a word. **T-shirt T-ball X-ray e-mail U-turn**

Dash

A **dash** is used to show a break in a sentence, to emphasize certain words, or to show that a speaker has been interrupted.

In a Sentence Break	Use a dash to show a sudden break in a sentence. **The skateboard—if you didn't notice—has a wheel missing.**
For Emphasis	Use a dash to emphasize a word, a series of words, a phrase, or a clause. **You can learn about many subjects—customs, careers, sports, weather—on the Internet.**
In Interrupted Speech	Use a dash to show that someone's speech is being interrupted by another person. **Well, hello—yes, I—that's right—yes, I—sure, I'd love to—I'll be there!**

Apostrophe

An **apostrophe** is used to form plurals, to form contractions, to show that a letter or letters have been left out of a word, or to show possession.

In Contractions	Use an apostrophe to show that one or more letters have been left out to form a contraction. The list below shows some common contractions.

Common Contractions

couldn't (could not)	**haven't** (have not)	**she's** (she is)
didn't (did not)	**I'll** (I will)	**they'll** (they will)
doesn't (does not)	**isn't** (is not)	**they're** (they are)
don't (do not)	**it's** (it is; it has)	**wouldn't** (would not)
hasn't (has not)	**I've** (I have)	**you'd** (you would)

To Form Plurals	Use an apostrophe and *s* to form the plural of a letter, a number, or a sign. **A's** (letter) **8's** (number) **+'s** (sign)
In Place of Omitted Numbers or Letters	Use an apostrophe to show that one or more letters or numbers have been left out or for a special pronunciation. **class of '99** (*19* is left out) **fixin' to go** (*g* is left out)
To Form Singular Possessives	Add an apostrophe and *s* to make the possessive form of most singular nouns. **My sister's hobby is jazz dancing.** When a singular noun ends with an *s* or *z* sound, you may form the possessive by adding just an apostrophe. **Lucas' hobby is collecting pencil stubs.** *Except:* When a singular noun is a one-syllable word, add both an apostrophe and an *s*. **Gus's father took him fishing.**
To Form Plural Possessives	Add just an apostrophe to make the possessive form of plural nouns ending in *s*. **the girls' logrolling team** For plural nouns not ending in *s*, add an apostrophe and *s*. **children's book**
To Form Shared Possessives	When possession is shared by more than one noun, add an apostrophe and *s* to the last noun. **Jim, Jeb, and Jerry's fish.**

Quotation Marks

Quotation marks are used to enclose the exact words of the speaker, to show that words are used in a special way, and to punctuate titles.

To Set Off Direct Quotations	Place quotation marks before and after the spoken words. **"Rosa Parks is a true American hero," the teacher reminded her students.**
Placement of Punctuation	Put periods and commas *inside* quotation marks. **Trev said, "Let's make tuna sandwiches."** **"Sounds good," said Rich.** Place question marks or exclamation points *inside* the quotation marks when they punctuate the quotation; place them *outside* when they punctuate the main sentence. **"Will we have tuna and apples?" asked Trev.** **"Yes!" replied Rich.** **Did you hear Mom say, "We're out of pickles"?**
For Special Words	Quotation marks may be used to set apart a word that is being discussed. **The word "scrumptious" is hard to spell.**
To Punctuate Titles	Place quotation marks around titles of songs, poems, short stories, essays, and chapters of books. Also use quotation marks with articles found in magazines, newspapers, encyclopedias, or electronic sources. (**SEE** page 388.) **"America the Beautiful"** (song) **"McBroom Tells the Truth"** (short story) **"Water, Water Everywhere"** (chapter) *Tip:* When you write a title, capitalize the first word, last word, and every word in between except for articles (*a, an, the*), short prepositions (*by, for, to*), and coordinating conjunctions (*and, or, but*).

Question Mark

A **question mark** is used after a direct question (an interrogative sentence) and to show doubt about the correctness of something.

Direct Question	Place a question mark at the end of a direct question. **Do you want to visit other galaxies?**
To Show Doubt	Place a question mark in parentheses to show that you aren't sure a fact is correct. **The ship arrived in Boston on July 23(?), 1652.**

Exclamation Point

An **exclamation point** is used to express strong feeling. It may be placed after a word, a phrase, or a sentence.

To Express Strong Feeling	**Surprise!** (word) **Happy birthday!** (phrase) **Wait for me!** (sentence) *Tip:* Never use double exclamation points in school writing assignments or in business letters.

Parentheses

Parentheses are used around words included in a sentence to add information or to help make an idea clearer.

To Add Information	Use parentheses to add information. **The map (figure 2) will help you understand the explorer's route.**
To Make an Idea Clearer	Use parentheses to make an idea clearer. **Five of the students provided background music (humming very quietly) for the singer.**

Italics and Underlining

Italics is a printer's term for type that is slightly slanted. Italics is used for titles and special words. **Note:** In handwritten material, each word or letter that should be in italics is <u>underlined</u>. If you use a computer, you should use italics.

For Titles	Use italics (or underlining) for titles of plays, books, newspapers, magazines, television programs, movies (videos), record albums (cassettes and CD's), and other complete works.

> *The Wiz* **OR** <u>**The Wiz**</u> (play)
> *Exploring an Ocean Tide Pool* (book)
> *Pinky and the Brain* (television program)
> *The Prince of Egypt* (movie)

For Specific Words	Use italics (or underlining) to indicate names of aircraft and ships.

> *Columbia* **OR** <u>**Columbia**</u> (spacecraft)
> <u>**Merrimac**</u> (Civil War ship)

Use italics (or underlining) to indicate foreign words.

> *E pluribus unum,* **meaning "one out of many," is written on many U.S. coins.**

Use italics (or underlining) to indicate words discussed as words, rather than for their meaning.

> **The word** *freedom* **means different things to different people.**

Punctuation Marks

é	Accent	,	Comma	( )	Parentheses
'	Apostrophe	—	Dash	.	Period
*	Asterisk	/	Diagonal/Slash	?	Question Mark
[ ]	Brackets	...	Ellipsis	" "	Quotation Marks
^	Caret	!	Exclamation Point	;	Semicolon
:	Colon	-	Hyphen	__	Underscore

Editing for Mechanics

Capitalization

Proper Nouns and Proper Adjectives	Capitalize all proper nouns and proper adjectives. A proper noun names a specific person, place, thing, or idea. A proper adjective is formed from a proper noun. Proper Nouns: **Beverly Cleary** **Golden Gate Bridge** **Utah Jazz** **Thanksgiving** Proper Adjectives: **American citizen** **Chicago skyline** **New Jersey shore**
Names of People	Capitalize the names of people and also the initials or abbreviations that stand for those names. **John Steptoe** **Harriet Tubman** **C. S. Lewis** **Sacagawea**
Words Used as Names	Capitalize words such as *mother, father, aunt,* and *uncle* when these words are used as names. **Ask Mother what we're having for lunch.** (*Mother* is used as a name; you could use her first name in its place.) **Ask my mother what we're having for lunch.** (In this sentence, *mother* describes someone but is not used as a name.)

Capitalization (continued)

Geographic Names

Capitalize geographic names that are either proper nouns or proper adjectives.

Planets and heavenly bodies	**Earth, Jupiter, Milky Way**
Continents.	**Europe, Asia, South America, Australia, Africa**
Countries	**Chad, Haiti, Greece, Chile, Jordan**
States	**New Mexico, Alabama, West Virginia, Delaware, Iowa**
Provinces.	**Alberta, British Columbia, Québec, Ontario**
Cities	**Montreal, Portland**
Counties	**Wayne County, Dade County**
Bodies of water	**Hudson Bay, North Sea, Lake Geneva, Saskatchewan River, Indian Ocean, Gulf of Mexico**
Landforms	**Appalachian Mountains, Bitterroot Range, Capitol Reef**
Public areas	**Vietnam Memorial, Sequoia National Forest**
Roads and highways	**New Jersey Turnpike, Interstate 80, Central Avenue, Adam's Apple Road**
Buildings.	**Pentagon, Oriental Theater, Empire State Building**

Titles Used with Names	Capitalize titles used with names of persons. **President Carter**　　**Dr. Martin Luther King, Jr.** **Mayor Sharon Sayles-Belton** *Tip:* Do not capitalize titles when they are used alone: the president, the doctor, the mayor.
Historical Events	Capitalize the names of historical events, documents, and periods of time. **Boston Tea Party**　　**Stone Age** **Emancipation Proclamation**
Abbreviations	Capitalize abbreviations of titles and organizations. **M.D.** (doctor of medicine) **ADA** (American Dental Association)
Organizations	Capitalize the name of an organization, an association, or a team and its members. **Girl Scouts of America**　**the Democratic Party** **Chicago Bulls**　　　　　**Republicans**
Titles	Capitalize the first word of a title, the last word, and every word in between except articles (*a, an, the*), short prepositions, and coordinating conjunctions. ***National Geographic World*** [magazine] **"The Star-Spangled Banner"** [song] ***Beauty and the Beast*** [movie] ***In My Pocket*** [book] *Tip:* Don't lowercase every short word in a title. Although *my* is a short word, it is not an article, a preposition, or a coordinating conjunction.
First Words	Capitalize the first word of every sentence. **Our first basketball game is on Monday.** Capitalize the first word of a direct quotation. **Jamir shouted, "Keep that ball moving."**

Capitalization (continued)

Days and Months	Capitalize the names of days of the week, months of the year, and holidays.
	
	   Wednesday **March** **Easter**
	   Arbor Day **Passover** **Juneteenth Day**
	
	Tip: Do not capitalize the seasons.
	
	   winter **spring** **summer** **fall** (or **autumn**)

Names of Religions, Nationalities, Languages	Capitalize the names of religions, nationalities, and languages.
	
	   Christianity, Hinduism, Islam [religions]
	   Australian, Somalian, Chinese [nationalities]
	   English, Spanish, Hebrew [languages]

Official Names	Capitalize the names of businesses and the official names of their products. (These are called trade names.)
	
	   Budget Mart **Crispy Crunch cereal**
	   Choconut candy **Smile toothpaste**
	
	Tip: Do not capitalize a general descriptive word like *toothpaste* when it follows the product name.

Capitalize	**Do Not Capitalize**
January, March	**winter, spring**
Grandpa (as a name)	**my grandpa** (describing him)
Mayor Sayles-Belton	**Ms. Sayles-Belton, the mayor**
President Washington	**George Washington, our first president**
Ida B. Wells Elementary School	**the local elementary school**
Lake Ontario	**the lake area**
the South (section of the country)	**south** (a direction)
planet Earth	**the earth we live on**

Numbers

Numbers 1 to 9	Numbers from one to nine are usually written as words; all numbers 10 and over are usually written as numerals. **one three 10 115 2,000** *Except:* Numbers being compared should be kept in the same style. **Students from 8 to 11 years old are invited.** **Students from eight to eleven years old are invited.**
Very Large Numbers	You may use a combination of numbers and words for very large numbers. **15 million 1.2 billion** You may spell out large numbers that can be written as two words. **three million seven thousand** If you need more than two words to spell out a number, write it as a numeral. **3,275,100 7,418**
Sentence Beginnings	Use words, not numerals, to begin a sentence. **Fourteen new students joined the jazz band.**
Numerals Only	Use numerals for numbers in the following forms: money . . . . **$3.97** decimals . . . . **25.5** percentages. **6 percent** chapters. . . . . **chapter 8** pages . . . . **pages 17-20** addresses . . . . **445 E. Acorn Dr.** dates . . . . **June 19** times . . . . **1:30 p.m.** statistics . . . . **a vote of 5 to 2** identification numbers. . . . . **Highway 50**

Plurals

Nouns Ending in a Consonant	Form the plurals of most nouns by adding *s*.
	    balloon → balloons **shoe → shoes**
	
	Form the plurals of nouns ending in *sh, ch, x, s,* and *z* by adding *es* to the singular.
	    brush → brushes **bunch → bunches**
	    box → boxes **dress → dresses**
	    buzz → buzzes

Nouns Ending in *o*	Form the plurals of most words ending in *o* by adding *s*.
	    patio → patios **rodeo → rodeos**
	
	Form the plurals of most nouns ending in *o*, with a consonant letter just before the *o*, by adding *es*.
	    echo → echoes **hero → heroes**
	
	Except: Musical terms and words of Spanish origin form plurals by adding *s;* check your dictionary for other words of this type.
	    piano → pianos **solo → solos**
	    taco → tacos **burrito → burritos**

Nouns Ending in *ful*	Form the plurals of nouns that end with *ful* by adding an *s* at the end of the word.
	    two spoonfuls **three tankfuls**
	    four bowlfuls **five cupfuls**

Nouns Ending in *f* or *fe*	Form the plurals of nouns that end in *f* or *fe* in one of two ways.
	1. If the final *f* is still heard in the plural form of the word, simply add *s*.
	    goof → goofs **chief → chiefs** **safe → safes**
	2. If the final *f* has the sound of *v* in the plural form, change the *f* to *v* and add *es*.
	    calf → calves **loaf → loaves** **knife → knives**

Nouns Ending in y

Form the plurals of common nouns that end in y (with a consonant letter just before the y) by changing the y to i and adding es.

sky → skies	bunny → bunnies
story → stories	musky → muskies

Form the plurals of nouns that end in y (with a vowel before the y) by adding only s.

donkey → donkeys	monkey → monkeys
key → keys	day → days

Form the plurals of proper nouns that end in y by adding only s.

Two Penny Candys are opening in our city.

Compound Nouns

Form the plurals of most compound nouns by adding s or es to the important word in the compound.

sisters-in-law	maids of honor
secretaries of state	houses of assembly
life jackets	

Irregular Nouns

Some nouns form plurals by taking on an irregular spelling.

child → children	goose → geese
man → men	woman → women
foot → feet	tooth → teeth
ox → oxen	mouse → mice
cactus → cacti or cactuses	

Adding an 's

The plurals of symbols, letters, numerals, and words discussed as words are formed by adding an *apostrophe* and s.

two ?'s and two !'s	five 7's
x's and y's	a's and an's

Tip: For information on forming plurals and plural possessives, see page 385.

Abbreviations

An **abbreviation** is the shortened form of a word or phrase.

Common Abbreviations	Most abbreviations begin with a capital letter and end with a period. *Tip:* The following abbreviations are always acceptable in both formal and informal writing: **Mr. Mrs. Ms. Dr. Jr.** **M.D. B.C.E. C.E. a.m. p.m. (A.M., P.M.)** In formal writing, do not abbreviate the names of states, countries, months, days, or units of measure. Also do not use signs or symbols (%, &) in place of words.
Acronyms	An acronym is a word formed from the first letter or letters of words in a phrase. Acronyms do not end with a period. **SADD** (**S**tudents **A**gainst **D**estructive **D**ecisions) **CARE** (**C**ooperative for **A**merican **R**elief **E**verywhere) **PIN** (**p**ersonal **i**dentification **n**umber) **radar** (**ra**dio **d**etecting **a**nd **r**anging)
Initialisms	An initialism is like an acronym except the letters that form the abbreviation are pronounced individually. **TV** (**t**ele**v**ision) **CD** (**c**ompact **d**isc) **PSA** (**p**ublic **s**ervice **a**nnouncement) **CIA** (**C**entral **I**ntelligence **A**gency) **ASAP** (**a**s **s**oon **a**s **p**ossible)

State Abbreviations

	Standard	Postal		Standard	Postal		Standard	Postal
Alabama	**Ala.**	**AL**	Kentucky	**Ky.**	**KY**	North Dakota	**N.D.**	**ND**
Alaska	**Alaska**	**AK**	Louisiana	**La.**	**LA**	Ohio	**Ohio**	**OH**
Arizona	**Ariz.**	**AZ**	Maine	**Maine**	**ME**	Oklahoma	**Okla.**	**OK**
Arkansas	**Ark.**	**AR**	Maryland	**Md.**	**MD**	Oregon	**Ore.**	**OR**
California	**Calif.**	**CA**	Massachusetts	**Mass.**	**MA**	Pennsylvania	**Pa.**	**PA**
Colorado	**Colo.**	**CO**	Michigan	**Mich.**	**MI**	Rhode Island	**R.I.**	**RI**
Connecticut	**Conn.**	**CT**	Minnesota	**Minn.**	**MN**	South Carolina	**S.C.**	**SC**
Delaware	**Del.**	**DE**	Mississippi	**Miss.**	**MS**	South Dakota	**S.D.**	**SD**
District of			Missouri	**Mo.**	**MO**	Tennessee	**Tenn.**	**TN**
Columbia	**D.C.**	**DC**	Montana	**Mont.**	**MT**	Texas	**Tex.**	**TX**
Florida	**Fla.**	**FL**	Nebraska	**Neb.**	**NE**	Utah	**Utah**	**UT**
Georgia	**Ga.**	**GA**	Nevada	**Nev.**	**NV**	Vermont	**Vt.**	**VT**
Hawaii	**Hawaii**	**HI**	New			Virginia	**Va.**	**VA**
Idaho	**Idaho**	**ID**	Hampshire	**N.H.**	**NH**	Washington	**Wash.**	**WA**
Illinois	**Ill.**	**IL**	New Jersey	**N.J.**	**NJ**	West Virginia	**W. Va.**	**WV**
Indiana	**Ind.**	**IN**	New Mexico	**N.M.**	**NM**	Wisconsin	**Wis.**	**WI**
Iowa	**Iowa**	**IA**	New York	**N.Y.**	**NY**	Wyoming	**Wyo.**	**WY**
Kansas	**Kan.**	**KS**	North Carolina	**N.C.**	**NC**			

Address Abbreviations

	Standard	Postal		Standard	Postal		Standard	Postal
Avenue	**Ave.**	**AVE**	Lake	**L.**	**LK**	Rural	**R.**	**R**
Boulevard	**Blvd.**	**BLVD**	Lane	**Ln.**	**LN**	South	**S.**	**S**
Court	**Ct.**	**CT**	North	**N.**	**N**	Square	**Sq.**	**SQ**
Drive	**Dr.**	**DR**	Park	**Pk.**	**PK**	Station	**Sta.**	**STA**
East	**E.**	**E**	Parkway	**Pky.**	**PKY**	Street	**St.**	**ST**
Expressway	**Expy.**	**EXPY**	Place	**Pl.**	**PL**	Terrace	**Ter.**	**TER**
Heights	**Hts.**	**HTS**	Plaza	**Plaza**	**PLZ**	Turnpike	**Tpke.**	**TPKE**
Highway	**Hwy.**	**HWY**	Road	**Rd.**	**RD**	West	**W.**	**W**

Common Abbreviations

AC alternating current
a.m. ante meridiem
B.C.E. before the
    common era
C.E. the common era
C.O.D. cash on delivery
D.A. district attorney
DC direct current

tc. and so forth
FM frequency modulation
kg kilogram
km kilometer
kw kilowatt
lb. pound
M.D. doctor of medicine
m.p.g. miles per gallon

m.p.h. miles per hour
oz. ounce
pd. paid
pg. page (or p.)
p.m. post meridiem
qt. quart
R.S.V.P. please reply

Checking Your Spelling

■ **Check your spelling** by using a dictionary or a list of commonly misspelled words (like the one that follows).

■ **Check a dictionary for the correct pronunciation** of each word you are trying to spell. Knowing how to pronounce a word will help you remember how to spell it.

■ **Look up the meaning of each word.** Knowing how to spell a word is of little use if you don't know what it means.

■ **Practice seeing the word in your mind's eye.** Look away from the dictionary page and write the word on a piece of paper. Check the spelling in the dictionary. Repeat this process until you can spell the word correctly.

■ **Make a spelling dictionary.** Include any words you misspell in a special notebook. (**SEE** page 307.)

■ **Practice.** Learning to become a good speller takes time.

A

	address	already	anybody	athletic
	adventure	although	apartment	attention
	advertisement	always	apologize	attitude
about	advise	American	application	attractive
above	afraid	among	appreciate	audience
absent	after	amount	April	August
accept	against	ancient	aren't	aunt
accident	agreement	angel	argument	author
accompany	allowance	angle	arithmetic	automobile
accurate	all right	animal	around	autumn
ache	almost	anniversary	arrival	avenue
achieve	alone	anonymous	article	awful
across	along	another	artificial	awhile
actual	a lot	answer	athlete	

B

baggage
balloon
banana
bargain
basement
beautiful
because
become
been
before
beginning
behind
believe
belong
between
bicycle
birthday
biscuit
blanket
blizzard
bought
breakfast
brilliant
brother
brought
bruise
buckle
building
built
burglar
business
busy
button
buy

C

cafeteria
calendar
called
campaign
candidate
canoe
canyon
captain
careful
careless
casserole
caterpillar
caught
celebration
cemetery
century
certain
certificate
change
character
chief
children
chimney
chocolate
choir
choose
Christmas
church
city
civilization
classmates
classroom
climate
closet
cocoa
cocoon
color

come
coming
committee
community
company
complete
concert
congratulate
cooperate
cough
could
couldn't
country
courage
courteous
courtesy
cousin
criticize
cupboard
curious
customer

D

dairy
dangerous
daughter
day
dear
December
decorate
definition
delicious
describe
desert
dessert
developed
didn't
different
difficulty

disappear
disastrous
discover
discussion
distance
divide
division
doctor
does
done
doubt

E

early
earth
Easter
easy
edge
either
electricity
elephant
emergency
encourage
enormous
enough
entertain
environment
every
everybody
exactly
excellent
exercise
exhausted
expensive
experience
explain
expression
eyes

F

face
familiar
family
famous
fashion
faucet
favorite
February
fierce
fifty
finally
first
football
foreign
forty
forward
found
fountain
fourth
fragile
Friday
friend
from
front
fuel
full

G

gadget
generally
generous
genius
gentle
geography
getting
goes
gone
government
grade
graduation
grammar
grateful
great
grocery
group
guarantee
guard
guardian
guess
gymnasium

H

half
handkerchief
handsome
happened
happiness
haven't
having
hazardous
heard
heavy
height
history
holiday
honor
horrible
hospital
hour
humorous
hundreds

I

icicle
ideal
identical
imagine
immediately
immigrant
impatient
important
impossible
incredible
independent
individual
influence
innocent
instead
intelligent
interested
island

J

January
jewelry
journal
journey
judgment
juicy
July
June

K

kitchen
knew
knife
knives
know
knowledge

L

language
laughed
league
leave
length
lesson
letter
light
lightning
likely
listen
literature
little
loose
lovable

M

magazine
making
manufacture
many
March
marriage
material
mathematics
May
maybe
mayor
might
millions
minute
mirror
Monday
money
morning
mountain
music
musician
mysterious

N

natural
necessary
neighborhood
neither
never
nice
noisy
none
no one
nothing
November
nuclear
number

obey
occasion
o'clock
October
office
often
once
operate
opposite
other
outside
own

package
paragraph
parallel
party
pasture
patience
peace
people
picture
piece
place
played
pleasant
please
pleasure
point
poison
practice
prejudice
preparation
present
president

pretty
principal
privilege
problem
products
psychology
pumpkin

Q

quarter
quickly
quiet
quit
quite
quotient

R

raise
ready
really
reason
receive
recognize
remember
responsibilities
restaurant
right
rough
route

S

safety
said
salad
salary
sandwich
Santa Claus
Saturday

says
scared
scene
school
sentence
September
several
shoes
should
since
skiing
something
sometimes
soon
special
started
store
straight
studying
suddenly
sugar
summer
Sunday
suppose
sure
surprise
surround
swimming
system

table
teacher
tear
temperature
terrible
Thanksgiving
their
there

they're
though
thought
thousands
through
Thursday
tired
together
tomorrow
tonight
toys
traveling
trouble
truly
Tuesday
turn

unconscious
unfortunately
until
unusual
upon
use
usually

V

vacation
vacuum
vegetable
vehicle
very
violence
visitor
voice
volume

wasn't
weather
Wednesday
weight
weird
welcome
welfare
were
we're
what
when
where
which
while
whole
whose
women
world
wouldn't
write
writing
wrote

Y

yellow
yesterday
young
your
you're
yourself

Using the Right Word

You need to use "the right words" in your writing and speaking, and this section will help you do that. First, look over the commonly misused words on the next 10 pages. Then, whenever you have a question about which word is the *right* word, come back to this section for help. (Remember to look for your word in a dictionary if you don't find it here.)

a, an	**I played a joke on my dad.** (Use *a* before words beginning with a consonant sound.) **I placed an ugly rubber chicken under his pillow.** (Use *an* before words beginning with a vowel sound.)
accept, except	**Please accept my apology.** (*Accept* means "to receive.") **Everyone except me finished the race.** (*Except* means "other than.")
allowed, aloud	**We are allowed to read to partners in class.** (*Allowed* means "permitted.") **We may not read aloud in the library, however.** (*Aloud* is an adverb meaning "clearly heard.")
a lot	**A lot of my friends like jeans with holes in them.** (*A lot* is always two words.)

already, all ready	I **already** finished my homework. (*Already* is an adverb telling when.) Now I'm **all ready** to play some buckets. (*All ready* is a phrase meaning "completely ready.")
ant, aunt	An **ant** is an insect. An **aunt** is a close relative.
ate, eight	I **ate** a bowl of popcorn. He had **eight** pieces of licorice.
bare, bear	She put her **bare** feet into the cool stream. She didn't see the **bear** fishing on the other side.
blew, blue	I **blew** on my cold hands. The tips of my fingers looked almost **blue**.
board, bored	A **board** is a piece of wood. You feel **bored** when there's nothing to do.
brake, break	Pump the **brake** to slow down. You don't want to **break** a bone.
bring, take	Please **bring** me my glasses. (*Bring* means "to move toward the speaker.") **Take** your dishes to the kitchen. (*Take* means "to carry away.")
by, buy	Did a hawk just fly **by** my window? I better **buy** some new glasses.
can, may	**Can** I go off the high dive? (I am asking if I have the "ability" to do it.) **May** I go off the high dive? (I am asking for "permission" to do something.)

capital, capitol	The **capital** city of Texas is Austin. Be sure to begin Austin with a **capital** letter. My uncle works in the **capitol** building. (*Capitol,* with an "ol," is used when writing about a government building.)
cent, scent, sent	Each rose costs 99 **cents**. The **scent** (smell) of the flowers is sweet. Dad **sent** Mom a dozen roses.
chose, choose	David **chose** to take drum lessons last year. He will **choose** a different instrument this year. (*Chose* [chōz] is the past tense of the verb *choose* [chōoz].)
close, clothes	**Close** the window. Then put the **clothes** in the dryer.
coarse, course	A cat's tongue feels **coarse**, like sandpaper. I took a **course** called "Caring for Cats."
creak, creek	Old houses **creak** when the wind blows hard. The water in the nearby **creek** is clear and cold.
dear, deer	Amber is my **dear** friend. The **deer** enjoyed the sweet corn in her garden.
desert, dessert	Cactuses grow in the **desert** near our house. My favorite **dessert** is strawberry pie.
dew, do, due	The **dew** on the grass got my new shoes wet. I **do** my homework right after school. The report is **due** on Wednesday.
die, dye	The plant will **die** if it isn't watered. The red **dye** in the sweatshirt turned everything in the wash pink.

doesn't, don't	She doesn't like green bananas. (doesn't = does not) I don't either. (don't = do not)
fewer, less	We had fewer snow days this winter. (*Fewer* refers to something you can count.) That meant less time for ice-skating. (*Less* refers to something you cannot count.)
find, fined	Did you find your book? Yes, but I was fined because it was overdue.
fir, fur	Fir trees are evergreen trees. Polar bears have thick fur coats.
for, four	You may eat the kiwis for a snack. The four of you may also share the crackers.
good, well	Ling looks good in that outfit. (*Good* is an adjective modifying "Ling.") It fits her well. (*Well* is an adverb modifying "fits.")
hare, hair	A hare looks like a large rabbit. My hair looks like a wet rabbit.
heal, heel	It takes a long time for a blister to heal. Gracie has a blister on her heel.
hear, here	I couldn't hear your directions. I was over here, and you were way over there.
heard, herd	We heard the noise, all right! It sounded like a herd of charging elephants.
heir, air	An heir is a person who inherits something. Air is what we breathe.

hi, high	**Say hi to the pilot for me.** **How high is this plane flying?**
hole, whole	**A donut has a hole in the middle of it.** **Montel ate a whole donut.**
hour, our	**It takes one hour to ride to the beach.** **Let's pack our lunches and go.**
its, it's	**This backpack is no good; its zipper is stuck.** (*Its* shows possession.) **It's also ripped.** (*It's* is the contraction of "it is.")
knew, new	**I knew it was going to rain.** **I still wanted to wear my new shoes.**
knight, night	**The knight stood guard by the iron gates.** **Torches were lit for the long night.**
knot, not	**I have a knot in my shoelaces.** **I am not able to untie the tangled mess.**
know, no	**Do you know all the dates for our history test?** **No, let's study them together.**
knows, nose	**Mr. Beck knows at least a billion historical facts.** **His nose is always in a book.**
lay, lie	**Just lay the sleeping bags on the floor.** (*Lay* means "to place.") **After the hike, we'll lie down and rest.** (*Lie* means "to recline.")
lead, led	**Some old paint contains lead.** **I get to lead the ponies around the show ring.** **Yesterday the drill team led the parade past the arena.**

learn, teach	I need to learn these facts about the moon. (*Learn* means "to get information.")
	Tomorrow I have to teach the science lesson. (*Teach* means "to give information.")
loose, lose	Lee's pet tarantula is loose! (*Loose [lōōs]* means "free or untied.")
	No one but Lee could lose a big, fat spider. (*Lose [lōōz]* means "to misplace or fail to win.")
made, maid	Yes, I have made a big mess.
	I need a maid to help me clean it up.
mail, male	Many people receive mail on their computers.
	Men are male; women are female.
meat, meet	I think meat can be a part of a healthful diet.
	We were so excited to finally meet the senator.
metal, medal	Gold is a precious metal.
	Is the Olympic first-place medal actually made of gold?
miner, minor	Some coal miners suffer from black lung disease.
	Minors are young people who are not legally adults.
oar, or, ore	You use an oar to row a boat.
	Either Kim or Makaila will do the rowing.
	Iron ore is a mineral.

one, won	Markus bought one raffle ticket. He won the bike with that single ticket.
pain, pane	Cuts, bruises, and broken bones cause pain. I can finally see through the pane of clean glass.
pair, pare, pear	A pair (two) of pigeons roosted on our windowsill. To pare an apple means to peel it. A ripe pear is sweet and juicy.
passed, past	The school bus passed a stalled truck. In the past, most children walked to school.
peace, piece	Ms. Brown likes peace and quiet in her room. I like a piece of cake in my lunch.
plain, plane	Toni wanted a plain (basic) white dress. The coyote ran across the flat plain. A stunt plane can fly upside down.
pore, pour, poor	A pore is a tiny opening in the skin. Please pour me another glass of juice. Rich is the opposite of poor.
principal, principle	Our principal is a strong leader. (The noun *principal* is a school administrator; the adjective *principal* means "most important.") She asks students to follow this principle: Respect each other, and I'll respect you. (*Principle* means "idea" or "belief.")
quiet, quit, quite	Libraries should be quiet places. Quit talking, please. I hear quite a bit of whispering going on.

raise, **rays,** **raze**	Please don't raise (lift) the shades. The sun's rays are very bright this afternoon. To raze means "to tear something down."
read, **red**	Have you read any books by Betsy Byars? Why are most barns painted red?
right, **write,** **rite**	Is this the right (correct) place to turn right? I'll write the directions on a note card. The pastor performed the marriage rite (ceremony).
road, **rode,** **rowed**	My house is one block from the main road. I rode my bike to the pond. Then I rowed the boat to my favorite fishing spot.
scene, **seen**	The movie has a great chase scene. Have you seen it yet?
sea, **see**	A sea is a body of salty water. I see a tall ship on the horizon.
seam, **seem**	The seam in my jacket is ripped. I seem to always catch my sleeve on the door handle.
sew, **so,** **sow**	Shauna loves to sew her own clothes. She saves her allowance, so she can buy fabric. I'd rather sow seeds and watch my garden grow.
sit, **set**	May I sit on one of those folding chairs? Yes, if you help me set them up first.
some, **sum**	I have some math problems to do. What is the sum of 58 + 17?
son, **sun**	Joe Jackson is the son of Kate Jackson. The sun is the source of the earth's energy.

sore, soar	Our feet and legs were sore after the long hike. We watched hawks soar above us.
stationery, stationary	Wu designs his own stationery (paper) on the computer. A stationary bike stays in place while you pedal it.
steal, steel	You can steal third base, but don't take it home! Many knives are made of steel.
tail, tale	A snake uses its tail to move its body. "Sammy the Spotted Snake" is my favorite tall tale.
than, then	Jana's card collection is bigger than Erica's. (*Than* is used in a comparison.) When Jana is finished, then we can play. (*Then* tells when.)
their, there, they're	What should we do with their cards? (*Their* shows ownership.) Put them over there for now. They're going to pick them up later. (they're = they are)
threw, through	He threw the ball at the basket. It swished through the net.
to, too, two	Josie passed the ball to Shannon. Lea was too tired to guard her. (*Too* means "very.") The fans jumped and cheered, too. (*Too* means "also.") Maria easily scored two points.

waist, waste	My little sister's waist is tiny.
	No part of the buffalo went to waste.
wait, weight	I can't wait for the field trip.
	My brother lifts weights to get strong.
way, weigh	Show me the way to the gym.
	Birds weigh very little because of their hollow bones.
weak, week	The opposite of strong is weak.
	There are seven days in a week.
wear, where	The crossing guards wear yellow ponchos.
	Where do you think they got them?
weather, whether	I like rainy weather.
	My dad goes golfing whether it's nice out or not.
which, witch	Which book should I read?
	You'll like *The Lion, the Witch, and the Wardrobe.*
who, which, that	The man who answered the door was my dad.
	The movie, which was very funny, ended too soon.
	The puppy that I really wanted was sold already.
who, whom	Who ordered this pizza?
	The pizza was ordered by whom?
who's, whose	Who's that knocking at the door? (**Who's** = who is)
	Whose door are you talking about?
wood, would	Some baseball bats are made of wood.
	Would you like to play baseball after school?
you're, your	You're talking to the right person! (**You're** = you are)
	You can pick up your pizzas after school.

Understanding Sentences

A **sentence** is made up of one or more words that express a complete thought. A sentence begins with a capital letter. It ends with a period, a question mark, or an exclamation point.

 **Note**   Find more information about sentences in "Writing Basic Sentences," pages 113-117, and in "Combining Sentences," pages 118-121.

Parts of a Sentence

SUBJECT

A **subject** is the part of a sentence that does something.

> Marisha **baked a chocolate cake.**

A subject can also be the word that is talked about.

> She **is a marvelous cook.**

Simple Subject	A simple subject is the subject without the words that describe or modify it.
	Marisha's little sister likes to help.
Complete Subject	The complete subject is the simple subject and all the words that describe it.
	Marisha's little sister likes to help.
	(*Marisha's little sister* is the complete subject.)
Compound Subject	A compound subject has two or more simple subjects.
	Marisha and her sister frosted the cake.

PREDICATE

A **predicate** (verb) is the part of the sentence that says something about the subject.

Marisha baked the cake for my birthday.
(*Baked* tells what the subject did.)

Simple Predicate	A simple predicate (verb) is the predicate without the words that modify or complete it. **Marisha baked the cake yesterday.**
Complete Predicate	The complete predicate is the simple predicate with all the words that modify or complete it. **Marisha baked the cake yesterday.** (The complete predicate is *baked the cake yesterday.*)
Compound Predicate	A compound predicate has two or more simple predicates, or verbs. **She decorated it and hid it in the cupboard.**

MODIFIER

A **modifier** is a word or a group of words that describes another word.

My family planned a surprise party.
(*My* modifies *family; a* and *surprise* modify *party.*)

They hid behind the door and waited quietly.
(*Behind the door* modifies *hid; quietly* modifies *waited.*)

Subject-Verb Agreement

The subject and verb of a sentence must "agree" with one another. If you use a singular subject, use a singular verb. If you use a plural subject, use a plural verb. (**SEE** page 116.)

Anthony helps Miss Park.
(The singular subject *Anthony* agrees with the singular verb *helps.*)

The boys help Miss Park.
(The plural subject *boys* agrees with the plural verb *help.*)

CLAUSES

A **clause** is a group of words that has a subject and a predicate. A clause can be independent or dependent.

Independent Clause	An independent clause expresses a complete thought and can stand alone as a sentence. **I ride my bike to school**
Dependent Clause	A dependent clause does not express a complete thought and cannot stand alone as a sentence. Dependent clauses usually begin with a subordinating conjunction like *when*. (**SEE** page 435.) **when the weather is nice** *Tip:* Some dependent clauses begin with a relative pronoun like *who* or *that*. (**SEE** page 424.) An **independent clause** plus a dependent clause form a complex sentence. **I ride my bike to school when the weather is nice.**

PHRASES

A **phrase** is a group of related words. Phrases cannot stand alone as sentences.

Noun Phrase	This is a noun phrase. It lacks a predicate. **the student**
Verb Phrase	This is a verb phrase. It lacks a subject. **wrote a report**
Prepositional Phrase	This is a prepositional phrase. (**SEE** page 434.) **about George Washington**
Appositive Phrase	This is an appositive phrase. **our first president**

Note: When you put these phrases together, they become a sentence.

The student wrote a report about George Washington, our first president.

Types of Sentences

Simple Sentences	A simple sentence has only one independent clause (and states only one complete thought). However, it may have a compound subject or a compound predicate, and still be a simple sentence.

> **My** knees ache.
> (Simple subject, simple predicate)
>
> Cory **and** I skated **for two hours.**
> (Compound subject, simple predicate)
>
> **My** face **and** neck look **red and** feel **hot.**
> (Compound subject, compound predicate)

Compound Sentences	A compound sentence is made up of two or more simple sentences joined by a comma and a coordinating conjunction (*and, but, or*), or by a semicolon. (**SEE** page 435 for more about coordinating conjunctions.)

> **I've skated in Los Angeles, but I have only seen a picture of New York.**
> (The conjunction *but* connects two independent clauses.)
>
> **Los Angeles is 30 miles from my home; New York is 3,000 miles away.**
> (A semicolon connects two independent clauses.)

Complex Sentences	A complex sentence contains one independent clause (in **black**) and one or more dependent clauses (in red). Dependent clauses begin with a subordinating conjunction like *because* or a relative pronoun like *who* or *that*.

> Because it was raining**, the game was called off.**
>
> **The students,** who were wet and cold**, got back on the bus.**

Kinds of Sentences

Declarative Sentences	Declarative sentences make statements. They tell something about a person, a place, a thing, or an idea. **The capital of Florida is Tallahassee.** **Lisha swims in the ocean.**
Interrogative Sentences	Interrogative sentences ask questions. **Did you know that Florida's major industry is tourism?** **Have you ever gone snorkeling?**
Imperative Sentences	Imperative sentences give commands. **You must never swim alone.** *Tip:* Imperative sentences sometimes use an understood subject (you). **Never swim alone. Stay here.**
Exclamatory Sentences	Exclamatory sentences communicate strong emotion or surprise. **I just saw a dolphin!** **Watch out for sharks!**

Sentence Sense

- A sentence is one or more words that express a complete thought.
- A sentence has two basic parts—a subject and a predicate (verb).
- A sentence makes a statement, asks a question, gives a command, or shows strong emotion.
- A sentence begins with a capital letter and ends with a period, a question mark, or an exclamation point.
- More information on sentences is included in "Writing Basic Sentences," pages 113-117, and in "Combining Sentences," pages 118-121.

Understanding Our Language

All the words in our language have been divided into eight groups. These word groups are called the *parts of speech,* and each group includes words that are used in the same way in a sentence.

Parts of Speech

Nouns Words that name a person, a place, a thing, or an idea. *(Bill, office, billboard, confusion)*

Pronouns Words used in place of nouns. *(I, me, her, them, who, which, those, myself, some)*

Verbs Words that express action or state of being. *(is, are, run, jump)*

Adjectives Words that describe a noun or pronoun. *(tall, quiet, three, the, neat)*

Adverbs Words that describe a verb, an adjective, or another adverb. *(gently, easily, fast, very)*

Interjections Words (set off by commas or exclamation points) that show emotion or surprise. *(Wow, Oh, Yikes!)*

Prepositions Words that show position or direction and introduce prepositional phrases. *(on, near, over, on top of)*

Conjunctions Words that connect words or groups of words. *(and, or, because)*

Nouns

A **noun** is a word that names a person, a place, a thing, or an idea.

Person: **Nadia, friend, Josh, parent**
Place: **home, Miami, city, backyard**
Thing: **baseball, homework, secret**
Idea: **happiness, trouble, friendship**

KINDS OF NOUNS

Common Nouns	A common noun is any noun that does not name a specific person, place, thing, or idea. Common nouns are not capitalized. **man park team holiday**
Proper Nouns	A proper noun names a specific person, place, thing, or idea. Proper nouns are capitalized. **Reggie White Lincoln Park Eagles Labor Day**
Concrete Nouns	A concrete noun names a thing that can be seen or touched. Concrete nouns are either common or proper. **magazine cactus Washington Monument**
Abstract Nouns	An abstract noun names something that cannot be seen or touched. Abstract nouns are either common or proper. **love democracy Christianity Judaism**

NUMBER OF NOUNS

Singular Nouns	A singular noun names one person, place, thing, or idea. **room paper pen pal hope**
Plural Nouns	A plural noun names more than one person, place, thing, or idea. **rooms papers pen pals hopes**

SPECIAL TYPES OF NOUNS

Compound Nouns	A compound noun is made up of two or more words.
	busboy (written as one word)
	blue jeans (written as two words)
	two-wheeler (written as a hyphenated word)
	sister-in-law (written as a hyphenated word)

Collective Nouns	A collective noun names a collection of persons, animals, or things.
	Persons:
	class **team** **clan** **group** **family**
	Animals:
	herd **flock** **litter** **pack** **colony**
	Things:
	bunch **batch** **collection**

Specific Nouns	Specific nouns make your writing come to life.
	Tip: **SEE** page 66 in "Editing and Proofreading."

GENDER OF NOUNS

The gender of a noun refers to its being feminine *(female)*, masculine *(male)*, neuter *(neither male nor female)*, or indefinite *(male or female)*.

Gender of Nouns	**Feminine** (female):
	cow **hen** **mother** **sister** **women**
	Masculine (male):
	bull **rooster** **father** **brother** **men**
	Neuter (neither male nor female)
	tree **closet** **cobweb**
	Indefinite (male or female):
	child **pilot** **parent** **dentist**

USES OF NOUNS

Subject Nouns	A noun may be the subject of a sentence. The subject is the part of the sentence that does something or is being talked about. **Joe gave Nadia a note.** (The noun *Joe* did something, *gave Nadia a note.*)
Predicate Nouns	A predicate noun follows a form of the verb "be" (*is, are, was, were,* etc.) and renames the subject. **The book is a mystery.** (The noun *mystery* renames the subject *book*; it is another name for the subject.)
Possessive Nouns	A possessive noun shows ownership. Use an apostrophe and *s* to form possessive nouns. **The book's ending is a big surprise.** (The *'s* added to *book* shows that the *ending* is part of the book.)

NOUNS AS OBJECTS

Direct Objects	A noun is a direct object when it receives the action of the verb. **Nadia read the book.** (*Book* is the direct object because it receives the action of the verb *read.*)
Indirect Objects	A noun is an indirect object when it names the person to whom or for whom something is done. **Joe gave Nadia the book.** (The book is given "to whom"? The book is given to "Nadia," the indirect object.)
Objects of a Preposition	A noun is an object of a preposition when it is part of a prepositional phrase. (**SEE** page 434.) **Nadia put the book on the shelf.** (The noun *shelf* is the object of the preposition *on.*)

Pronouns

A **pronoun** is a word used in place of a noun.

Carlotta rescued an injured sandpiper.

She took it to a veterinarian.

(*She* is a pronoun that replaces the noun *Carlotta*. *It* is a pronoun that replaces the noun *sandpiper*.)

Antecedents	An antecedent is the noun that a pronoun refers to or replaces. All pronouns have antecedents. **Anju's skateboard glides easily now that it is oiled.** (*Skateboard* is the antecedent of the pronoun *it*.)
Agreement of Pronouns	The pronouns in your sentences must *agree* with their antecedents in number and person. **Anju's skateboard works great now that it is oiled.** (The pronoun *it* and its antecedent *skateboard* are both singular, so they agree.) **The other kids' boards look like they could use some oil, too.** (The pronoun *they* and its antecedent *boards* are both plural, so they agree.)
Number of Pronouns	Pronouns can be either singular or plural. **I flipped a skateboard.** **We flipped the skateboards.**

Personal Pronouns

Singular: I, me, you, he, she, him, her, it

Plural: we, us, you, they, them

PERSON OF PRONOUNS

The person of a pronoun tells whether the pronoun is speaking, being spoken to, or being spoken about.

First-Person Pronouns	A first-person pronoun is used in place of the name of the speaker. **I like blue-moon ice cream.** (*I* replaces the speaker's name.)
Second-Person Pronouns	A second-person pronoun is used to name the person or thing spoken to. **Su, have you decided on a flavor?** (*You* replaces the name *Su,* the person being spoken to.)
Third-Person Pronouns	A third-person pronoun is used to name the person or thing spoken about. **Jon said that he wants pumpkin ice cream.** (*He* replaces *Jon,* the person being spoken about.)

Singular Pronouns

	Subject Pronouns	Possessive Pronouns	Object Pronouns
First Person	I	my, mine	me
Second Person	you	your, yours	you
Third Person	he she it	his her, hers its	him her it

Plural Pronouns

	Subject Pronouns	Possessive Pronouns	Object Pronouns
First Person	we	our, ours	us
Second Person	you	your, yours	you
Third Person	they	their, theirs	them

USES OF PRONOUNS

Subject Pronouns

A subject pronoun is used as the subject of a sentence.

I can tell jokes well.

They really make people laugh.

> **Singular:** I, you, he, she, it
> **Plural:** we, you, they

Object Pronouns

An object pronoun is used as a direct object, an indirect object, or in a prepositional phrase.

Mr. Otto encourages me.
(*Me*, a direct object, receives the action of the verb *encourages*.)

Mr. Otto often gives us extra help with math.
(*Us*, an indirect object, names the people for whom something is done.)

My friends made a funny card for him.
(*Him* is the object in the prepositional phrase *for him*.)

> **Singular:** me, you, him, her, it
> **Plural:** us, you, them

Possessive Pronouns

A possessive pronoun shows ownership. It can be used before a noun, or it can stand alone.

Gloria finished writing her story.
(*Her* comes before the noun *story*.)

The idea for the plot was mine.
(*Mine* can stand alone.)

> **Before a noun:**
> my, your, his, her, its, our, their
> **Stand alone:**
> mine, yours, his, hers, its, ours, theirs

OTHER TYPES OF PRONOUNS

Relative Pronouns	A relative pronoun connects one part of a sentence with a word in another part of the sentence. **Any fifth grader who wants to join our music group should see Carlos.**
Interrogative Pronouns	An interrogative pronoun asks a question. **Who is going to play the keyboard?**
Demonstrative Pronouns	A demonstrative pronoun points out or identifies a noun without naming it. **That sounds like a great idea!**
Intensive and Reflexive Pronouns	An intensive pronoun stresses the word it refers to. A reflexive pronoun refers back to the subject. **Carlos himself taught the group.** (intensive) **Carlos enjoyed himself.** (reflexive)
Indefinite Pronouns	An indefinite pronoun refers to people or things that are not named or known. **Nobody is here to videotape the practice.**

Types of Pronouns

Relative
who, whom, whose, which, what, that, whoever, whatever, whichever

Interrogative
who, whose, whom, which, what

Demonstrative
this, that, these, those

Intensive and Reflexive
myself, himself, herself, itself, yourself, themselves, ourselves

Indefinite

all	anything	everybody	most	no one	some
another	both	everyone	much	nothing	somebody
any	each	everything	neither	one	someone
anybody	each one	few	nobody	other	something
anyone	either	many	none	several	such

Verbs

A **verb** shows action or links the subject to another word in the sentence. The verb is the main word in the predicate part of the sentence.

> **The boys hike along the river.**
> (The verb *hike* shows action.)

> **I am happy about that.**
> (The verb *am* links the subject *I* to the word *happy*.)

ACTION VERBS

An action verb tells what the subject is doing.

> **I watched most of the game.**

> **I left after the third quarter.**

Transitive Verbs	An action verb is called a transitive verb if it is followed by an object (*noun* or *pronoun*). The object makes the meaning of the verb complete. **Ann Cameron writes books about Julian.** (The meaning of the verb *writes* is completed by the noun *books*.)
Verbs Followed by a Direct Object	A direct object receives the action of a transitive verb. The direct object answers the question *what?* or *whom?* after the verb. **Raffi composes songs for little children.** (The noun *songs* is a direct object. *Composes* is a transitive verb.)
Verbs Followed by an Indirect Object	An indirect object receives the action of a transitive verb, indirectly. An indirect object names the person *to whom* or *for whom* something is done. **Books give children enjoyment.** (*Children* is an indirect object. *Give* is a transitive verb, and *enjoyment* is a direct object.)

LINKING AND HELPING VERBS.

Linking Verbs	A linking verb links a subject to a noun or an adjective in the predicate part of the sentence. **That car is a convertible.** (The verb *is* links the subject *car* to the noun *convertible*.) **My new car looks shiny.** (The verb *looks* links the subject *car* to the adjective *shiny*.)
Helping Verbs	Helping verbs (also called auxiliary verbs) include *has, had,* and *have; do* and *did;* and forms of the verb "be" (*is, are, was, were,* etc.). **Lee will write in his journal.** (The verb *will* helps state a future action, *will write.*) **Lee has been writing in his journal.** (The verbs *has* and *been* help state a continuing action, *has been writing.*)

Linking Verbs

The most common linking verbs are forms of the verb *be:*
is, are, was, were, am, being, been

Other linking verbs include the following:
smell, look, taste, remain, feel, appear, sound, seem, become, grow, stand, turn

Helping Verbs

The most common helping verbs are listed below:
shall, will, should, would, could, must, can, may, have, had, has, do, did

The forms of the verb *be* are also helping verbs:
is, are, was, were, am, being, been

TENSES OF VERBS

The time of a verb is called its tense. Tense is shown by endings *(talked)*, by helping verbs *(did talk)*, or by both *(have talked)*.

Present Tense Verbs	The present tense of a verb states an action that is *happening now* or that *happens regularly*. **I like soccer.** **We practice every day.**
Past Tense Verbs	The past tense of a verb states an action or state of being that *happened at a specific time in the past*. **Anne kicked the soccer ball.** **She was the goalie.**
Future Tense Verbs	The future tense of a verb states an action that *will take place*. It is formed by using *will* or *shall* before the main verb. **I will like soccer forever.** **We shall practice every day.**

PERFECT TENSES

Present Perfect Tense Verbs	The present perfect tense states an action that *is still going on*. Add *has* or *have* before the past participle form of the main verb. **Alexis has slept for two hours.**
Past Perfect Tense Verbs	The past perfect tense states an action that *began and was completed in the past*. Add *had* before the past participle form of the main verb. **Jondra had slept for eight hours.**
Future Perfect Tense Verbs	The future perfect tense states an action that *will begin in the future and end at a specific time*. Add *will have* before the past participle form of the main verb. **Riley will have slept for 12 hours.**

FORMS OF VERBS

Singular and Plural Verbs	A singular verb is used when the subject in a sentence is singular.
	Ben likes cream cheese and olive sandwiches. (The subject *Ben* and the verb *likes* are both singular.)
	A plural verb is used when the subject is plural.
	Black olives taste like wax. (The subject *olives* and the verb *taste* are both plural.)
	Tip: When a subject and verb are both singular or plural, they agree in number. (**SEE** page 413.)
Active and Passive Verbs	A verb is active if the subject is doing the action.
	Kara threw a fastball. (*Threw* is active because the subject *Kara* is doing the action.)
	A verb is passive if the subject does not do the action.
	A fastball was thrown by Kara. (*Was thrown* is passive because the subject *fastball* is not doing the action.)
Regular Verbs	Most verbs in the English language are regular. Add *ed* to regular verbs to state a past action; use *has, have,* or *had* with the *ed* form to make perfect tenses.
	I play. Yesterday I played. I have played.
	He calls. Yesterday he called. He has called.
Irregular Verbs	Some verbs in the English language are irregular. Instead of adding *ed*, the word changes to state a past action. (**SEE** the chart on page 429.)
	I speak. Yesterday I spoke. I have spoken.
	She runs. Yesterday she ran. She has run.

Common Irregular Verbs

The principal parts of some common irregular verbs are listed below. The part used with the helping verbs *has, have,* or *had* is called the past participle.

Present Tense I hide.	She hides
Past Tense Yesterday I hid.	Yesterday she hid.
Past Participle I have hidden.	She has hidden.

Present Tense	Past Tense	Past Participle	Present Tense	Past Tense	Past Participle
am, are	was, were	been	lie (recline)	lay	lain
begin	began	begun	make	made	made
bite	bit	bitten	ride	rode	ridden
blow	blew	blown	ring	rang	rung
break	broke	broken	rise	rose	risen
bring	brought	brought	run	ran	run
burst	burst	burst	see	saw	seen
catch	caught	caught	set	set	set
come	came	come	shake	shook	shaken
dive	dove, dived	dived	shine (light)	shone	shone
do	did	done	shrink	shrank	shrunk
draw	drew	drawn	sing	sang, sung	sung
drink	drank	drunk	sink	sank, sunk	sunk
drive	drove	driven	sit	sat	sat
eat	ate	eaten	speak	spoke	spoken
fall	fell	fallen	spring	sprang, sprung	sprung
fight	fought	fought	steal	stole	stolen
fly	flew	flown	swear	swore	sworn
freeze	froze	frozen	swim	swam	swum
give	gave	given	swing	swung	swung
go	went	gone	take	took	taken
grow	grew	grown	tear	tore	torn
hang	hung	hung	throw	threw	thrown
hide	hid	hidden, hid	wake	woke	woken
know	knew	known	wear	wore	worn
lay (place)	laid	laid	weave	wove	woven
lead	led	led	write	wrote	written

Adjectives

Adjectives are words that modify (describe) nouns or pronouns. Adjectives tell *what kind, how many,* or *which one.*

> Male peacocks have beautiful feathers.
> The feathers are colorful.

(An adjective after a linking verb is called a *predicate adjective.*)

Articles	The words *a, an,* and *the* are special adjectives called articles.
	Owlet is the name for a baby owl.
Proper and Common Adjectives	Proper adjectives (in red) are formed from proper nouns. They are always capitalized. Common adjectives (in blue) are any adjectives that are not proper.
	On a cold Wisconsin day, a Hawaiian vacation sounds wonderful.

FORMS OF ADJECTIVES

Positive Adjectives	The positive (base) form of an adjective describes a noun without comparing it to another noun.
	A hummingbird is small.
Comparative Adjectives	The comparative form of an adjective compares two people, places, things, or ideas.
	A hummingbird is smaller than a sparrow.
	(The ending *er* is added to one-syllable adjectives.)
	Hummingbirds are more colorful than sparrows.
	(*More* is added before most adjectives with two or more syllables.)
Superlative Adjectives	The superlative form of an adjective compares three or more people, places, things, or ideas.
	The hummingbird is the smallest bird I've seen.
	(The ending *est* is added to one-syllable adjectives.)
	The parrot is the most colorful bird in the zoo.
	(*Most* is added before most adjectives with two or more syllables.)

Irregular Forms of Adjectives

Positive	Comparative	Superlative
good	better	best
bad	worse	worst
many	more	most
little	less	least

Note: Do not use *more* or *most* with forms of *good* and *bad*.

SPECIAL KINDS OF ADJECTIVES

Compound Adjectives

Compound adjectives are made up of more than one word. Some compound adjectives are spelled as one word; others are hyphenated.

Many white-throated sparrows live in our evergreen bushes.

Demonstrative Adjectives

Demonstrative adjectives point out specific nouns. For example, *this* and *these* point out nouns that are nearby, and *that* and *those* point out nouns that are distant.

This nest has four eggs and that nest has two.
These eggs will hatch before those eggs will.

Indefinite Adjectives

Indefinite adjectives tell approximately (not exactly) how many or how much.

Most students love summer.
Some days are rainy, but few days are boring.

Predicate Adjectives

Predicate adjectives follow linking verbs and describe subjects.

The apples are juicy. They taste sweet.

Two-Syllable Adjectives

Some two-syllable adjectives show comparisons either by their *er / est* endings or by modifiers like *more* and *most*.

friendly	friendlier	friendliest
friendly	more friendly	most friendly

Adverbs

Adverbs are words that modify (describe) verbs, adjectives, or other adverbs. Adverbs tell *how, when, where, how often,* and *how much.*

> **The softball team practices faithfully.**
> (*Faithfully* modifies the verb *practices.*)

> **Yesterday's practice was extra long.**
> (*Extra* modifies the adjective *long.*)

> **Last night the players slept quite soundly.**
> (*Quite* modifies the adverb *soundly.*)

TYPES OF ADVERBS

Adverbs of Time	Adverbs of time tell *when, how often,* or *how long.* **Max batted first.** (when) **Katie's team played weekly.** (how often) **Her team was in first place briefly.** (how long)
Adverbs of Place	Adverbs of place tell *where.* **The first pitch curved inside.** (where) **The batter leaned forward.** (where)
Adverbs of Manner	Adverbs of manner tell *how* something is done. **Max waited eagerly for the next pitch.** (how)
Adverbs of Degree	Adverbs of degree tell *how much* or *how little.* **The catcher was totally surprised.** (how much) **He scarcely saw the fastball coming.** (how little) *Tip:* Adverbs often end in *ly,* but not always. Words like *not, never, very,* and *always* are common adverbs.

FORMS OF ADVERBS

Positive Adverbs	The positive (base) form of an adverb does not make a comparison. **Max plays hard from the first pitch to the last out.**
Comparative Adverbs	The comparative form of an adverb is formed by adding *er* to one-syllable adverbs or the word *more* or *less* before longer adverbs. **He plays harder than his cousin plays.** **He plays more often than his cousin does.**
Superlative Adverbs	The superlative form of an adverb is formed by adding *est* to one-syllable adverbs or the word *most* or *least* before longer adverbs. **Max plays hardest in close games.** **Max plays most often in center field.**

Irregular Forms of Adverbs

Positive	Comparative	Superlative
well	better	best
badly	worse	worst
quickly	more quickly	most quickly
fairly	less fairly	least fairly

Tip: Do not confuse *well* and *good*. *Good* is an adjective and *well* is usually an adverb. (**SEE** page 431.)

Interjections

Interjections are words or phrases that express strong emotion. Commas or exclamation marks are used to separate interjections from the rest of the sentence.

> **Wow, look at those mountains!**

> **Hey! Keep your eyes on the road!**

Prepositions

Prepositions are words that show position or direction and introduce prepositional phrases.

Our cats do what they please in our house.

Object of a Preposition	The object of the preposition is the noun or pronoun that comes after the preposition. **Smacker watches from the desk drawer.** (The noun *drawer* is the object of the preposition *from*.) **Then Smacker ducks inside it.** (The pronoun *it* is the object of the preposition *inside*. The antecedent of the pronoun *it* is the noun *drawer* in the previous sentence.)
Prepositional Phrases	Prepositional phrases include a preposition, the object of the preposition (a noun or a pronoun), and any words that modify the object. **Jo-jo sneaks toward the gerbil cage.** (*Toward* is a preposition, *cage* is the object of the preposition, and *the* and *gerbil* modify *cage*.)

Common Prepositions

aboard	below	in	through
about	beneath	inside	throughout
above	beside	into	till
across	besides	like	to
across from	between	near	toward
after	beyond	of	under
against	but	off	underneath
along	by	on	until
along with	down	onto	up
among	during	out	up to
around	except	outside	upon
at	except for	over	with
before	for	past	within
behind	from	since	without

Conjunctions

Conjunctions connect individual words or groups of words.

The river is wide and deep.

We can fish in the morning or in the evening.

Coordinating Conjunctions	A coordinating conjunction connects equal parts: two or more words, phrases, or clauses. **The river rushes down the valley, and then it winds through the prairie.** (The conjunction *and* connects two independent clauses to make a compound sentence.)
Correlative Conjunctions	A correlative conjunction is used in pairs. **Either snow or wind can make the trip dangerous.** (*Either* and *or* work as a pair in this sentence to connect two words.)
Subordinating Conjunctions	A subordinating conjunction often introduces the dependent clause in a complex sentence. **Our trip was delayed when the snowstorm hit.** **We stayed in town until the snow stopped.**

Common Conjunctions

Coordinating	and, but, or, nor, for, so, yet
Correlative	either/or, neither/nor, not only/but also, both/and, whether/or, as/so
Subordinating	after, although, as, as if, as long as, as though, because, before, if, in order that, since, so, so that, that, though, unless, until, when, where, whereas, while

Tip: Relative pronouns can also connect clauses. (**SEE** page 424.)

Student Almanac

Using Language

In this section, you will find information about the history of the English language. You will also find charts of foreign terms, sign language, Braille, the cursive alphabet, as well as a chart of editing and proofreading marks.

The History of the English Language

An early form of English was first spoken more than 2,000 years ago among a tribe of people in Britain called the Celts. Then people from other countries came to Britain, and the English language used by the Celts mixed with the other languages to form the English of today.

0-1000 C.E. The Romans invaded Britain in the first century, bringing with them the same alphabet we use today. About 500 years later, three Germanic tribes (the Angles, Saxons, and Jutes) crossed the North Sea to Britain. The result was a mixture of the German and Celtic languages.

1066 In 1066, the Normans from France invaded England. They began to use English and added some French words like *hotel* and *nation*. Priests and scholars who used Greek and Latin also began to add some of their words to the language.

1400s At first, people in different places had different ways of speaking English. The invention of printed books in the 1400s helped to change that. As people read more, they began to use a similar kind of English.

English from Around the World

Words from many cultures have been added to English. This chart shows you some of these words.

Old English	man, woman, morning, night, day, month, year, cat, dog, house, red, yellow, at, in, by, from, cow, calf, pig
Scandinavian	they, them, their, knife, sky, ski, happy, scare, egg
French	constitution, city, state, nation, congress, mayor, poetry, art, court, medicine, dance, fashion, tailor, physician, beef, veal, pork
Greek	paragraph, school, alphabet, stomach
Latin	camp, wine, paper, perfume, umbrella, mile, senator, legislator
Native American	canoe, toboggan, opossum, moose, chipmunk, pecan, hickory, igloo, kayak
Spanish	cigar, mosquito, tornado, rodeo, canyon
Italian	spaghetti, pizza, macaroni, balcony, bank, piano, balloon, tarantula, volcano
Dutch	cookie, coleslaw, deck, dock, boss, pump
German	hamburger, kindergarten, pretzel, book
Asian	pepper, panther, shampoo, silk, jungle, tea, ketchup
Australian	kangaroo, boomerang, koala, outback
African	chimpanzee, banana, banjo, okra
Middle Eastern	candy, cotton, coffee, sugar, spinach, tiger

Foreign Words

There are more than 200 major languages in the world today. No wonder people sometimes have trouble communicating, especially when they travel. Here are some foreign words that may help you bridge the "communication gap."

LANGUAGE	HELLO OR GOOD DAY	GOOD-BYE
Chinese (Mandarin dialect)	dzău	dzàijyàn
Danish	hallo	farvel
Farsi (Iran)	salaam ‎سلام	khoda hafez ‎خدا حافظ
French	bonjour	au revoir
German	Guten Tag	Auf Wiedersehen
Hawaiian	aloha	aloha
Hebrew	shalom	shalom
Italian	buon giorno	addio
Polish	hallo	żegnam
Portuguese	alô	adeus
Russian pronunciation	Здравствуйте ZDRAHST-vooy-tyeh	до свидания daw svee-DA-nee-ya
Spanish	hola	adiós
Swahili	neno la kusalimu rafiki au mtani	kwa heri
Swedish	god dag	adjö
Tagalog (Philippines)	kumusta	paalám
Thai	sa wat dee ka	la kone na ka

Note Notice that several languages have similar words for greetings, like the French "bonjour" and the Italian "buon giorno." That's because many languages of today began as the same language thousands of years ago.

Manual Alphabet (Sign Language)

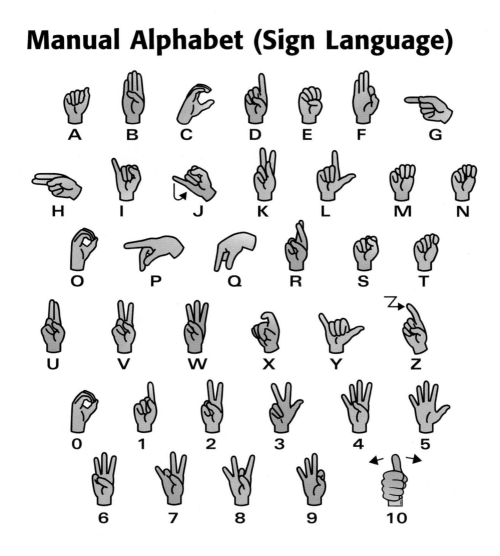

Braille Alphabet and Numbers

Cursive Alphabet

Aa Bb Cc Dd Ee
Ff Gg Hh Ii Jj
Kk Ll Mm Nn
Oo Pp Qq Rr Ss
Tt Uu Vv Ww Xx
Yy Zz 1234567890

Editing and Proofreading Marks

agr.	agreement	*n.c.*	not clear
awk.	awkward expression	⁋	new paragraph
cap. (≡)	capitalization	RO	run-on sentence
ꝺ	delete (take out)	◯ *sp.*	spelling
d. neg.	double negative	TS	topic sentence
frag.	sentence fragment	*u.*	usage
⊙	insert (add) a period	*w.c.*	word choice
∧	insert here	*wordy*	too many words
l.c. (/)	make lowercase	X	find and correct error

Exploring Science

The charts of facts and information in this chapter, from animal facts to metric measurements, will help you throughout the school day.

The World of Science

Animal Facts

Animal	Male	Female	Young	Group	Gestation (days)	Longevity (years)
Bear	He-bear	She-bear	Cub	Sleuth	180-240	18-20 (34)*
Cat	Tom	Queen	Kitten	Clutter/Clowder	52-65	10-17 (30)
Cattle	Bull	Cow	Calf	Drove/Herd	280	9-12 (25)
Chicken	Rooster	Hen	Chick	Brood/Flock	21	7-8 (14)
Deer	Buck	Doe	Fawn	Herd	180-250	10-15 (26)
Dog	Dog	Bitch	Pup	Pack/Kennel	55-70	10-12 (24)
Donkey	Jack	Jenny	Foal	Herd/Pace	340-385	18-20 (63)
Duck	Drake	Duck	Duckling	Brace/Herd	21-35	10 (15)
Elephant	Bull	Cow	Calf	Herd	515-760	30-60 (98)
Fox	Dog	Vixen	Cub/Kit	Skulk	51-60	8-10 (14)
Goat	Billy	Nanny	Kid	Tribe/Herd	135-163	12 (17)
Goose	Gander	Goose	Gosling	Flock/Gaggle	30	25-30
Horse	Stallion	Mare	Filly/Colt	Herd	304-419	20-30 (50+)
Lion	Lion	Lioness	Cub	Pride	105-111	10 (29)
Monkey	Male	Female	Boy/Girl	Band/Troop	149-179	12-15 (29)
Rabbit	Buck	Doe	Bunny	Nest/Warren	27-36	6-8 (15)
Sheep	Ram	Ewe	Lamb	Flock/Drove	121-180	10-15 (16)
Swan	Cob	Pen	Cygnet	Bevy/Flock	30	45-50
Swine	Boar	Sow	Piglet	Litter/Herd	101-130	10 (15)
Tiger	Tiger	Tigress	Cub		105	19
Whale	Bull	Cow	Calf	Gam/Pod/Herd	276-365	37
Wolf	Dog	Bitch	Pup	Pack	63	10-12 (16)

* ( ) Record for oldest animal of this type

Periodic Table of the Elements

Atomic Number	2
Symbol	**He**
	Helium
Atomic Weight (or Mass Number of most stable isotope if in parentheses)	**4.00260**

Legend:
- Alkali metals
- Alkaline earth metals
- Transition metals
- Lanthanide series
- Actinide series
- Other metals
- Nonmetals
- Noble gases

1a	2a	3b	4b	5b	6b	7b	8	8	8	1b	2b	3a	4a	5a	6a	7a	0
1 **H** Hydrogen 1.00797																	2 **He** Helium 4.00260
3 **Li** Lithium 6.941	4 **Be** Beryllium 9.0128											5 **B** Boron 10.811	6 **C** Carbon 12.01115	7 **N** Nitrogen 14.0067	8 **O** Oxygen 15.9994	9 **F** Fluorine 18.9984	10 **Ne** Neon 20.179
11 **Na** Sodium 22.9898	12 **Mg** Magnesium 24.305											13 **Al** Aluminum 26.9815	14 **Si** Silicon 28.0855	15 **P** Phosphorus 30.9738	16 **S** Sulfur 32.064	17 **Cl** Chlorine 35.453	18 **Ar** Argon 39.948
19 **K** Potassium 39.0983	20 **Ca** Calcium 40.08	21 **Sc** Scandium 44.9559	22 **Ti** Titanium 47.88	23 **V** Vanadium 50.94	24 **Cr** Chromium 51.996	25 **Mn** Manganese 54.9380	26 **Fe** Iron 55.847	27 **Co** Cobalt 58.9332	28 **Ni** Nickel 58.69	29 **Cu** Copper 63.546	30 **Zn** Zinc 65.39	31 **Ga** Gallium 69.72	32 **Ge** Germanium 72.59	33 **As** Arsenic 74.9216	34 **Se** Selenium 78.96	35 **Br** Bromine 79.904	36 **Kr** Krypton 83.80
37 **Rb** Rubidium 85.4678	38 **Sr** Strontium 87.62	39 **Y** Yttrium 88.905	40 **Zr** Zirconium 91.224	41 **Nb** Niobium 92.906	42 **Mo** Molybdenum 95.94	43 **Tc** Technetium (98)	44 **Ru** Ruthenium 101.07	45 **Rh** Rhodium 102.906	46 **Pd** Palladium 106.42	47 **Ag** Silver 107.868	48 **Cd** Cadmium 112.41	49 **In** Indium 114.82	50 **Sn** Tin 118.71	51 **Sb** Antimony 121.75	52 **Te** Tellurium 127.60	53 **I** Iodine 126.905	54 **Xe** Xenon 131.29
55 **Cs** Cesium 132.905	56 **Ba** Barium 137.33	57-71* Lanthanides	72 **Hf** Hafnium 178.49	73 **Ta** Tantalum 180.948	74 **W** Tungsten 183.85	75 **Re** Rhenium 186.207	76 **Os** Osmium 190.2	77 **Ir** Iridium 192.22	78 **Pt** Platinum 195.08	79 **Au** Gold 196.967	80 **Hg** Mercury 200.59	81 **Tl** Thallium 204.383	82 **Pb** Lead 207.19	83 **Bi** Bismuth 208.980	84 **Po** Polonium (209)	85 **At** Astatine (210)	86 **Rn** Radon (222)
87 **Fr** Francium (223)	88 **Ra** Radium 226.025	89-103** Actinides	104 **Rf** Rutherfordium (261)	105 **Db** Dubnium (262)	106 **Sg** Seaborgium (263)	107 **Bh** Bohrium (262)	108 **Hs** Hassium (265)	109 **Mt** Meitnerium (266)	110 (269)	111 (272)							

(Of elements 110–121, some are still unknown, and some are recently claimed but unnamed. They have temporary systematic names.)

*Lanthanides	57 **La** Lanthanum 138.906	58 **Ce** Cerium 140.12	59 **Pr** Praseodymium 140.908	60 **Nd** Neodymium 144.24	61 **Pm** Promethium (145)	62 **Sm** Samarium 150.36	63 **Eu** Europium 151.96	64 **Gd** Gadolinium 157.25	65 **Tb** Terbium 158.925	66 **Dy** Dysprosium 162.50	67 **Ho** Holmium 164.930	68 **Er** Erbium 167.26	69 **Tm** Thulium 168.934	70 **Yb** Ytterbium 173.04	71 **Lu** Lutetium 174.967
**Actinides	89 **Ac** Actinium 227.028	90 **Th** Thorium 232.038	91 **Pa** Protactinium 231.036	92 **U** Uranium 238.029	93 **Np** Neptunium 237.048	94 **Pu** Plutonium (244)	95 **Am** Americium (243)	96 **Cm** Curium (247)	97 **Bk** Berkelium (247)	98 **Cf** Californium (251)	99 **Es** Einsteinium (252)	100 **Fm** Fermium (257)	101 **Md** Mendelevium (258)	102 **No** Nobelium (259)	103 **Lr** Lawrencium (260)

Sun

Mercury

Venus

Earth

Mars

Jupiter

Saturn

Our Solar System

There are thousands of galaxies in the universe. Our solar system is in the Milky Way Galaxy, which is 150,000 light-years in diameter. Though this galaxy contains nearly one trillion stars, our solar system has only one star—the sun—and nine planets.

Mercury has the shortest year. It is 88 days long.

Venus spins the slowest. It takes 243 days to spin around once.

Earth supports life for plants, animals, and people.

Mars has less gravity than Earth. A 100-pound person would weigh about 38 pounds on Mars.

Jupiter is the largest planet. It is more than 10 times bigger than Earth.

Saturn has seven rings. It also has the most moons—23.

Uranus has the most rings—15.

Neptune is three times as cold as Earth.

Pluto is the smallest planet and the farthest from the sun.

Uranus

Neptune

Pluto

	Sun	Moon	Mercury	Venus	Earth	Mars	Jupiter	Saturn	Uranus	Neptune	Pluto
Orbital Speed (in miles per second)		0.6	29.8	21.8	18.5	15.0	8.1	6.0	4.2	3.4	3.0
Rotation on Axis	24 days 16 hrs. 48 min.	27 days 7 hrs. 43 min.	59 days	243 days	23 hrs. 56 min.	24 hrs. 37 min.	9 hrs. 55 min.	10 hrs. 39 min.	17 hrs. 8 min.	16 hrs. 7 min.	6 days
Mean Surface Gravity (Earth = 1.00)		0.16	0.38	0.9	1.00	0.38	2.53	1.07	0.91	1.14	0.07
Density (times that of water)	100 (core)	3.3	5.4	5.3	5.5	3.9	1.3	0.7	1.27	1.6	2.03
Mass (times that of Earth)	333,000	0.012	0.056	0.82	6×10^{21} metric tons	0.10	318	95	14.5	17.2	0.0026
Approx. Weight of a 100-Pound Human		16	39	90	100	38	253	107	91	114	7
Number of Satellites	9 planets	0	0	0	1	2	16	23	15	8	1
Mean Distance to Sun (in millions of miles)		93.0	36.0	67.24	92.96	141.7	483.8	887.1	1,783.9	2,796.4	3,666
Revolution Around Sun (in Earth days or years)		365.25 days	88.0 days	224.7 days	365.25 days	687 days	11.86 years	29.46 years	84.0 years	165 years	248 years
Approximate Surface Temperature (degrees Fahrenheit)	10,000° (surface) 27,000,000° (center)	lighted side 260° dark side -280°	-346° to 950°	850°	-126.9° to 136°	-191° to -24°	-236°	-203°	-344°	-360°	-342° to -369°
Diameter (in miles)	865,400	2,155	3,032	7,519	7,926	4,194	88,736	74,978	32,193	30,775	1,423

The Metric System

Even though the metric system is not the official system of measurement in the United States, it is used in science, medicine, and some other fields.

The metric system is a simple form of measurement. It is based on the decimal system (units of 10), so there are no fractions. The table below lists the basic measurements in the metric system.

Linear Measure (Length or Distance)

1 centimeter	= 10 millimeters	= ....0.3937 inch
1 decimeter	= 10 centimeters	= ....3.937 inches
1 meter	= 10 decimeters	= ......39.37 inches or 3.28 feet
1 dekameter	= 10 meters	= ....393.7 inches
1 kilometer	= 1,000 meters	= ....0.621 mile

Square Measure (Area)

1 square centimeter	= 100 square millimeters	= ....0.155 square inch
1 square decimeter	= 100 square centimeters	= ....15.5 square inches
1 square meter	= 100 square decimeters	= 1,549.9 sq. inches or 1.196 sq. yards
1 square dekameter	= 100 square meters	= ....119.6 square yards
1 square kilometer	= 100 square hectometers	= ....0.386 square mile

Capacity Measure

1 centiliter	= 10 milliliters	= ....0.338 fluid ounce
1 deciliter	= 10 centiliters	= ....3.38 fluid ounces
1 liter	= 10 deciliters	= 1.057 liquid qts. or 0.908 dry qt.
1 kiloliter	= 1,000 liters	= 264.18 gallons or 35.315 cubic feet

Land Measure

1 centare	= 1 square meter	= ....1,549.9 square inches
1 hectare	= 100 ares	= ....2.471 acres
1 square kilometer	= 100 hectares	= ....0.386 square mile

Volume Measure

1 cubic centimeter	= 1,000 cubic millimeters	= ....0.061 cubic inch
1 cubic decimeter	= 1,000 cubic centimeters	= ....61.023 cubic inches
1 cubic meter	= 1,000 cubic decimeters	= ....35.314 cubic feet

Weights

1 centigram	= 10 milligrams	= ....0.1543 grain
1 decigram	= 10 centigrams	= ....1.5432 grains
1 gram	= 10 decigrams	= ....15.432 grains
1 dekagram	= 10 grams	= ....0.3527 ounce
1 kilogram	= 1,000 grams	= ....2.2046 pounds

American to Metric Table

The following table shows you what the most common U.S. measurements are in the metric system. You probably already know that 1 inch equals 2.54 centimeters. But did you know that 1 gallon equals 3.7853 liters?

Linear Measure (Length or Distance)

1 inch	=			2.54 centimeters
1 foot	=	12 inches	=	0.3048 meter
1 yard	=	3 feet	=	0.9144 meter
1 mile	=	1,760 yards or 5,280 feet	=	1,609.3 meters

Square Measure (Area)

1 square inch	=			6.452 square centimeters
1 square foot	=	144 square inches	=	929 square centimeters
1 square yard	=	9 square feet	=	0.8361 square meter
1 acre	=	4,840 sq. yards	=	0.4047 hectare
1 square mile	=	640 acres	=	259 hectares or 2.59 sq. kilometers

Cubic Measure

1 cubic inch	=			16.387 cubic centimeters
1 cubic foot	=	1,728 cubic inches	=	0.0283 cubic meter
1 cubic yard	=	27 cubic feet	=	0.7646 cubic meter
1 cord	=	8 cord feet	=	3.625 cubic meters

Dry Measure

1 pint	=			0.5505 liter
1 quart	=	2 pints	=	1.1012 liters
1 peck	=	8 quarts	=	8.8096 liters
1 bushel	=	4 pecks	=	35.2383 liters

Liquid Measure

4 fluid ounces	=	1 gill	=	0.1183 liter
1 pint	=	4 gills	=	0.4732 liter
1 quart	=	2 pints	=	0.9463 liter
1 gallon	=	4 quarts	=	3.7853 liters

Five Ways to Measure When You Don't Have a Ruler

1. Many floor tiles are 12-inch by 12-inch squares.
2. U.S. paper currency is 6-1/8 inches long by 2-5/8 inches wide.
3. A quarter is approximately 1 inch wide.
4. A penny is approximately 3/4 inch wide.
5. A standard sheet of paper is 8-1/2 inches by 11 inches.

Conversion Table

You can use the following table to change, or convert, one unit of measurement into another.

To change	to	multiply by
acres	square miles	0.001562
Celsius	Fahrenheit	1.8*
	*(Multiply Celsius by 1.8; then add 32)	
cubic meters	cubic yards	1.3079
cubic yards	cubic meters	0.7646
Fahrenheit	Celsius	0.55*
	*(Multiply Fahrenheit by 0.55 after subtracting 32)	
feet	meters	0.3048
feet	miles	0.0001894
feet/sec.	miles/hr.	0.6818
grams	ounces	0.0353
grams	pounds	0.002205
inches	centimeters	2.5400
kilowatts	horsepower	1.341
liters	gallons (U.S.)	0.2642
liters	pints (dry)	1.8162
liters	pints (liquid)	2.1134
liters	quarts (dry)	0.9081
liters	quarts (liquid)	1.0567
meters	miles	0.0006214
meters	yards	1.0936
metric tons	tons	1.1023
miles	kilometers	1.6093
miles	feet	5,280
miles/hr.	feet/min.	88
millimeters	inches	0.0394
ounces	grams	28.3495
ounces	pounds	0.0625
pounds	kilograms	0.45359
pounds	ounces	16
quarts (dry)	liters	1.1012
quarts (liquid)	liters	0.94634
square feet	square meters	0.0929
square kilometers	square miles	0.3861
square meters	square feet	10.7639
square miles	square kilometers	2.5900
square yards	square meters	0.8361
tons	metric tons	0.9072
tons	pounds	2,000
yards	meters	0.9144
yards	miles	0.0005682

Other Units of Measure

Below are some additional units of measure that you may come across in or out of school. They are used to measure everything from boards to "light." The ones in the blue box at the bottom of the page are used in shipbuilding, in the military, and with horses.

Astronomical Unit (A.U.) • 93,000,000 miles, the average distance of the earth from the sun (Used in astronomy)

Board Foot (bd. ft.) • 144 cubic inches (12 in. × 12 in. × 1 in.) (Used for measuring lumber)

Bolt • 40 yards (Used for measuring cloth)

Btu • British thermal unit—amount of heat needed to increase the temperature of one pound of water by one degree Fahrenheit (252 calories)

Gross • 12 dozen or 144

Knot • Not a distance, but a rate of speed—one nautical mile per hour

Light, Speed of • 186,281.7 miles per second

Light-year • 5,878,000,000,000 miles—the distance light travels in a year

Pi (π) • 3.14159265+ —the ratio of the circumference of a circle to its diameter

Roentgen • Dosage unit of radiation exposure produced by X rays

Score • 20 units

Sound, Speed of • Usually placed at 1,088 feet per second at 32° Fahrenheit at sea level

Miscellaneous Measurements

3 inches . . = . . 1 palm	18 inches . . . = ... 1 cubit
4 inches . . = . . 1 hand	21.8 inches . . = ... 1 Bible cubit
6 inches . . = . . 1 span	2-1/2 feet . . . = . . 1 military pace

Improving Math Skills

The Language of Math

What's your favorite subject? Your least favorite? Chances are you answered "Math" to one of these questions. Most students either like math a lot or *not at all!* One reason for this is that math has its own language. Some students pick up this language (mostly signs and symbols) very easily; other students don't pick it up so easily. Either way, the following chapter can help you.

In this chapter, you will find step-by-step guidelines for solving word problems, a list of the most common math symbols, and a variety of math tables.

Solving Math Word Problems

In a sense, math word problems are like everyday problems. First you have to understand just what the problem is, and then you can solve it. Using the five-step process on page 452 will also help. The following constellation project will teach you how to use the five steps.

An Everyday Problem

Your class is making pictures of the Big Dipper in science, and it's your job to cut out enough stars for everyone.

At first, this seems easy. But how will you accomplish this task? You won't know until you turn it into a word problem. You can do this by *filling in the numbers* and then *identifying the problem:*

- ■ **First, fill in the numbers:** You need to know how many stars there are in the Big Dipper (7), and how many students there are in your classroom (let's say, 29).

- ■ **Second, identify the problem:** How many stars do you need to cut out altogether so that every student has seven? (29 x 7)

Note When it comes to solving this problem, or any other word problem, be sure to follow all of the steps in the process. It's just too easy to miss important details if you try to take shortcuts.

The Steps in the Process

1 **Read or listen to the problem carefully.** Pay attention to key words and phrases, such as "in all" or "how many." In the Big Dipper problem on page 451, the phrases "how many" and "altogether" appear.

2 **Collect the information.** Gather all the information you need to solve the problem. The information you need to solve the Big Dipper problem includes the numbers 7 and 29. (Don't forget, sometimes numbers are written as words.)

Hint: Study any maps, charts, or graphs that go along with the problem. They often contain important information.

3 **Set up the problem.** Decide whether you need to add, subtract, multiply, or divide.

- The following words tell you to add or multiply:
  in all, in total, altogether.
- These phrases tell you to subtract:
  how many more than, how many less than, find the difference, how many are left, how much younger than.
- These phrases tell you to divide:
  how much ... each, how many ... each.

4 **Solve the problem.** Show all of your work so you can check it later. Here's the Big Dipper problem again:

$$\begin{array}{ll} 29 & \text{students} \\ \times\ 7 & \text{stars for each student} \\ \hline 203 & \text{stars altogether} \end{array}$$

5 **Check your answer.** Here are several ways: Do the problem again, do it a different way, use a calculator, or start with your answer and work backward. For example, the answer (product) to the Big Dipper problem was 203. If you divide 203 by 7, you should get 29. Or if you divide 203 by 29, you should get 7.

Word Problem Practice

1 **Read the problem carefully.** The soccer team parents bought 48 cans of cola, 36 cans of root beer, and 36 cans of lemon-lime soda to sell at the soccer match. Only 42 cans of soda were sold. How many cans were left?

2 **Collect the information.** After you read the problem, you know how many cans of soda were purchased—48, 36, and 36. You also know how many cans were sold—42.

3 **Set up the problem.**

$$
\begin{array}{r}
2 \\
48 \\
36 \\
+36 \\
\hline
120
\end{array}
$$

Discussion: This is really a two-step problem. Before you can find out how many cans of soda were left, you have to find out how many cans there were to begin with. So you add 48, 36, and 36 for a total of 120.

4 **Solve the problem.**

$$
\begin{array}{r}
1\ 10 \\
1\cancel{2}0 \\
-\ 42 \\
\hline
78
\end{array}
$$

Discussion: Then subtract the 42 cans sold in order to find out the number of cans remaining.

5 **Check your answer.**

$$
\begin{array}{r}
1 \\
78 \\
+\ 42 \\
\hline
120
\end{array}
$$

Discussion: Check your work. You can check a subtraction problem by adding your answer to the second number in the subtraction problem. Make sure your answer makes sense.

(**Answer:** 78 cans of soda were left.)

Symbols, Numbers, and Tables

The following two pages will help you with your basic math work. The first list includes common symbols and their meanings; the second list includes more advanced symbols. The other tables include prime numbers, multiplication facts, decimal equivalents, and Roman numerals.

Common Math Symbols

+	plus (addition)
−	minus (subtraction)
×	multiplied by
÷	divided by
=	is equal to
≠	is not equal to
%	percent
¢	cents
$	dollars
°	degree
′	minute (also foot)
″	second (also inch)

Advanced Math Symbols

<	is less than
>	is greater than
±	plus or minus
:	is to (ratio)
π	pi
$\sqrt{}$	square root
≥	is greater than or equal to
≤	is less than or equal to
∠	angle
⊥	is perpendicular to
‖	is parallel to
∴	therefore

A Chart of Prime Numbers Less than 500

2	3	5	7	11	13	17	19	23	29
31	37	41	43	47	53	59	61	67	71
73	79	83	89	97	101	103	107	109	113
127	131	137	139	149	151	157	163	167	173
179	181	191	193	197	199	211	223	227	229
233	239	241	251	257	263	269	271	277	281
283	293	307	311	313	317	331	337	347	349
353	359	367	373	379	383	389	397	401	409
419	421	431	433	439	443	449	457	461	463
467	479	487	491	499					

Table of Basic Multiplication Facts

X	0	1	2	3	4	5	6	7	8	9	10
0	0	0	0	0	0	0	0	0	0	0	0
1	0	1	2	3	4	5	6	7	8	9	10
2	0	2	4	6	8	10	12	14	16	18	20
3	0	3	6	9	12	15	18	21	24	27	30
4	0	4	8	12	16	20	24	28	32	36	40
5	0	5	10	15	20	25	30	35	40	45	50
6	0	6	12	18	24	30	36	42	48	54	60
7	0	7	14	21	28	35	42	49	56	63	70
8	0	8	16	24	32	40	48	56	64	72	80
9	0	9	18	27	36	45	54	63	72	81	90
10	0	10	20	30	40	50	60	70	80	90	100

Decimal Equivalents of Common Fractions

1/2	.5000	1/32	.0313	3/11	.2727	6/11	.5455
1/3	.3333	1/64	.0156	4/5	.8000	7/8	.8750
1/4	.2500	2/3	.6667	4/7	.5714	7/9	.7778
1/5	.2000	2/5	.4000	4/9	.4444	7/10	.7000
1/6	.1667	2/7	.2857	4/11	.3636	7/11	.6364
1/7	.1429	2/9	.2222	5/6	.8333	7/12	.5833
1/8	.1250	2/11	.1818	5/7	.7143	8/9	.8889
1/9	.1111	3/4	.7500	5/8	.6250	8/11	.7273
1/10	.1000	3/5	.6000	5/9	.5556	9/10	.9000
1/11	.0909	3/7	.4286	5/11	.4545	9/11	.8182
1/12	.0833	3/8	.3750	5/12	.4167	10/11	.9091
1/16	.0625	3/10	.3000	6/7	.8571	11/12	.9167

Roman Numerals

I	1	**VII**	7	**XL**	40	**C**	100	$\overline{\text{C}}$	100,000
II	2	**VIII**	8	**L**	50	**D**	500	$\overline{\text{D}}$	500,000
III	3	**IX**	9	**LX**	60	**M**	1,000	$\overline{\text{M}}$	1,000,000
IV	4	**X**	10	**LXX**	70	$\overline{\text{V}}$	5,000		
V	5	**XX**	20	**LXXX**	80	$\overline{\text{X}}$	10,000		
VI	6	**XXX**	30	**XC**	90	$\overline{\text{L}}$	50,000		

Using Maps

All About Maps

Maps have many uses. There are different kinds of maps for each of the different uses. Your handbook uses one kind of map, the *political map*. Political maps show how the earth is divided into countries and states. They also show the capitals and major cities. Usually, the most important names on a map are typed in the largest print.

In this section, you will learn how to use maps. You will learn how to find the countries of the world, as well as interesting facts about the continents, oceans, and rivers.

Map Symbols

Mapmakers use many special marks and symbols. Below you'll find the most common ones.

The Compass Rose

The *compass rose* is used to show direction (north, south, east, and west). On most maps, north is at the top. But you should always check the *compass rose* to make sure you know where north is. If there is no symbol, you can assume that north is at the top of the page.

The Legend

The *legend,* or *key,* is a box printed on a map that contains important marks and symbols. The legend will help you understand and use the map. This map legend, which goes with the United States map on page 461, includes symbols, cities, and state boundaries.

UNITED STATES

⊛	National Capitals	———	International Boundaries
Austin ⊙	State Capitals	- - - - -	State Boundaries
Dallas •	Cities	**TEXAS**	State Names

0   100   200   300   400 Miles

The Map Scale

The *map scale* shows you how far it really is between places. For example, a scale might show that one inch on the map equals 400 miles on the earth. If two cities are shown three inches apart, then they are really 1200 miles apart. A ruler makes using a scale easy. Here is the scale from the map of the United States.

0   100   200   300   400 Miles

Hint: If you don't have a ruler, use a piece of paper. Put a dot on your paper at "0." Put another dot on your paper at the 100-, 200-, 300-, and 400-mile marks. Your paper can now be used to measure the distance between points on the map. (Map scales differ, so always check the scale on the map you are using.)

Latitude and Longitude

Latitude and *longitude* lines are another feature of most maps. These imaginary lines, placed on a map by mapmakers, are used to locate any point on the earth.

Latitude • The lines that go from east to west around the earth are called lines of **latitude.** The line of latitude that goes around the earth exactly halfway between the North Pole and the South Pole is called the *equator.* Latitude is measured in degrees, with the equator being 0 degrees (0°).

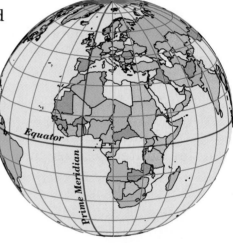

Above the equator, the lines are called *north latitude* and measure from 0° to 90° north (the North Pole). Below the equator, the lines are called *south latitude* and measure from 0° to 90° south (the South Pole). On a map, latitude numbers are printed along the sides.

Longitude • The lines that run from the North Pole to the South Pole are lines of **longitude.** Longitude is also measured in degrees, beginning with 0 degrees. The north-south line measuring 0° passes through Greenwich, England. It is called the *prime meridian.*

Lines east of the prime meridian are called *east longitude.* Lines west of the prime meridian are called *west longitude.* On a map, longitude numbers are printed at the top and bottom.

Coordinates • The latitude and longitude numbers of a country or other place are called its **coordinates.** In each set of coordinates, latitude is given first, then longitude. To locate a place on a map using its coordinates, find the point where the two lines cross. (**SEE** pages 469-471.)

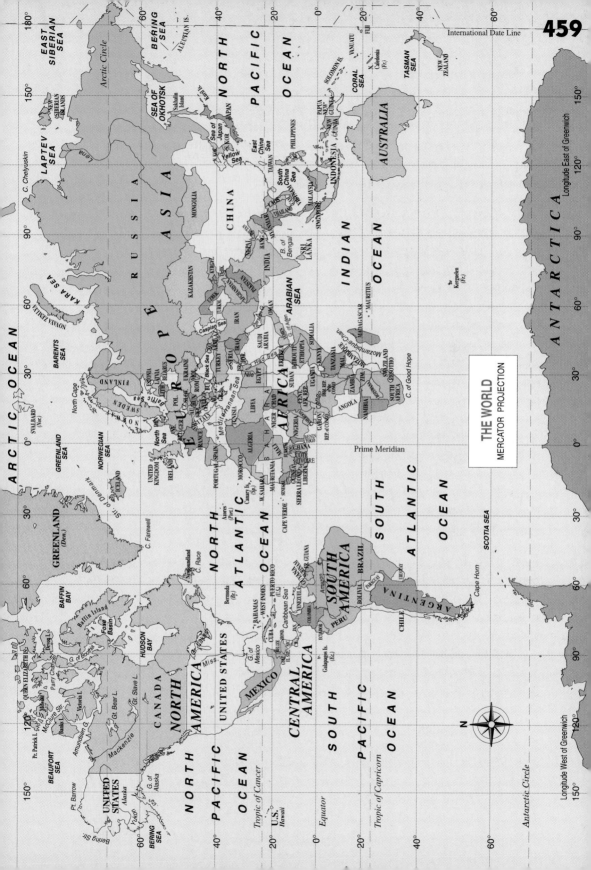

THE WORLD

MERCATOR PROJECTION

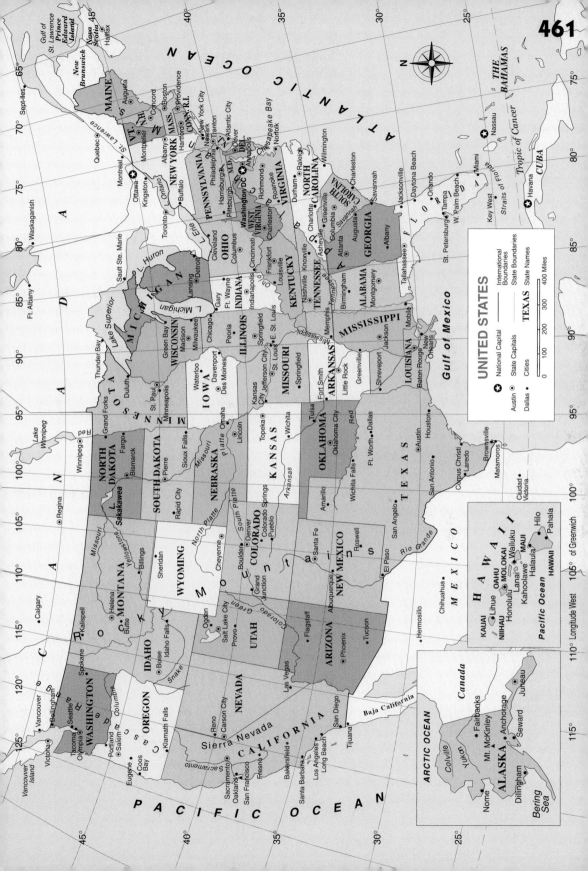

GULF OF MEXICO

NORTH ATLANTIC OCEAN

Straits of Florida

Tropic of Cancer

U.S.A.

MEXICO

Yucatan Channel

Grand Bahama
Great Bahama
Freeport
Bimini Islands
Andros Island
New Providence
Nassau
Eleuthera
Great Abaco
THE BAHAMAS
Cat Island
San Salvador
Rum Cay
Long Island
Great Exuma
Crooked Island
Acklins Island
Mayaguana
Great Inagua

TURKS AND CAICOS ISLANDS (U.K.)
Grand Turk

Pinar del Río
Havana
Matanzas
Santa Clara
Cienfuegos
Isla de la Juventud
CUBA
Camaguey
Holguín
Santiago de Cuba
Guantanamo

Cayman Islands (U.K.)
George Town

JAMAICA
Kingston

Santiago
Cap-Haïtien
HAITI
Port-au-Prince
DOM. REP.
Santo Domingo

GREATER ANTILLES

Anguilla (U.K.)

WEST INDIES

British Virgin Islands (U.K.)
Virgin Islands
San Juan
Puerto Rico (U.S.)
St. Croix (U.S.)

St. Barthelemy (FRANCE)
St. Martin (FRANCE and NETH.)
Neth. Antilles (U.S.)
Basseterre
ST. KITTS & NEVIS
Montserrat (U.K.)
ANTIGUA
St. Johns
BARBUDA &
GUADELOUPE (FRANCE)
Basse-Terre
Marie Galante
DOMINICA
Roseau
MARTINIQUE (FRANCE)
Fort-de-France
Castries
ST. LUCIA
BARBADOS
Bridgetown
ST. VINCENT &
THE GRENADINES
Kingstown
GRENADA
St. George's
Tobago
TRINIDAD & TOBAGO
Port-of-Spain
Trinidad

LESSER ANTILLES

NETHERLAND ANTILLES (NETH.)
Aruba
Curaçao
Bonaire
Willemstad

GUYANA

VENEZUELA

COLOMBIA

CARIBBEAN SEA

N

La Palma
Colon
Panama Canal
Panama
PANAMA
Santiago
David
Gulf of Panama

Puerto Limon
Sag. Jose
San Jose
COSTA RICA
Liberia
Golfito

Puerto Cabezas
Bluefields
NICARAGUA
Matagalpa
Coco
Puerto
Lempira
Lago de Managua
Lago de Nicaragua
Managua
León
Granada
Rivas
San Juan

HONDURAS
San Pedro Sula
Tegucigalpa
Islas de la Bahia
Patuca
Ulua

BELIZE
Belize City
Belmopan
Gulf of Honduras

GUATEMALA
Puerto Barrios
Coban
Motagua
Quezaltenango
Guatemala City
Flores
Usumacinta

EL SALVADOR
San Salvador
San Miguel

NORTH PACIFIC OCEAN

CENTRAL AMERICA

Longitude West of Greenwich

CENTRAL AMERICA
0   200 Km
0   200 Mi.
Capitals of Countries
International Boundaries

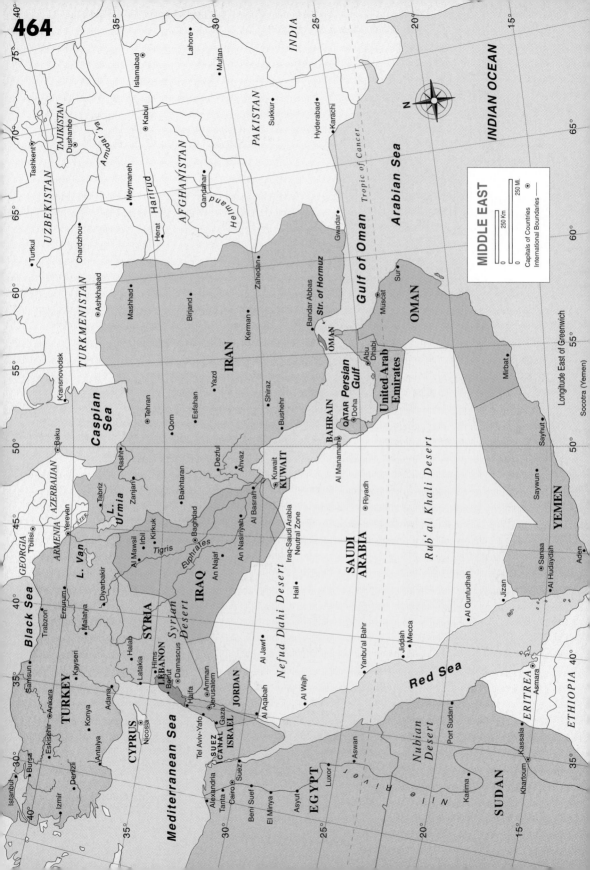

MIDDLE EAST

INDIAN OCEAN

Arabian Sea

Gulf of Oman

Str. of Hormuz

Tropic of Cancer

INDIA

Lahore •
• Multan

PAKISTAN

Hyderabad •
• Karachi

Sukkur •

AFGHANISTAN

Islamabad ⊙
• Kabul

Dushanbe ⊙

TAJIKISTAN

Tashkent ⊙

UZBEKISTAN

Turkul •

Amu Dar'ya

Meymaneh •

Herat •

Qandahar •

Harirud

Helmand

Chardzhou •

Ashkhabad ⊙

TURKMENISTAN

Kransnovodsk •

Baku ⊙

AZERBAIJAN

Yerevan ⊙

ARMENIA

Tbilisi ⊙

GEORGIA

Rasht •

Caspian Sea

Mashhad •

Birjand •

IRAN

Tehran •

Qom •

Esfahan •

Yazd •

Kerman •

Shiraz •

Bushehr •

Zahedan •

Gwadar •

Bandar Abbas •

OMAN

Sur •

Muscat ⊙

OMAN

Abu Dhabi ⊙

United Arab Emirates

Mirbat •

Sayhut •

Saywun •

YEMEN

Sanaa •

Aden •

Al Hudaydah •

Jizan •

Al Qunfudhah •

Socotra (Yemen)

Longitude East of Greenwich

Rub' al Khali Desert

SAUDI ARABIA

Riyadh ⊙

Doha ⊙

QATAR *Persian Gulf*

BAHRAIN

Al Manamah ⊙

Kuwait •

KUWAIT

Al Basrah •

An Nasiriyah •

An Najaf •

Baghdad •

Euphrates

Tigris

Kirkuk •

Irbil •

Al Mawsil •

IRAQ

Deztul •

Ahvaz •

Bakhtaran •

Zanjan •

Tabriz •

Urmia

L. Urmia

L. Van

Diyarbakir •

Malatya •

Erzurum •

Trabzon •

Samsun •

TURKEY

Ankara ⊙

Eskişehir •

Kayseri •

Konya •

Adana •

Antalya •

Denizli •

Izmir •

Bursa •

Istanbul •

Black Sea

Mediterranean Sea

CYPRUS

Nicosia ⊙

Latakia •

Halab •

Hims •

SYRIA

Damascus ⊙

LEBANON

Beirut ⊙

Syrian Desert

Haifa •

Tel Aviv-Yafo •

Gaza

Jerusalem ⊙

ISRAEL

Amman ⊙

JORDAN

Al Aqabah •

Al Jawf •

Nefud Dahi Desert

Haïl •

Iraq-Saudi Arabia
Neutral Zone

Al Wajh •

Yanbu'al Bahr •

Jiddah •

Mecca •

Red Sea

Nubian Desert

Port Sudan •

Kassala •

Khartoum ⊙

Katima •

SUDAN

ERITREA

Asmara ⊙

ETHIOPIA

Aswan •

Luxor •

Asyut •

El Minya •

Beni Suef •

Cairo ⊙

Suez •

SUEZ CANAL

Tanta •

Alexandria •

EGYPT

Nile River

N

0   250 Km
0   250 Mi.

⊙ Capitals of Countries
—— International Boundaries

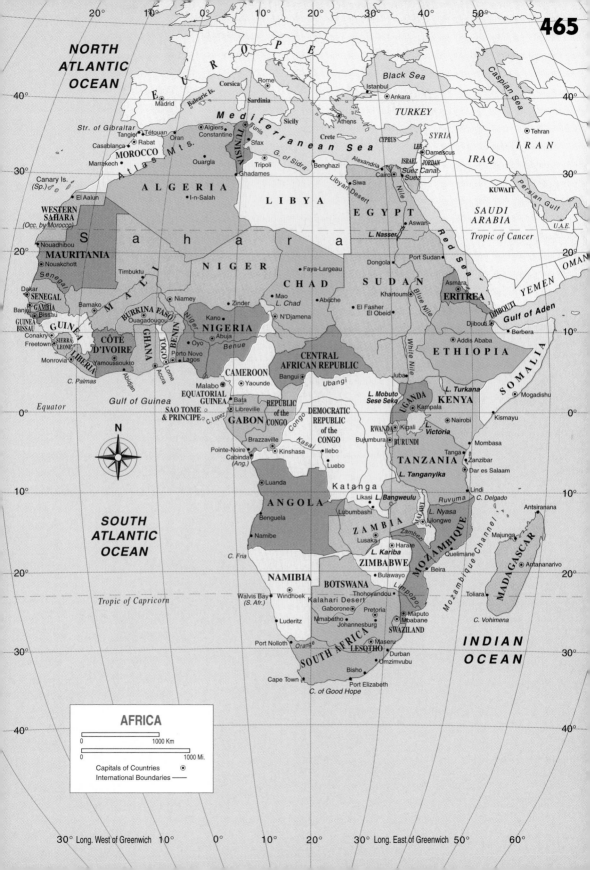

ATLANTIC
OCEAN

GREENLAND

UNITED STATES
(Alaska)

ARCTIC
North Pole
OCEAN

ICELAND

BERING
SEA

BRITISH ISLES

EAST
SIBERIAN
SEA

ALEUTIAN IS.

Anadyr

BARENTS
SEA

SVALBARD

NOVAYA ZEMLYA

SEVERNAYA
ZEMLYA

Komandorskiye Is.

London
NORTH
SEA

KARA SEA

LAPTEV SEA

Kolyma

Srednekolymsk

Magadan

Kamchatka Pen.

Petropavlovsk-
Kamchatskiy

Paris

Berlin

BALTIC SEA

St. Petersburg

Nordvik

R

Dudinka

Arctic Circle

Lena

Yakutsk

SEA OF
OKHOTSK

Vienna

Warsaw

Moscow

Salekhard

Yenisey

Tura

Nikolayevsk

Sakhalin I.

KURIL IS.

Kiev

U

S

S

I

A

Khanty-Mansiysk

L.
Baykal

Komsomol'sk
Skovorodino

Amur

Khabarovsk

Hokkaido

Perm'

Yekaterinburg
Chelyabinsk
Magnitogorsk

Ob'

Tomsk

Krasnoyarsk

Kirensk

Irkutsk

Chita

Qiqihar
Changchun

Hakodate

Vladivostok

Sendai
Honshu

EUROPE

Ural'sk

Omsk

Novosibirsk

Ulan-Ude

Shenyang

SEA
OF
JAPAN

Istanbul

BLACK SEA

Gur'yev

KAZAKHSTAN

Barnaul

Semipalatinsk

Uliastay

Hovd

Ulaanbaatar

MONGOLIA

Gobi

Beijing

Dandong

KOREA

Seoul

KOREA

Tokyo

Nagoya

Izmir

Ankara

Karaganda

ARAL SEA

L. Balkhash

INNER MONGOLIA

Great Wall

Tianjin

Pyongyang

Hiroshima
Shikoku

TURKEY

Erzurum

CASPIAN SEA

Bishkek

KYRGYZ.

Urumqi

Huang

GRAND CANAL

Jinan

YELLOW
SEA

Kyushu

Nagasaki

MED.
SEA

Adana

Aleppo

Tabriz

Krasnovodsk

Tashkent

Alma-Ata

SINKIANG

Yumen

Lanzhou

Kaifeng

Shanghai

EAST
CHINA
SEA

RYUKYUS
(Jap.)

Tropic of Cancer

CYPRUS

LEBANON

Beirut

Damascus

SYRIA

Ashkhabad

UZBEK.

Kokand

Aksu

Xi'an

Wuhan

Jerusalem

ISRAEL

Amman

IRAQ

Baghdad

Tehran

TURKMENISTAN

TAJIK.

Shache

Hotan

CHINA

Chongqing

Changsha

Fuzhou

Taipei

JORDAN

Basra

IRAN

Mashad

Herat

Kabul

TIBET

Lhasa

Chang (Yangtze)

TAIWAN

KUWAIT

AFGHANISTAN

Islamabad

HIMALAYA

Thimphu

Guangzhou

HONG KONG

BAHRAIN

Shiraz

Quetta

Srinagar

NEPAL

BHUTAN

Brahmaputra

QATAR

Bandar
Abbas

PAKISTAN

New Delhi

Kathmandu

Luzon

PHILIPPINES

Mecca

Riyadh

U.N. ARAB
EMIR.

Muscat

Gwadar

Indus

Kanpur

Mandalay

Myitkyina

Hanoi

Hainan

Manila

Samar

SAUDI
ARABIA

OMAN

Karachi

INDIA

Dhaka

BANGLA-
DESH

MYANMAR

LAOS

G. of Tonkin

SOUTH
CHINA
SEA

Mindoro

Leyte

Sanaa

YEMEN

Ahmadabad

Calcutta

Vientiane

Rangoon

THAILAND

VIETNAM

Palawan

Negros

Davao

Aden

G. of Aden

ARABIAN
SEA

Daman

Bombay

Hyderabad

Yanam

Bangkok

CAMBODIA

Phnom Penh

Mindanao

Socotra

BAY OF
BENGAL

Ho Chi Minh City
(Saigon)

Kota Kinabalu

SABAH

Bangalore

Madras

Mahe

Karikal

G. of
Thailand

BRUNEI

SARAWAK

CELEBES
SEA

Manado

Madurai

SRI LANKA
(CEYLON)

George Town

MALAYA

MALAYSIA

Kuching

Celebes

SEYCHELLES

Colombo

Kandy

Medan

Kuala Lumpur

SINGAPORE

Borneo

Banjarmasin

Ujung Pandang

BANDA
SEA

MALDIVES

Male

Sumatra

Str. of Malacca

Makassar Str.

Timor

Equator

Palembang

Jakarta

JAVA

Surabaya

INDONESIA

JAVA SEA

Sumbawa

FLORES SEA

Flores

TIMOR
SEA

N

MADAGASCAR

SUNDA IS.

INDIAN OCEAN

AUSTRALIA

Tropic of Capricorn

Broome

Perth

ASIA

0   1200 Km

0   1200 Mi.

⊙ Capitals of Countries

—— International Boundaries

Longitude East of Greenwich

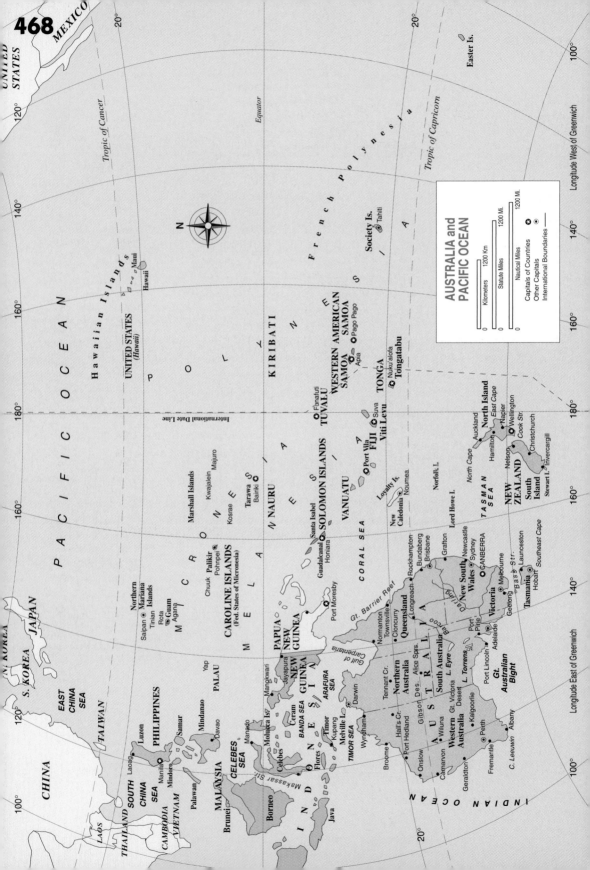

MEXICO

UNITED STATES

CHINA

N. KOREA

S. KOREA

JAPAN

TAIWAN

THAILAND

CAMBODIA

VIETNAM

LAOS

PHILIPPINES

Luzon

Laoag

Mindoro

Manila

Samar

Mindanao

Davao

MALAYSIA

Brunei

Borneo

Palawan

Celebes

Manado

Java

Flores

EAST
CHINA
SEA

SOUTH
CHINA
SEA

CELEBES
SEA

BANDA SEA

TIMOR SEA

ARAFURA
SEA

Makassar Str.

PACIFIC OCEAN

Tropic of Cancer

Equator

Tropic of Capricorn

Hawaiian Islands

Maui

Hawaii

UNITED STATES
(Hawaii)

P O L Y N E S I A

French Polynesia

Society Is.

Tahiti

Easter Is.

Longitude West of Greenwich

Longitude East of Greenwich

International Date Line

KIRIBATI

Fanafuti

TUVALU

Suva

FIJI

Viti Levu

WESTERN
SAMOA

AMERICAN
SAMOA

Pago Pago

Apia

TONGA

Nuku'alofa

Tongatabu

Marshall Islands

Kwajalein

Majuro

Kosrae

Tarawa

Bairiki

NAURU

Chuuk

Palikir

Pohnpei

CAROLINE ISLANDS
(Fed. States of Micronesia)

Yap

PALAU

Northern
Mariana
Islands

Saipan

Tinian Islands

Rota

Agana

Guam

M I C R O N E S I A

M E L A N E S I A

SOLOMON ISLANDS

Santa Isabel

Guadalcanal

Honiara

VANUATU

Port Vila

New
Caledonia

Noumea

Loyalty Is.

Norfolk I.

Lord Howe I.

CORAL
SEA

Gt. Barrier Reef

PAPUA
NEW
GUINEA

Manokwari

Jayapura

NEW
GUINEA

Port Moresby

Gulf of
Carpentaria

Moluca Isl.

Ceram

Timor

Kupang

Melville I.

Bathurst I.

Darwin

Wyndham

Broome

Port Hedland

Hall's Cr.

Onslow

Carnarvon

Geraldton

Wiluna

Western
Australia

Kalgoorlie

C. Leeuwin

Fremantle

Perth

Gt. Victoria
Desert

Gibson Des.

Great Sandy Des.

Alice Sprs.

Tennant Cr.

Northern
Australia

Normanton

Townsville

Cloncurry

Longreach

Queensland

Rockhampton

Bundaberg

Brisbane

Grafton

Newcastle

Sydney

New South
Wales

CANBERRA

Melbourne

Victoria

Geelong

South Australia

L. Eyre

L. Torrens

Port
Augusta

Port Pirie

Port Lincoln

Adelaide

Gt.
Australian
Bight

A U S T R A L I A

Flinders R.

Darling

Murray

Gt. Dividing Ra.

Bass Str.

Tasmania

Hobart

Launceston

Southeast Cape

TASMAN
SEA

NEW
ZEALAND

North Cape

North Island

East Cape

Auckland

Hamilton

Napier

Wellington

Cook Str.

Nelson

Christchurch

South Island

Invercargill

Stewart I.

INDIAN OCEAN

INDONESIA

Index to World Maps

Country	Latitude	Longitude	Country	Latitude	Longitude
Afghanistan	33° N	65° E	Comoros	12° S	44° E
Albania	41° N	20° E	Congo,		
Algeria	28° N	3° E	Dem. Rep. of the	4° S	25° E
Andorra	42° N	1° E	Congo,		
Angola	12° S	18° E	Rep. of the	1° S	15° E
Antigua and			Costa Rica	10° N	84° W
Barbuda	17° N	61° W	Côte d'Ivoire	8° N	5° W
Argentina	34° S	64° W	Croatia	45° N	16° E
Armenia	41° N	45° E	Cuba	21° N	80° W
Australia	25° S	135° E	Cyprus	35° N	33° E
Austria	47° N	13° E	Czech Republic	50° N	15° E
Azerbaijan	41° N	47° E	Denmark	56° N	10° E
Bahamas	24° N	76° W	Djibouti	11° N	43° E
Bahrain	26° N	50° E	Dominica	15° N	61° W
Bangladesh	24° N	90° E	Dominican Republic	19° N	70° W
Barbados	13° N	59° W	Ecuador	2° S	77° W
Belarus	54° N	25° E	Egypt	27° N	30° E
Belgium	50° N	4° E	El Salvador	14° N	89° W
Belize	17° N	88° W	Equatorial Guinea	2° N	9° E
Benin	9° N	2° E	Eritrea	17° N	38° E
Bhutan	27° N	90° E	Estonia	59° N	26° E
Bolivia	17° S	65° W	Ethiopia	8° N	38° E
Bosnia-			Fiji	19° S	174° E
Herzegovina	44° N	18° E	Finland	64° N	26° E
Botswana	22° S	24° E	France	46° N	2° E
Brazil	10° S	55° W	Gabon	1° S	11° E
Brunei Darussalam	4° N	114° E	The Gambia	13° N	16° W
Bulgaria	43° N	25° E	Georgia	43° N	45° E
Burkina Faso	13° N	2° W	Germany	51° N	10° E
Burundi	3° S	30° E	Ghana	8° N	2° W
Cambodia	13° N	105° E	Greece	39° N	22° E
Cameroon	6° N	12° E	Greenland	70° N	40° W
Canada	60° N	95° W	Grenada	12° N	61° W
Cape Verde	16° N	24° W	Guatemala	15° N	90° W
Central African			Guinea	11° N	10° W
Republic	7° N	21° E	Guinea-Bissau	12° N	15° W
Chad	15° N	19° E	Guyana	5° N	59° W
Chile	30° S	71° W	Haiti	19° N	72° W
China	35° N	105° E	Honduras	15° N	86° W
Colombia	4° N	72° W	Hungary	47° N	20° E

Country	Latitude	Longitude	Country	Latitude	Longitude
Iceland	65° N	18° W	Montenegro	43° N	19° E
India	20° N	77° E	Morocco	32° N	5° W
Indonesia	5° S	120° E	Mozambique	18° S	35° E
Iran	32° N	53° E	Myanmar	22° N	98° E
Iraq	33° N	44° E	Namibia	22° S	17° E
Ireland	53° N	8° W	Nauru	1° S	166° E
Israel	31° N	35° E	Nepal	28° N	84° E
Italy	42° N	12° E	The Netherlands	52° N	5° E
Jamaica	18° N	77° W	New Zealand	41° S	174° E
Japan	36° N	138° E	Nicaragua	13° N	85° W
Jordan	31° N	36° E	Niger	16° N	8° E
Kazakhstan	45° N	70° E	Nigeria	10° N	8° E
Kenya	1° N	38° E	Northern Ireland	55° N	7° W
Kiribati	0° N	175° E	Norway	62° N	10° E
North Korea	40° N	127° E	Oman	22° N	58° E
South Korea	36° N	128° E	Pakistan	30° N	70° E
Kuwait	29° N	47° E	Palau	8° N	138° E
Kyrgyzstan	42° N	75° E	Panama	9° N	80° W
Laos	18° N	105° E	Papua New Guinea	6° S	147° E
Latvia	57° N	25° E	Paraguay	23° S	58° W
Lebanon	34° N	36° E	Peru	10° S	76° W
Lesotho	29° S	28° E	The Philippines	13° N	122° E
Liberia	6° N	10° W	Poland	52° N	19° E
Libya	27° N	17° E	Portugal	39° N	8° W
Liechtenstein	47° N	9° E	Qatar	25° N	51° E
Lithuania	56° N	24° E	Romania	46° N	25° E
Luxembourg	49° N	6° E	Russia	60° N	80° E
Macedonia	43° N	22° E	Rwanda	2° S	30° E
Madagascar	19° S	46° E	St. Kitts and Nevis	17° N	62° W
Malawi	13° S	34° E	Saint Lucia	14° N	61° W
Malaysia	2° N	112° E	Saint Vincent and		
Maldives	2° N	70° E	the Grenadines	13° N	61° W
Mali	17° N	4° W	San Marino	44° N	12° E
Malta	36° N	14° E	São Tomé and		
Marshall Islands	7° N	172° E	Príncipe	1° N	7° E
Mauritania	20° N	12° W	Saudi Arabia	25° N	45° E
Mauritius	20° S	57° E	Scotland	57° N	5° W
Mexico	23° N	102° W	Senegal	14° N	14° W
Micronesia	5° N	150° E	Serbia	45° N	21° E
Moldova	47° N	28° E	Seychelles	5° S	55° E
Monaco	43° N	7° E	Sierra Leone	8° N	11° W
Mongolia	46° N	105° E	Singapore	1° N	103° E

Country	Latitude	Longitude	Country	Latitude	Longitude
Slovakia	49° N	19° E	Tunisia	34° N	9° E
Slovenia	46° N	15° E	Turkey	39° N	35° E
Solomon Islands	8° S	159° E	Turkmenistan	40° N	55° E
Somalia	10° N	49° E	Tuvalu	8° S	179° E
South Africa	30° S	26° E	Uganda	1° N	32° E
Spain	40° N	4° W	Ukraine	50° N	30° E
Sri Lanka	7° N	81° E	United Arab		
Sudan	15° N	30° E	Emirates	24° N	54° E
Suriname	4° N	56° W	United Kingdom	54° N	2° W
Swaziland	26° S	31° E	United States	38° N	97° W
Sweden	62° N	15° E	Uruguay	33° S	56° W
Switzerland	47° N	8° E	Uzbekistan	40° N	68° E
Syria	35° N	38° E	Vanuatu	17° S	170° E
Taiwan	23° N	121° E	Venezuela	8° N	66° W
Tajikistan	39° N	71° E	Vietnam	17° N	106° E
Tanzania	6° S	35° E	Wales	53° N	3° W
Thailand	15° N	100° E	Western Samoa	10° S	173° W
Togo	8° N	1° E	Yemen	15° N	44° E
Tonga	20° S	173° W	Yugoslavia	44° N	19° E
Trinidad and			Zambia	15° S	30° E
Tobago	11° N	61° W	Zimbabwe	20° S	30° E

Geographic Facts

CONTINENTS	Area (Sq Km)	Percent of Earth's Land
Asia	44,026,000	29.7
Africa	30,271,000	20.4
North America	24,258,000	16.3
South America	17,823,000	12.0
Antarctica	13,209,000	8.9
Europe	10,404,000	7.0
Australia	7,682,000	5.2

MAJOR ISLANDS	Area (Sq Km)
Greenland	2,175,600
New Guinea	792,500
Borneo	725,500
Madagascar	587,000
Baffin	507,500
Sumatra	427,300
Honshu	227,400
Great Britain	218,100

LONGEST RIVERS	Length (Km)
Nile, *Africa*	6,671
Amazon, *South America*	6,437
Chang Jiang (Yangtze), *Asia*	6,380
Mississippi-Missouri	5,971
Ob-Irtysk, *Asia*	5,410

OCEANS	Area (Sq Km)	Percent of Earth's Water
Pacific	166,241,000	46.0
Atlantic	86,557,000	23.9
Indian	73,427,000	20.3
Arctic	9,485,000	2.6

Making History

This section of your handbook includes a close look at the United States Constitution, a chart of presidents and vice presidents, and a historical time line.

The U.S. Constitution

Of the many history-making events in United States history, none is more important than the convention held in Philadelphia in 1787. It was held to revise the Articles of Confederation. Instead, the delegates decided to write a new plan for the government.

By the time the convention ended, George Washington and the other delegates had passed the United States Constitution. Through the years, this Constitution has been changed (amended) several times, but it is still the "law of the land," just as it was 200 years ago.

The Parts of the Constitution

The U.S. Constitution has three main parts: a **preamble,** 7 **articles,** and 27 **amendments.** The *preamble* states the purpose of the Constitution, the *articles* explain how the government works, and the 10 original *amendments* list the basic rights guaranteed to all American citizens. Together, these parts contain the laws and guidelines necessary to set up and run a successful national government.

But the Constitution doesn't give power just to the national government. It also gives some power to the states and some to the people. Remember this when you study the Constitution.

The Preamble • We the people of the United States, in order to form a more perfect Union, establish justice, insure domestic tranquility, provide for the common defense, promote the general welfare, and secure the blessings of liberty to ourselves and our posterity, do ordain and establish this Constitution for the United States of America.

The Articles of the Constitution • The articles of the Constitution explain how each branch of government works and what each can and cannot do. The articles also explain how the federal and state governments must work together, and how the Constitution can be amended or changed.

ARTICLE 1 explains the legislative branch, how laws are made, and how Congress works.

ARTICLE 2 explains the executive branch, the offices of the president and vice president, and the powers of the executive branch.

ARTICLE 3 explains the judicial branch, the Supreme Court and other courts, and warns people against trying to overthrow the government.

ARTICLE 4 describes how the United States federal government and the individual state governments work together.

ARTICLE 5 tells how the Constitution can be amended, or changed.

ARTICLE 6 states that the United States federal government and the Constitution are the law of the land.

ARTICLE 7 outlines how the Constitution must be adopted.

The Bill of Rights

To get the necessary votes to approve the Constitution, a number of changes (amendments) had to be made. These 10 original amendments are called the Bill of Rights. They guarantee all Americans some very basic rights, including the right to worship, to speak freely, and to have a jury trial.

AMENDMENT 1 People have the right to worship, to speak freely, to gather together, and to question the government.

AMENDMENT 2 People have the right to bear arms.

AMENDMENT 3 The government cannot have soldiers stay in people's houses without their permission.

AMENDMENT 4 People and their property cannot be searched without the written permission of a judge.

AMENDMENT 5 People cannot be tried for a serious crime without a jury. They cannot be tried twice for the same crime or be forced to testify against themselves. Also, they cannot have property taken away while they are on trial. Any property taken for public use must receive a fair price.

AMENDMENT 6 In criminal cases people have a right to a trial, to be told what they are accused of, to hear witnesses against them, to get witnesses in their favor, and to have a lawyer.

AMENDMENT 7 In cases involving more than $20, people have the right to a jury trial.

AMENDMENT 8 People have a right to fair bail (money given as a promise the person will return for trial), fines, and punishments.

AMENDMENT 9 People have rights that are not listed in the Constitution.

AMENDMENT 10 Powers not given to the federal government are given to the states or to the people.

The Other Amendments

The Constitution and the Bill of Rights were ratified in 1791. Since that time, more than 7,000 amendments to the Constitution have been proposed. Because three-fourths of the states must approve an amendment before it becomes law, just 27 amendments have been passed. The first 10 are listed under the Bill of Rights; the other 17 are listed below.

AMENDMENT 11 A person cannot sue a state in federal court. (1795)

AMENDMENT 12 President and Vice President are elected separately. (1804)

AMENDMENT 13 Slavery is abolished, done away with. (1865)

AMENDMENT 14 All persons born in the United States or those who have become citizens enjoy full citizenship rights. (1868)

AMENDMENT 15 Voting rights are given to all citizens regardless of race, creed, or color. (1870)

AMENDMENT 16 Congress has the power to collect income taxes. (1913)

AMENDMENT 17 United States Senators are elected directly by the people. (1913)

AMENDMENT 18 Making, buying, and selling alcoholic beverages is no longer allowed. (1919)

AMENDMENT 19 Women gain the right to vote. (1920)

AMENDMENT 20 The President's term begins January 20; Senators' and Representatives' terms begin January 3. (1933)

AMENDMENT 21 (Repeals Amendment 18) Alcoholic beverages can be made, bought, and sold again. (1933)

AMENDMENT 22 The President is limited to two elected terms. (1951)

AMENDMENT 23 District of Columbia residents gain the right to vote. (1961)

AMENDMENT 24 All voter poll taxes are forbidden. (1964)

AMENDMENT 25 If the Presidency is vacant, the Vice President takes over. If the Vice Presidency is vacant, the President names someone, and the Congress votes on the choice. (1967)

AMENDMENT 26 Citizens 18 years old gain the right to vote. (1971)

AMENDMENT 27 No law changing the pay for members of Congress will take effect until after an election of Representatives. (1992)

U.S. Presidents and Vice Presidents

(*Did not finish term)

	President	Term	Vice President	
1	George Washington	Apr. 30, 1789 - Mar. 3, 1797	John Adams	1
2	John Adams	Mar. 4, 1797 - Mar. 3, 1801	Thomas Jefferson	2
3	Thomas Jefferson	Mar. 4, 1801 - Mar. 3, 1805	Aaron Burr	3
	Thomas Jefferson	Mar. 4, 1805 - Mar. 3, 1809	George Clinton	4
4	James Madison	Mar. 4, 1809 - Mar. 3, 1813	George Clinton	
	James Madison	Mar. 4, 1813 - Mar. 3, 1817	Elbridge Gerry	5
5	James Monroe	Mar. 4, 1817 - Mar. 3, 1825	Daniel D. Tompkins	6
6	John Quincy Adams	Mar. 4, 1825 - Mar. 3, 1829	John C. Calhoun	7
7	Andrew Jackson	Mar. 4, 1829 - Mar. 3, 1833	John C. Calhoun	
	Andrew Jackson	Mar. 4, 1833 - Mar. 3, 1837	Martin Van Buren	8
8	Martin Van Buren	Mar. 4, 1837 - Mar. 3, 1841	Richard M. Johnson	9
9	William H. Harrison*	Mar. 4, 1841 - April 4, 1841	John Tyler	10
10	John Tyler	Apr. 6, 1841 - Mar. 3, 1845		
11	James K. Polk	Mar. 4, 1845 - Mar. 3, 1849	George M. Dallas	11
12	Zachary Taylor*	Mar. 5, 1849 - July 9, 1850	Millard Fillmore	12
13	Millard Fillmore	July 10, 1850 - Mar. 3, 1853		
14	Franklin Pierce	Mar. 4, 1853 - Mar. 3, 1857	William R. King	13
15	James Buchanan	Mar. 4, 1857 - Mar. 3, 1861	John C. Breckinridge	14
16	Abraham Lincoln	Mar. 4, 1861 - Mar. 3, 1865	Hannibal Hamlin	15
	Abraham Lincoln*	Mar. 4, 1865 - Apr. 15, 1865	Andrew Johnson	16
17	Andrew Johnson	Apr. 15, 1865 - Mar. 3, 1869		
18	Ulysses S. Grant	Mar. 4, 1869 - Mar. 3, 1873	Schuyler Colfax	17
	Ulysses S. Grant	Mar. 4, 1873 - Mar. 3, 1877	Henry Wilson	18
19	Rutherford B. Hayes	Mar. 4, 1877 - Mar. 3, 1881	William A. Wheeler	19
20	James A. Garfield*	Mar. 4, 1881 - Sept. 19, 1881	Chester A. Arthur	20
21	Chester A. Arthur	Sept. 20, 1881 - Mar. 3, 1885		
22	Grover Cleveland	Mar. 4, 1885 - Mar. 3, 1889	Thomas A. Hendricks	21
23	Benjamin Harrison	Mar. 4, 1889 - Mar. 3, 1893	Levi P. Morton	22
24	Grover Cleveland	Mar. 4, 1893 - Mar. 3, 1897	Adlai E. Stevenson	23
25	William McKinley	Mar. 4, 1897 - Mar. 3, 1901	Garret A. Hobart	24
	William McKinley*	Mar. 4, 1901 - Sept. 14, 1901	Theodore Roosevelt	25
26	Theodore Roosevelt	Sept. 14, 1901 - Mar. 3, 1905		
	Theodore Roosevelt	Mar. 4, 1905 - Mar. 3, 1909	Charles W. Fairbanks	26
27	William H. Taft	Mar. 4, 1909 - Mar. 3, 1913	James S. Sherman	27
28	Woodrow Wilson	Mar. 4, 1913 - Mar. 3, 1921	Thomas R. Marshall	28
29	Warren G. Harding*	Mar. 4, 1921 - Aug. 2, 1923	Calvin Coolidge	29
30	Calvin Coolidge	Aug. 3, 1923 - Mar. 3, 1925		
	Calvin Coolidge	Mar. 4, 1925 - Mar. 3, 1929	Charles G. Dawes	30
31	Herbert C. Hoover	Mar. 4, 1929 - Mar. 3, 1933	Charles Curtis	31

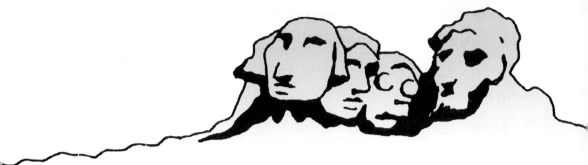

Order of Presidential Succession

1. Vice president
2. Speaker of the House
3. President pro tempore of the Senate
4. Secretary of state
5. Secretary of the treasury
6. Secretary of defense
7. Attorney general
8. Secretary of the interior
9. Secretary of agriculture
10. Secretary of commerce
11. Secretary of labor
12. Secretary of health and human services
13. Secretary of housing and urban development
14. Secretary of transportation
15. Secretary of energy
16. Secretary of education
17. Secretary of veterans affairs

| 1500 | 1520 | 1540 | 1560 | 1580 |

United States History

1492
Columbus lands in the West Indies.

1513
Ponce de Léon explores Florida.

1565
Spain settles St. Augustine, Florida, the first permanent European colony.

1519
Magellan begins three-year voyage around the world.

1570
League of Iroquois Nations is formed.

1519
Aztec empire dominates Mexico.

1588
England defeats the Spanish Armada and rules the seas.

Science and Inventions

1507
Glass mirrors are greatly improved.

1543
Copernicus challenges beliefs by claiming sun-centered universe.

1530
Bottle corks are invented.

1558
The magnetic compass is invented by John Dee.

1596
The thermometer is invented.

1509
Watches are invented.

Literature and Life

1536
The first songbook is used in Spain.

1580
The first water closet is designed in Bath, England.

1500
The game of Bingo is developed.

1538
Mercator draws map with America on it.

1507
Book on surgery is developed.

1564
The first horse-drawn coach is used in England.

1599
Copper coins are first made.

U.S. POPULATION: (Native American)
approximately 1,100,000

(Spanish)
1,021

1600   1620   1640   1660   1680   1700

1607
The first English settlement is established at Jamestown, Virginia.

1629
Massachusetts Bay Colony is established.

1619
First African slaves are brought to Virginia.

1620
Plymouth Colony is founded by Pilgrims.

1673
Marquette and Joliet explore the Mississippi River for France.

1664
The Dutch colony of New Netherlands becomes the English colony of New York.

1682
William Penn founds Pennsylvania.

1608
The telescope is invented.

1643
Torricelli invents the barometer.

1671
The first calculation machine is invented.

1629
Human temperature is measured by a physician in Italy.

1609
Galileo makes the first observations with a telescope.

1668
Reflecting telescope is invented by Sir Isaac Newton.

1682
Halley's Comet is studied by Edmund Halley and named for him.

1687
Newton describes gravity.

1600
William Shakespeare's plays are performed at the Globe Theatre in London.

1630
Popcorn is introduced to the Pilgrims by Native Americans.

1658
The first illustrated book for children, *World of Visible Objects,* is written by John Comenius.

1622
The year begins on January 1, instead of March 25.

1653
The first postage stamps are used in Paris.

1685
The first drinking fountain is used in England.

1697
Charles Perrault writes *Tales of Mother Goose.*

| (English) 350 | 2,302 | 26,634 | 75,058 | 151,507 |

1700	1710	1720	1730	1740

United States History

1705
The Virginia Act establishes public education.

1718
New Orleans is founded by France.

1707
England (English) and Scotland (Scots) become Great Britain (British).

1733
The British Molasses Act places taxes on sugar and molasses.

1735
Freedom of the press is established during trial of John Peter Zenger.

1747
The Ohio Company is formed to settle the Ohio River Valley.

Science and Inventions

1701
Seed drill that plants seeds in a row is invented by Jethro Tull.

1709
The pianoforte (first piano) is invented by Christofori Bartolommeo.

1712
Thomas Newcomen develops the first practical steam engine.

1728
The first dental drill is used by Pierre Fauchard.

1735
Rubber is found in South America.

1732
Sedatives for operations are discovered by Thomas Dover.

1742
Benjamin Franklin invents the efficient Franklin stove.

Literature and Life

1700
The Selling of Joseph by Samuel Sewall is the first book against slavery of Africans.

1726
Jonathan Swift writes *Gulliver's Travels.*

1731
Benjamin Franklin begins the first public library.

1704
The *Boston News-Letter* is the first successful newspaper in the American colonies.

1737
An earthquake in Calcutta, India, kills 300,000 people.

U.S. POPULATION: (English Colonies)

250,888	331,711	466,185	629,445	905,563

| 1750 | 1760 | 1770 | 1780 | 1790 | 1800 |

1750
Flatbed boats and Conestoga wagons begin moving settlers west.

1763
Britain wins the French and Indian War.

1765
The Stamp Act tax is imposed on the colonies by Britain.

1775
The first battles of the Revolutionary War are fought.

1776
The Declaration of Independence is signed on July 4.

1787
The U.S. Constitution is signed.

1789
George Washington becomes the first U.S. president.

1781
United colonies adopt Articles of Confederation as first government.

1781
The British surrender at Yorktown.

1752
Benjamin Franklin discovers that lightning is a form of electricity.

1770
The first steam carriage is invented.

1764
"Spinning jenny," a machine for spinning cotton, is invented.

1783
The first hot-air balloon is flown.

1793
Eli Whitney invents the cotton gin to remove the seeds from cotton.

1796
The smallpox vaccine is developed.

1752
The first American hospital is established in Philadelphia.

1757
Streetlights are installed in Philadelphia.

1764
Mozart writes his first symphony.

1782
The American bald eagle is first used as a symbol of the United States.

1786
The first ice-cream company in America begins production.

1790
The U.S. government takes its first official census.

1795
Food canning is introduced.

| 1,170,760 | 1,593,625 | 2,148,076 | 2,780,369 | 3,929,157 |

1800	1810	1820	1830	1840

United States History

1800
Washington, D.C., becomes the U.S. capital.

1814
U.S. defeats Britain in the War of 1812.

1836
Texans defend the Alamo.

1803
The Louisiana Purchase doubles the size of the U.S.

1819
The U.S. acquires Florida from Spain.

1830
Native Americans are forced west by the Indian Removal Act.

1838
The Cherokee Nation is forced west on the "Trail of Tears."

1804
Lewis and Clark explore the Louisiana Territory and the Northwest.

1848
Gold is discovered in California.

Science and Inventions

1800
The battery is invented by Count Volta.

1816
The stethoscope is invented.

1839
Kirkpatrick Macmillan invents the bicycle.

1816
Joseph Niépce takes the first photograph.

1836
Samuel Morse invents the telegraph.

1844
Safety matches are produced.

1802
Robert Fulton builds the first steamboat.

1817
Erie Canal is begun.

1846
Elias Howe invents the sewing machine.

Literature and Life

1804
The first book of children's poems is published.

1812
Uncle Sam becomes a symbol of the U.S.

1820
Rip Van Winkle is written by Washington Irving.

1828
The first *Webster's Dictionary* is published.

1834
Louis Braille perfects a writing system for the blind.

1806
Gas lighting is first used in homes.

1814
Francis Scott Key writes "The Star-Spangled Banner."

1835
Hans Christian Andersen publishes *Tales Told to Children*.

1849
The safety pin is invented.

U.S. POPULATION:

5,308,080	7,240,102	9,638,453	12,860,702	17,063,353

| 1850 | 1860 | 1870 | 1880 | 1890 | 1900 |

1860
Abraham Lincoln is elected president.

1865
The Civil War ends, and the 13th Amendment to the Constitution ends slavery.

1876
Custer is defeated at the Battle of Little Big Horn.

1892
An immigration station is opened at Ellis Island, N.Y.

1861
The Civil War begins.

1869
Immigrant workers complete the coast-to-coast railroad in Utah.

1898
The U.S. defeats Spain in the Spanish-American War.

1862
Lincoln proclaims abolition of slavery in U.S.

1870
The 15th Amendment gives African American men the right to vote.

1857
Atlantic cable is completed.

1876
Alexander Graham Bell invents the telephone.

1893
Charles and Frank Duryea build the first successful U.S. gasoline-powered automobile.

1877
Thomas Edison invents the phonograph.

1860
Jean Lenoir builds an internal combustion engine.

1879
Thomas Edison invents the lightbulb.

1851
Isaac Singer produces a sewing machine.

1865
Antiseptic practices are introduced by Joseph Lister.

1896
Marconi invents the wireless radio.

1850
Oscar Levi Strauss makes the first blue jeans.

1876
The National Baseball League is established.

1892
The "Pledge of Allegiance" is written by F. Bellamy.

1855
Alexander Parks produces the first synthetic plastic.

1883
Four U.S. time zones are established.

1852
Harriet Beecher Stowe's novel *Uncle Tom's Cabin* strengthens the anti-slavery movement.

1886
The Statue of Liberty is erected in New York harbor to welcome immigrants.

1896
The first movie is shown in the U.S.

23,191,876   31,443,321   38,558,371   50,189,209   62,979,766

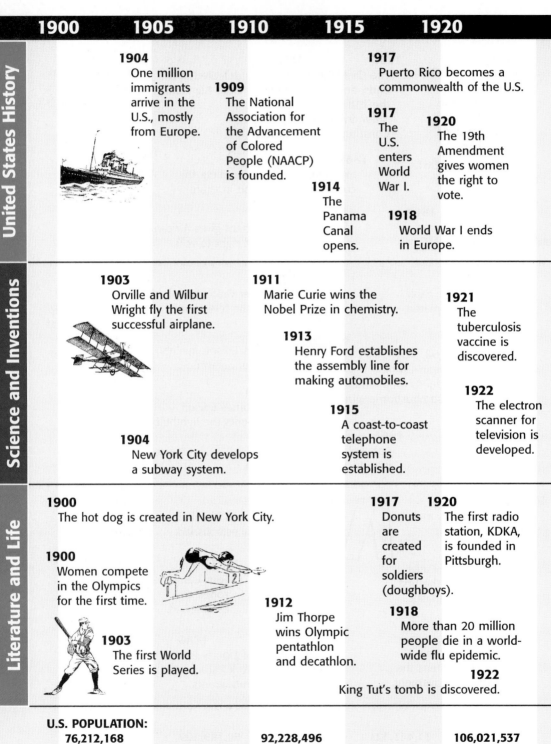

1900 **1905** **1910** **1915** **1920**

United States History

1904
One million immigrants arrive in the U.S., mostly from Europe.

1909
The National Association for the Advancement of Colored People (NAACP) is founded.

1914
The Panama Canal opens.

1917
Puerto Rico becomes a commonwealth of the U.S.

1917
The U.S. enters World War I.

1920
The 19th Amendment gives women the right to vote.

1918
World War I ends in Europe.

Science and Inventions

1903
Orville and Wilbur Wright fly the first successful airplane.

1904
New York City develops a subway system.

1911
Marie Curie wins the Nobel Prize in chemistry.

1913
Henry Ford establishes the assembly line for making automobiles.

1915
A coast-to-coast telephone system is established.

1921
The tuberculosis vaccine is discovered.

1922
The electron scanner for television is developed.

Literature and Life

1900
The hot dog is created in New York City.

1900
Women compete in the Olympics for the first time.

1903
The first World Series is played.

1912
Jim Thorpe wins Olympic pentathlon and decathlon.

1917
Donuts are created for soldiers (doughboys).

1918
More than 20 million people die in a world-wide flu epidemic.

1920
The first radio station, KDKA, is founded in Pittsburgh.

1922
King Tut's tomb is discovered.

U.S. POPULATION:
76,212,168   92,228,496   106,021,537

1925   **1930**   **1935**   **1940**   **1945**   **1950**

1927
Charles Lindbergh is the first to fly solo across the Atlantic.

1933
Franklin Roosevelt becomes president and enacts the New Deal to end the Depression.

1941
The U.S. enters World War II on Dec. 7 after the bombing of Pearl Harbor.

1948
Mahatma Gandhi assassinated.

1935
Dennis Chavez becomes the first Hispanic U.S. senator.

1945
World War II ends.

1929
Stock market crash causes Great Depression.

1945
The United States joins the United Nations.

1929
Alexander Fleming develops penicillin.

1938
Modern-type ballpoint pens are developed.

1930
First analog computer is invented by Vannevar Bush.

1935
Radar is invented.

1938
The photocopy machine is produced.

1947
Bell Lab scientists invent transistor.

1926
John Baird demonstrates his television system.

1931
The Empire State Building (102 stories, 1,250 feet) is completed as the tallest in the world.

1940
Enrico Fermi develops the nuclear reactor.

1925
Potato chips are produced in New York City.

1947
Jackie Robinson becomes the first African American major league baseball player.

1933
Albert Einstein immigrates to the U.S.

1927
Wings wins the first Academy Award for motion pictures.

1938
Superman "Action Comics" are created.

1931
"The Star-Spangled Banner" becomes the U.S. national anthem.

1947
Anne Frank's *Diary of a Young Girl* is published.

123,202,624   132,164,569

1950	1955	1960	1965	1970

United States History

1950
The United States enters the Korean War.

1955
The Civil Rights movement begins when Rosa Parks refuses to move to the back of the bus.

1955
Martin Luther King, Jr., begins organizing protests against black discrimination.

1959
Alaska and Hawaii become states.

1962
Cesar Chavez starts the National Farm Workers Association.

1963
President John F. Kennedy is assassinated.

1965
U.S. troops are sent to Vietnam.

1969
Neil Armstrong and Buzz Aldrin are the first men on the moon.

Science and Inventions

1951
Fluoridated water is discovered to prevent tooth decay.

1954
Jonas Salk develops the polio vaccine.

1957
Russia launches the first satellite, *Sputnik I.*

1958
Stereo long-playing records are produced.

1960
First laser is invented by Theodor Maiman.

1967
Cholesterol discovered as cause of heart disease.

1968
First U.S. heart transplant is performed by surgeon Norman Shumway.

1971
The space probe *Mariner* maps the surface of Mars.

Literature and Life

1950
New York City is the world's largest city, with 8 million people.

1951
Fifteen million American homes have televisions.

1955
Disneyland opens.

1957
Theodor "Dr. Seuss" Geisel's *Cat in the Hat* is published.

1957
Elvis Presley is the most popular rock 'n' roll musician in the U.S.

1964
The Beatles appear on *The Ed Sullivan Show.*

1969
Sesame Street television show with Jim Henson's muppets begins.

1970
The first Earth Day focuses on protecting the environment.

U.S. POPULATION:
151,325,798   179,323,175   203,302,031

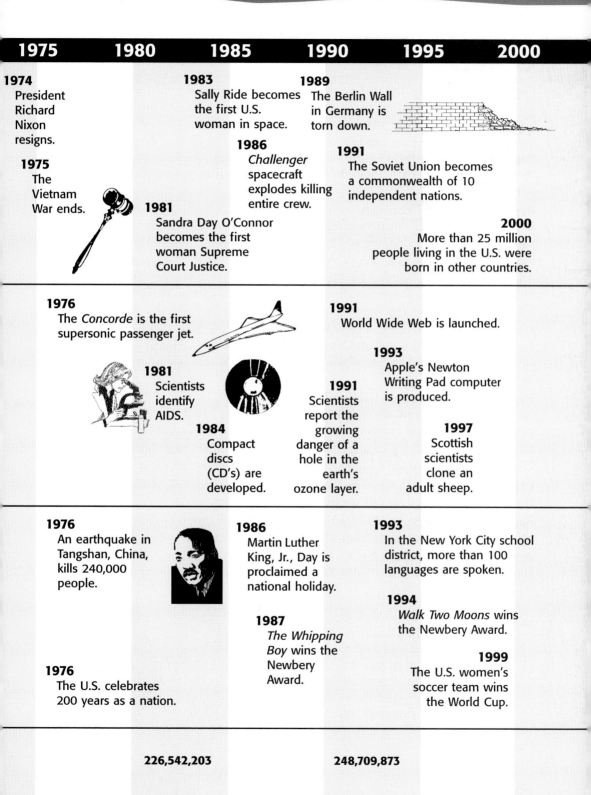

1975 **1980** **1985** **1990** **1995** **2000**

1974
President Richard Nixon resigns.

1975
The Vietnam War ends.

1983
Sally Ride becomes the first U.S. woman in space.

1989
The Berlin Wall in Germany is torn down.

1986
Challenger spacecraft explodes killing entire crew.

1991
The Soviet Union becomes a commonwealth of 10 independent nations.

1981
Sandra Day O'Connor becomes the first woman Supreme Court Justice.

2000
More than 25 million people living in the U.S. were born in other countries.

1976
The *Concorde* is the first supersonic passenger jet.

1991
World Wide Web is launched.

1981
Scientists identify AIDS.

1993
Apple's Newton Writing Pad computer is produced.

1991
Scientists report the growing danger of a hole in the earth's ozone layer.

1984
Compact discs (CD's) are developed.

1997
Scottish scientists clone an adult sheep.

1976
An earthquake in Tangshan, China, kills 240,000 people.

1986
Martin Luther King, Jr., Day is proclaimed a national holiday.

1993
In the New York City school district, more than 100 languages are spoken.

1994
Walk Two Moons wins the Newbery Award.

1987
The Whipping Boy wins the Newbery Award.

1976
The U.S. celebrates 200 years as a nation.

1999
The U.S. women's soccer team wins the World Cup.

226,542,203   248,709,873

Credits

Page 20: From "Dig It!" in *Images: Deep Down Underground* from *Heath Literacy* by Alvermann et al. Copyright © 1995 by D. C. Heath & Company. Reprinted by permission of Houghton Mifflin Company. All rights reserved.

Page 20: Text copyright © 1993 by Sneed B. Collard III from *Sea Snakes* by Sneed B. Collard III. Published by Boyds Mills Press, Inc. Reprinted by permission.

Page 21: From *Belinda's Hurricane* by Elizabeth Winthrop, copyright © 1984 by Elizabeth Winthrop Mahony. Used by permission of Dutton Children's Books, a division of Penguin Putnam Inc.

Page 21: From "Kilauea: Pete's Playground" in *Images: The Islands of Aloha* from *Heath Literacy* by Alvermann et al. Copyright © 1995 by D. C. Heath & Company. Reprinted by permission of Houghton Mifflin Company. All rights reserved.

Page 22: From "The Living Desert" in *Images: In the Desert* from *Heath Literacy* by Alvermann et al. Copyright © 1995 by D. C. Heath & Company. Reprinted by permission of Houghton Mifflin Company. All rights reserved.

Page 22: "Notes on Punctuation," copyright © 1979 by Lewis Thomas, from *The Medusa and the Snail* by Lewis Thomas. Used by permission of Viking Penguin, a division of Penguin Putnam Inc.

Page 58: Excerpt from *Charlotte's Web* by E. B. White, copyright © 1999. HarperCollins Children's Books. Reprinted by permission of the publisher.

Page 260: Excerpted from *The World Book Encyclopedia,* © 1997 World Book, Inc. Reprinted by permission of the publisher.

Page 291: Copyright © 1994 by Houghton Mifflin Company. Adapted and reproduced by permission from *The American Heritage Student Dictionary*.

Page 292: Copyright © 1994 by Houghton Mifflin Company. Adapted and reproduced by permission from *The American Heritage Student Thesaurus*.

Your Handbook Index

The index is your guide to using the *Writers Express* handbook. It will help you find specific information. For example, if you want to find a list of state abbreviations so you can address a letter, you can look under "abbreviations" or under "state." Both entries will tell you where to turn in your handbook to find the information.

Q

Quatrain, 247
Question,
  Crazy, 45
  Thinking move, 337
Question mark, 387
Questions, 387, 416
Quiet / quit / quite, 408
Quotation marks, 386
  Direct quotation, 386
  Special words, 386
  Titles, 386

R

Raise / rays / raze, 409
Rambling sentence, 115
Read / red, 409
Reader response journal, 136, 171

Reading,
  Context , 289
  Diagrams, 282
  Graphics, 280-287
  Graphs, 283-285
  Poetry, 239, 322-323
  Prefixes, suffixes, roots, 295-304
  Reviewing, 272
  Strategies, 271-279
  Symbols, 281
  Tables, 286-287
  Vocabulary, 289-305

Realistic stories, 220-225
  Sample, 225
Recalling information, 339, 345

Recipe stories, 143
Red / read, 409
Reference books, 260-262
  Parts of, 262
Reflexive pronoun, 424
Relative pronoun, 424
Repetition, 245

Report, classroom, 192-203
  Bibliography, 201, 203
  Gathering grid, 195
  Interactive, 206
  Multimedia, 204-207
  Observation, 188-191
  Outline, 197
  Sample note cards, 196
  Sample report, 202-203

Reporter, parts of a, 158
Request, letter of, 179
Research your subject, 46
Resolution, 276, 278
Responding to literature, 171
Response journal, 136, 171
Response sheet, 63
Review, book, 166-171
  Sample, 167
Revising, 9, 11, 25, 55-59, 131
  Checklist, 57
  With partners, 60-63
  Sample, 15
Rhyme, end, 245
Rhythm, 245

Riddles, writing, 250-253
Right / write / rite, 409
Rising action, 276, 278
Road / rode / rowed, 409
Roman numerals, 455
Roots, 294
  List of, 298-304
R.S.V.P., 148, 149, 397
Run-on sentence, 115

S

Salutation, 144, 145, 178, 179, 382
Save, computer, 27
Scene / seen, 409
Scent / cent / sent, 404
Scheduling work, 358
Science fiction, 279
Science reports,
  Sample observation, 191
Scoring a poem, 321
Scripting a poem, 320
Sea / see, 409
Seam / seem, 409
Search engine, 268
Second person,
  Point of view, 130, 278
  Pronoun, 422
Seen / scene, 409
Selecting subjects, 35-39, 95, 101
Semicolon, 381
Senses, graphic organizer, 48, 334
Sensory details, 83, 127
Sent / scent / cent, 404

Y